D0746629

BLOODSTOPPERS & BEARWALKERS

BLOODSTOPPERS

& BEARWALKERS

FOLK TRADITIONS OF
THE UPPER PENINSULA

RICHARD M. DORSON

HARVARD UNIVERSITY PRESS · CAMBRIDGE

To

STITH THOMPSON

FOREWORD TO THE PAPERBACK EDITION

Twenty-five years ago I ventured forth from the library stacks and the college classroom, where I had been studying and teaching American history, into the "field." As folklorists and anthropologists define the field, it represents an alien culture, a terra incognita far removed from their customary orbit. These itinerant scholars from a world of intellectuals come to reside among tribal peoples and folk communities and to learn their ways. One need not go very far to meet the folk—whoever they are; they may live just down the street. My colleague at Indiana University, the poet and novelist Sam Yellen, once wrote a memorable short story, "The Passionate Shepherd," about a college professor who grew tired of academe, donned workman's clothes, slipped out of his cubicle, strolled down to the town square—which we recognized as being in our town of Bloomington, Indiana—and crossed from the east side of the square where the university community shopped, to the west side, where on Saturdays the farmers and stone-quarry workers lounged. In no time at all the professor vanished from the university scene and took up his new life as a stonecutter, although he still dwelt in the same neighborhood.

The folklorist is crossing the square, or scaling the walls, that divide the book-learned from the tradition-oriented sectors of society, and in my foray into the Upper Peninsula of Michigan in 1946 I crossed the Straits of Mackinac by ferry to enter an uncharted world of folk societies. As I now realize, I could have found the folk anywhere, but at the time I needed a symbolic crossing in my voyage of discovery.

Five months in the field exhilarated and astonished me.

The bard and troubadours of Homer's day and King Arthur's court were all there, reciting in a variety of American accents their wondrous sagas. In the book I wrote about my journey and its revelations I tried to communicate my sense of the vitality and variety of the traditions I encountered. But a number of readers, who had never heard of the Upper Peninsula—as I had not, before I went to teach at Michigan State College—thought the subject narrow, regional, and "specialized." Others saw at once what I had in mind: a firsthand view of "co-existing cultures," as one reader wrote me. American folklore as a subject had just begun to make an impact on the public in the 1940's, through scissors-and-paste treasuries of what I called "fakelore." These compilations sought to cover the lore of the whole country, or large slabs of it, but instead of bona fide field materials they contained rewritten, fabricated, and sentimentalized reprints. No field collector can of course investigate all the United States, or even a succession of regions, in one lifetime. But fieldwork done in depth in a relatively limited area can illuminate the entire American scene.

This is what I hoped to do in the fabulous Upper Peninsula, by collecting the folk traditions of Indians, European ethnic groups, and occupational workers, three great strands of the oral lore to be found in the United States. The folklore I personally collected ran counter to many of the conventional notions of what folklore was supposed to be. Lumberjacks did not tell Paul Bunyan stories, for instance, but they did relish anecdotes about sly and eccentric camp bosses. Dialect stories, which are based on the language mistakes and cultural mishaps of first generation immigrants, proved to be a highly popular form of humorous storytelling, although never previously reported by folklorists.[*]

[*]See my article, with 84 texts, "Dialect Stories of the Upper Peninsula, A New Form of American Folklore," *Journal of American Folklore* 61 (1948): 113–150.

Today, two decades after the publication of *Bloodstoppers and Bearwalkers*, the public and the scholarly world increasingly recognize that folklore comes from the spoken word, and that such oral folklore is one of the chief avenues into the lives and minds of anonymous Americans. The red man, the black man, the immigrant, the laborer in the woods, mines, and factories, the man in the street, and the woman in the nursery may have left us little or nothing in the way of written records but they have bequeathed us absorbing verbal traditions of their experiences and concerns. I welcome the reissue of *Bloodstoppers and Bearwalkers* at a time when the nation is becoming more appreciative of the diversified folk cultures that have contributed vigor and strength to American life.

Richard M. Dorson

Bloomington, Indiana
24 September 1971

ACKNOWLEDGMENTS

A fellowship from the Library of Congress for Studies in the History of American Civilization enabled me to spend five months in the field in 1946 collecting the material for this volume. I am indebted to grants-in-aid from the All-College Research Fund of Michigan State College which made possible secretarial assistance in the preparation of the manuscript. Mr. Charles Angoff, to whom I am grateful for steady support, has kindly granted permission to reprint "The Lynching of the McDonald Boys" from the *American Mercury*. The illustrations following page 4 are from photographs by George T. Kolehmainen.

R. M. D.

CONTENTS

BLOODSTOPPERS & BEARWALKERS

THE BACKGROUND OF THIS BOOK

THIS book makes certain claims that distinguish it
from other folklore books. It deals with a variety of folk traditions, those of European stocks, of regional groups, of Indian
tribes, which all mingle on American soil. Usually a folklore collector confines himself to a single type, and the broad rich range
of American folk story never gets presented in one bundle.

Further, all the tales in this volume have been collected by me.
They are not taken from old books, or from students, or from
correspondents, or from youthful memories. They all came to me
in the very midst of "folk life," during a five-months trip I made
in 1946 to one of the richest storytelling regions in the United
States, the Upper Peninsula of Michigan.

I went to the Peninsula believing that one could uncover many
kinds of living folk stories in America, in a limited time and area,
and need not dream them up or copy them out in the library.
The quest succeeded most happily. This present collection could
be several times enlarged from my notebooks, and the abundance
and diversity of the oral traditions I found still stagger me. I
heard creation myths, fairy tales, tall tales, occult tales, legends,
romances, exploits, jests, anecdotes, noodle stories, dialect stories,
told by Ojibwa, Potawatomi, and Sioux Indians; by Finns, Swedes,
Poles, Germans, Italians, Irishmen, Frenchmen, Englishmen, even
by Luxemburgers, Slovenians, and Lithuanians; by farmers, lumberjacks, copper and iron miners, fishermen, sailors, railroaders,
bartenders, undertakers, authors, county officials, newspaper edi-
tors; by the senile and the juvenile, the educated and the illiterate; by family circles and boarding house cliques in full blast and
by solitary old-timers in tar paper shacks. I never spent a day in

the Peninsula without collecting tales, even when several hours went in driving, and although I literally knew not a soul in the area.

For my purposes the Upper Peninsula seemed made to order. Three of the Great Lakes ring it round, and the Wisconsin boundary blocks off its western base. There men have lived close to the earth, attracted by white pine timber, red copper and black iron ore, free farmland, and fishing grounds, and there they have written flaming chapters of frontier history. Exhausted and ravished, with no big cities and heavy industry to save her, the country lies dying now, but the free and easy ways and the wild and violent spirit still persist. Her old-timers have the materials and the leisure for spinning legends. This remote and rugged land has become a storytellers' paradise.

In addition, the Peninsula contains in miniscule the nation's varied folk culture. A dramatic century of land and water conquest, of mining and lumber booms, has generated a rich historical and local lore. On the European side, a dozen nationalities jostle each other in every town and provide a dazzling conglomeration of imported folkstuff, in contrast with the predominantly Yankee Lower Peninsula. The Indian element there, living now on scattered reservation villages, are the very Ojibwa from whom the great Schoolcraft had first gathered American Indian tales.

With these thoughts in mind I set out. From morning till night I chased after storytellers and ran into strange experiences and incredible personalities. Even on the very first day, driving two hundred miles due north to the Straits of Mackinac, I met a storytelling character. Alongside the highway a sign read, "Feed the Bears — Spike Horn."

Sure enough, in the pens blinked sleepy half-grown cubs and one formidable big fellow, who shook hands gravely with the dubious visitor. And now came an outrageously dressed, blasphemous, humped, and bearded old man, Spike himself, walking a little lamely.

"Why do you limp, Spike?"

"One night I shot two deer, both bucks, one in the light of the moon and the other in the dark of the moon. I skinned them and made me a pair of buckskin pants. The leg made from the deer I killed in the light of the moon kept stretching. The leg made from the deer I killed in the dark of the moon kept shrinking. I cut off the extra length and sewed it onto the short leg but still it shrunk faster than the other one grew, till it shriveled right up and I caught rheumatism from walking around bare."

So came the first story, and in time a thousand more. In five months I had harvested more than I could use and had settled down to the far longer task of digesting the discoveries. The stories in this book were written down in spiral notebooks in longhand,* just as I heard them. Many people ask, "How did you meet these storytellers, and how were you able to write down the stories?" In the fraternal Upper Peninsula towns, one can build up a list of potential informants quickly enough. Frequently I went to key persons in the town whose positions kept them in touch with the community: the newspaper editor, minister or priest, Chamber of Commerce secretary, school superintendent, county agricultural agent. They might themselves prove to be informants, and usually they could suggest a string of names. Or casual contacts could serve the same purpose, such as the hotel clerk, or a hitchhiker, or a fellow-boarder. Sometimes I ran into fine storytellers by accident; Bert Damour sat beside me in a lunch counter in L'Anse, Swan Olson was in the chair when I waited for a haircut in a Negaunee barbershop, John Hallen operated the hotel I stopped at in Manistique. The principal rule in the field is, talk to everybody and follow all the leads. When the collector becomes known in a town, the narrators may even seek him out, as happened when Chief Welsh stuck his head in the office of the Indian agent in L'Anse and asked for the professor fellow he had been reading about in the paper.

There are, of course, always blind alleys. The highly recommended informant turns out to be a popular lecturer with no

* I am depositing these notebooks in the Michigan State College Library.

fresh material; the local experts deny that the old Indian or French tales are still told. These wrong steers come largely from the gap between the so-called intelligentsia and the folk, and from the general misunderstanding of what folklore is. But the percentage runs favorably, for good talkers enjoy a wide reputation, and persistent inquiry soon leads you to their hangouts.

Collecting is very much a matter of timing, chance, and circumstance. No two days repeat themselves. Sometimes the single storyteller, sometimes the family or social group, provides the tales; the collector may act as interlocutor, or he may be a silent eavesdropper. One of the most dramatic story-swapping sessions I heard developed spontaneously among a group of boarders in a lodging house in Munising. On such an occasion all I could do was jot down a few notes and later get members of the group by themselves to retell their particular tales. Ordinarily I encountered no difficulty in the use of the notebook. People like to have their words taken down, and are quite willing to repeat a story slowly enough so that you can get it verbatim. Once the excitement of the story kindles the raconteurs, any sense of self-consciousness before a stranger or a pad and pencil disappears. The trick, of course, is to gain the confidence of each new acquaintance, to press the right stops and steer the talk along the desired lines. With the gifted or "natural" yarn-spinners talk flows easily enough, and I can only marvel at the luck that brought me in touch in a limited time with such superb narrators as Aunt Jane Goudreau, Swan Olson, Charlie Goodman, Trefflé Largenesse, Frank Valin, Joe Woods, Chief Welsh, Alec Philemon, George Cota, Burt Mayotte, to name only the stars.

Language barriers do not present a real difficulty to the American collector, for some bilingual interpreter will always be near at hand. Old John Pete of the Lac Vieux Desert reservation knew no English, but George Cadotte sat by his side and translated the stories fluently for me for hours on end. My Finnish friend, Aili Kolehmainen Johnson, translated the tales of Frank Valin, and Ariane de Félice from Paris, observing French folklore in Amer-

Alec Philemon of Hannahville, Potawatomi Indian and superb storyteller.

Mrs. Elizabeth Philemon and her son-in-law, Archie Megenuph of the Hannahville Reservation of Potawatomi Indians. At 94 she lives alone and weaves baskets. He is a former semi-pro baseball player.

Chief Herbert Welsh of L'Anse, Sioux Indian, said to be
a grandson of Sitting Bull.

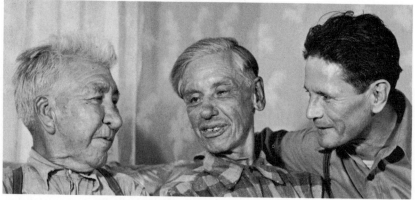

Pagan Chippewa Indians of the Lac Vieux Desert village. Old John Pete (left) is the
storyteller; George Cadotte (center) the interpreter.

Aunt Jane Goudreau of St. Ignace, French-Canadian and part Chippewa, teller of "roup-garou" legends.

Trefflé Largenesse and Charles Rivard of Marquette, illiterate French-Canadian conteurs of old fairy tales.

Frank Valin, the Finnish storyteller, outside his tar-paper shack at Rumeley.

Herman Maki of Palmer, teller of Finnish tall tales, locally celebrated humorist (in front of his Finnish-type summer home).

George Cota of Crystal Falls, French-Canadian and Irish, lumbercamp cook and woods storyteller.

Edwin T. Brown of Sault Ste. Marie, former chief clerk of the Soo locks, and a collector of photographs and stories of ships that sailed Lake Superior.

Swan Olson of Negaunee, Swedish, a mason by trade, a mild-mannered old man whose autobiographical sagas portray a ferocious swashbuckling hero.

ica, translated the contes of Trefflé Largenesse. The mere me-
chanics of running down your man, or woman, may prove the
chief difficulty; I spent the better part of a week chasing after
a highly recommended dialect reciter and prominent business
man in Hancock, who promised to give me some time and never
did. The Indians and lumberjacks I found to be much more available and coöperative than go-getting city merchants.

Different kinds of tales require differing methods of collection.
For a *conte* or *Märchen*, where the story is known *in extenso* to
the informant, he can proceed on his own once you have pressed
the right button. For a local legend, which has various shapes
and fragments lodged in the minds of the townspeople, the collector may have to ask several leading questions, much in the
form of an interview, and piece the data together into a connected whole, after he has queried many people in order to estab-
lish the group knowledge of the *Sage*. For the Lynching of the
McDonald Boys, I spoke to a number of people in Menominee
before I perceived the full outline. My first acquaintance with
the tradition came in a Munising boardinghouse, in the session
of spectral yarning I have just mentioned, when one hanger-on
referred to a lynch party who were all cursed to die with their
boots on. I starred his statement in my notebook, but when I
hunted up the speaker later he could add nothing further, except
to suggest I make inquiries in Menominee. Eventually I did so,
and the details multiplied richly and tantalizingly; for one thing,
I could not reconcile a continuous conflict in the accounts which
had the McDonalds hung in two different spots: both to the
railroad crossing sign in the center of town and to the jack pines
outside the sporting house; at length in the little village of Amasa
I met eighty-four-year-old George Premo, straight as a ramrod
and a character in his own right, who gave me the unexpurgated
version which explained that actually the McDonalds were strung
up twice. The final touches to the legend I gathered back in
Lansing, after a talk I gave to the Knights of Columbus, when

a Menominee man took me aside and told of the two lynchers who had sworn to beat the curse and failed to do so.

Occupational lore demands still another approach: the reminiscent conversational discourse. Only after I had talked with scores of old-time lumberjacks who would describe the experiences and incidents of woods life rather than any one consecutive narrative, did the patterns of tradition become visible.

With the collecting finished, the problem arose, how could my notebook tales be logically presented? The answer proved relatively simple because all that I had seen and heard supported my theory of folklore.

The key to the theory lay in the concept of *folk*. A fuzzy and much abused term, it could nevertheless convey a sharp and lucid meaning. It needed the indefinite article: *a* folk, not *the* folk. Any homogeneous group, any group that was vitally integrated, made a folk. Such groups were formed by places of residence, like the rural town or urban "neighborhood"; by racial and national stocks with a common culture; by occupations, whether herding cattle, or playing professional baseball, or attending school. These groups became sealed fraternities, possessing their own set of esoteric traditions, familiar as the sun to every member, bizarre as the jungle to any outsider. American society, because of its extreme complexity, was divisible into many such folks.

One can test this idea readily enough, if he equips himself with some small insight into the charmed circles. Quiz a lumberjack about barroom brawls, a Canadien about the *loup-garou*, an Ojibwa Indian about Winabijou, a native of Menominee about the lynching of the McDonald boys, a Wall Street broker about Chauncy Depew, a college coëd about Minnie the Mermaid — and notice the involuntary smile or grimace of recognition, and the anecdote or folk song that immediately follows. But the lumberjack and the Indian, even if they are neighbors, will be equally confounded at the other's trade hero; the coëd's mother doesn't know "Minnie the Mermaid" or "Flaming Mamie" from an operatic aria; the Finnish wife has never heard her husband's tales of Gustav Vasa, the Swedish George Washington. Yet each circle expresses astonishment that its commonplace topics arouse curiosity and that they should be called "folklore."

Folk traditions follow their own courses much like parallel railroad tracks which never meet. According to our background, age, job, and so on, we ride along one track, oblivious of the rest, unless circumstances cause us to switch. What I was doing in the Peninsula was to locate as many tracks as possible and ride along each for a while, with my storytellers as conductors, until I became familiar with the terrain.

If by folk then is meant a cohesive, like-minded group, what is lore? In its early usage the word suggested antiquities and survivals, as if lore were something stagnant or dead. But lore, while born in the past, lives in the present; it has a role to play; the old stories still entertain, the old customs please, the old beliefs awe men today.

Lore stands in contrast to learning. Learning is handed on through books and teachers; it is precise, factual, intellectual. Lore survives in fireside talk; it is nourished by fears and fancies. Learning belongs to the individual where lore clings to the group. We ask that lore live in people's mouths for at least several generations, that it be shared by many, that it bear the marks of much handling. Every folk breeds lore, in the process of living and imagining; floating lore always finds a home with a folk.

The stories in this book are folklore according to these specifications. They come by word of mouth, and they are told among closely knit groups. Most of the chapters represent such a folk group. By contrast, the gifted yarn spinner who glorifies his own past tells an individual, not a folk story, although even then he may be borrowing from someone else's saga. At any rate I isolated such tales within the chapter called "Sagamen."

When we consider the problem of defining *American* folktales, we encounter the quibble that Old World and Indian narratives collected on our soil derive from alien cultures. But our civilization has incorporated the immigrant and the red man, and the student of American folk culture should be interested in all the tales told within the United States. We may consider these variegated folk stories under three broad divisions, those preserved by the aboriginal inhabitants of the continent, those imported with the immigrant, and those that develop from American life. An urban American of the twentieth century can at once appreciate stories of tough lumberjacks. He can, with a wrench, get into the spirit of European peasant tales. But when it comes to Indian legends, he bogs down completely. This is the tradition farthest removed from his own outlook. As a result, the romancers and versifiers have altered and sweetened up Indian tales to fit white notions of the noble savage, so that today, in spite of the many careful collections by anthropologists, the average American knows nothing of the real Indian traditions.

This is the more regrettable because the Indians remain superb narrators of a pure oral heritage. While storytelling vanishes from modern, mechanized America, and peters out rapidly with the European stocks who become Americanized, it still thrives with the red man. Through stories he gets his religion, education, entertainment, and history. In spite of public schools, the Indian tribes remain largely nonliterate and must depend for knowledge on the spoken word. On the score of antiquity and supernaturalism and sheer volume, their pagan mythology ranks as the most exciting form of story art alive in our country.

A little effort to understand the Indian mind makes their tales sensible enough. Holding an animistic view of the universe, they believe that animals and plants possess spirits and can speak with men and give them special gifts. Being also shamanistic, they recognize that certain men can traffic with the greater spirits, for good or for ill, and the ordinary mortal must play one such wizard against another. This attitude toward the demon world is not confined to the red man. When Sam Colasacco, the Italian saloonkeeper, described the *fattura* enchantment, he said, "One fellow can tie you up and another what got more power can loosen you up." He could have been talking equally about medicine men or hoodoo doctors or priests. Christianity has not changed Indian ideas much, chiefly because the folk myths underlying the two cultures often dovetail.

American ways have nevertheless affected Indian traditions. They have created an underdog complex which finds a release in sly anecdotes of the red man outwitting the white and in bitter historical memories of massacres and reservation scandals. American slang and similes perforate the speech of bilingual raconteurs, who may consciously slant their tales for Yankee listeners. A Potawatomi told me why the silver dollar bears an eagle: out of respect to an Indian totem; a Sioux triumphantly described an Indian flying machine that preceded the Wright brothers, to prove that "you people got nothing on us." When it comes to fanciful storytelling, rich in natural scenery and comic plots, the Yankee has indeed nothing on the Indian.

Old World lore has moved to the United States with every fresh immigrant settlement. Some of it remains unchanged in its Old Country form, mainly hero legends and history traditions. Some becomes naturalized in the American scene, as when werewolf beliefs get attached to local persons or fairy tales incorporate modern gadgets. Some of the lore grows freshly from the impact of immigrant and native stocks, for example the highly popular dialect stories. And in still another category come certain Old World beliefs which spread widely among all groups and lose any specific ethnic tie: thus the prevalent ideas about bloodstopping and burnhealing. A good part of all this rich tradition continues to be told in the mother tongues, but the Old Country *Märchen* and *Sagen* are continually slipping over the line into English. Often the raconteur is bilingual, and when he is not, his audiences are. One Canadien family I met in Marquette has handed down fairy tales for four generations in French, but the fifth generation's storyteller has switched to English. The cultural crossroads can constantly be seen in the Peninsula children, who reply to their parents' mother tongue in English, or tack Finnish endings on to English verbs to form the hybrid jargon of Finglish.

Both the new American environment and novel juxtapositions of Old Country peoples reshape European tradition. A ragged Italian miner idling in front of a Crystal Falls saloon explained to me how the melting pot brewed in his town. "All kinds here, go to school together, marry each other. Cousin Jack marry Finn, Pole marry Swede, Italian marry Slovak. Now all one."

In the same town a staid, humorless Swedish lady from the Aland Islands produced another insight. "We never had anything to do with the Finns in Old Country. Their officials had to speak Swedish. It was a dishonor to talk with them. Russia had stolen Aland from Sweden and given it to Finland, you see. Then when we came over here and lived with them, we found they were as good people as we were."

The psychology of the Peninsula people in particular, and of American society in general, is bedded deep in this ethnic mix. America has grown from Europeans, and the Peninsula spectacularly illustrates the fact. All Europe commingles in her neighborly towns; besides the dominant Finns, French-Canadians and Cornishmen, you can find Belgians at St. Nicholas, Poles and Bohemians at Iron Mountain, Austrians and Armenians in Escanaba, Greeks in Marquette, Italians in Stambaugh, Danes in Norway, Swedes in Manistique, Czechs in Crystal Falls, Croats and Lithuanians in Ironwood, and even such tiny peoples as Luxemburgers at Escanaba, Slovenians at Shingleton, and Montenegrins at Wakefield. These colonies splotch the countryside with a cultural rainbow, and each contributes its own distinctive folk coloring.

Since folklore is international in many of its aspects, the collector sometimes finds close correspondences between Old World and New World traditions. The "tall tales" usually ascribed to the American genius turn up on the lips of many European storytellers. Peasant folk heroes, like Jussi the Finnish crofter or Janosek the Hungarian outlaw, perform rogueries and escapades very much like Davy Crockett and Jesse James. But for the most part, a native-born American finds himself in a strange world and a different century when he hears the stories of his fellow citizens from the Old Country.

He will feel far more at home in the local traditions that have grown upon his native land.

American history, in its personal and local setting, has flung up hundreds of local tales that linger on the lips of village sages, but never find their way into the printed record. For the most part the community cares little, and talks less, about past presidents and power politics; what concerns it deeply, and flavors its yarning, is the memory of the township crises and the neighborhood characters.

Listen to the talk that flows through the old-timers, and you will hear frequent references to local events that take on the proportion of epics, and to pioneers who loom as demigods. Solemn tales and sly anecdotes cluster around central topics: great disasters and conflagrations, mass panics and riots, odd characters and crackpots, fanatical cults and political frauds, success and failure in careers, infamous acts of outlawry and pioneering sagas of heroism, the hurly-burly of boom towns and the sad decay of ghost towns. This is the history told by the folk, so decorated and inflated in the retelling that the core of plain fact is soon swaddled in fancy, and no outsider dare winnow the truth from the fable.

Within this body of spoken history, special tales become endeared to the village family because of some twist or antic or oddness that capitivates the folk mind. Their mention always provokes knowing smiles or shudders, and any number of inconsistent recitals. Just why certain past events possess this folk appeal, no man can readily say, but the folk knows its taste and selects with fine discernment. The history legend must be salted with some humor, or tragedy, or mystery, it must be human and personal, tied to a familiar name or landmark, and yet slip over into a realm of mystery and wonder. For if the facts were completely known and arrayed, if there were no touch of hearsay and rumor, no element of marvel and even miracle, then there would be no reason to talk, and so no legend.

American society found story materials aplenty in the drama and necessities of frontier life. Each occupation bred its myth, as early exploits acquired the glamor of bygone times and early habits solidified into custom. The backwoods hunter, steamboat pilot, Lakes sailor, plains cowboy, mountain trapper, forty-niner, lumberjack, oil driller, railroader, all grew into myth types and entered American tradition.

The Upper Peninsula brims with such native legend. Her three centuries of history display the varieties of frontier experience, from French and Indian warfare to the wild pioneering surge for timber, ore, and homesteads. Memories of the heroic days burn brightly yet in her fraternal towns, along with the little homely incidents that stick in the mind and pass ultimately into folklore.

PART I
THE INDIAN TRADITION

1

INDIANS STUFFED AND LIVE

THE brightly colored map of Munising and the Pictured Rocks bears many intriguing place names — Caves of the Bloody Chiefs, Bridal Wreath Falls, Bathtub of the Gods, Virgin's Rocks. I asked the Chamber of Commerce secretary for the stories behind the names. "They're just some Indian legends we had to make up for the tourists," he said matter-of-factly.

Mackinac Island off St. Ignace, a tourist mecca, exhibits a Lovers' Leap, Devil's Kitchen, Skull's Cave, Manitou Rocks. Grace Franks Kane wrote some nauseous legends about them in a book called *Myths and Legends of the Mackinacs*. I asked wizened Pat Doud, who had lived his eighty-four years on the island, what about them. He answered indirectly. "A writer like you came here one time looking for material. He said the only Devil's Kitchen he could find was the Mackinac House kitchen." Pat knocked out Lover's Leap with a straight punch. "The warriors went across the water to fight; the beautiful maiden waited day after day; when her man didn't come back she jumped off the rock. I've never seen a beautiful Indian maiden and I've seen 'em all."

Then Pat uncorked some real folklore tales about early brawls between the Irish and the half-breeds. He told one about an Indian who had chased a white woman, was sentenced to jail for six months, and pleaded his own case. "White man come out, have all squaw he want. That all right, all right, all right. Indian try same thing and get hell kicked out of him. Now what's the matter, judge?"

Near Manistique a rectangular body of water framed by the forest attracts thousands of summer visitors, who have seen pictures and postcards of the "Big Spring." The tourist literature describing the Big Spring plays up "legends" of an Indian romance blighted on this spot, and the details are narrated to young and adult audiences by George Bishop, the genial, snowy-haired, impressive-looking director of the Upper Peninsula Development Bureau. His tale, recited with dramatic modulations that range from a deep boom to a stage whisper, contains an unbroken series of sweet clichés. The beauteous Onnandacie (little firefly) and the stalwart Kitchitikipi (I love you) paddled up a stream and came to the Big Spring, where they moored their birchen canoe. "And there, in the moonlight, dreaming, planning, whispering to each other the sweet mouthings of his love, they pledged their troth." But in a playful mood the gal ran out on the trunk of an overhanging tree, and the brave, following hard after, lost his balance and plunked in. When he failed to arise, Little Firefly went off her nut, mumbled "Kitchitikipi" all day long, and eventually took a running jump into the spring, so she could join her dream man in the Happy Hunting Ground. "And to this day, my friends, if you will visit the Spring, of a moonlight evening, in the month of May, when the gentle breezes are moving through the overhanging pine trees and rippling its surface, if you will listen intently, you will hear the waters of the spring murmuring the name of the Indian lover — Kitchitikipi, Kitchitikipi, Kitchitikipi."

The Indians, however, do have a legend about the Big Spring. The Thunder pulled the Serpent up into the sky, leaving a big hole in the ground, which filled with water. Chippewa mythology centers around the conflict between sky and underwater powers.

"Whence these stories, whence these legends and traditions?" Chiefly from the poet himself, even though Longfellow based "Hiawatha" on the genuine Chippewa tales of Schoolcraft (which

I found still flourishing in the same area a hundred years later). But he suppressed the earthy and knavish elements in the tradition, and stressed scenery and sentiment for a public that knew nothing about trickster heroes and thunder birds, and all about sylvan glades and noble savages. Minnehaha and Hiawatha became the models for cliff-leaping lovers in soupy legends localized throughout the country, often served up by the town poetess. Hiawatha (who is an Iroquois, not a Chippewa hero to begin with) and Paul Bunyan represent the same kind of childish pseudo legends fabricated by money-writers and Chambers of Commerce for a gullible public. Ironically, both figures are claimed for their area by Upper Peninsula businessmen, unaware that all about them lies an amazing wealth of living folklore. But the same error exists in the nation at large.

Even the whites who live side by side with the Peninsula Chippewa do not know Indian traditions any more than they know the Finnish or the French Canadian or the Cornish. Most whites despise the red men as whisky-crazed loafers and beggars. A few profess an ethnological interest. In Escanaba I asked the local Indianist, who had made a stir turning up old arrow heads and cave drawings, whether the nearby Indians still told their old tales. I had come fifty years too late, he informed me. But a few days later Alec Philemon dictated stories to me for an unbroken ten hours. At L'Anse I asked the resident Indian agent the same question. Alas, if only I had come a generation sooner, he said, and he began to read from an old Ojibwa history. While he was reading, an enormous Indian stuck his head through the office window and wanted to know if the professor he had heard was in town would like to come to a storytelling social. I went to the social and heard the husky Sioux match lengthy narratives with a fragile Chippewa grandmother until early in the morning.

If the public knows little about Indian folklore, and that mostly nonsense, the specialist knows a great deal. Anthropologists have assembled vast data on the tribal cultures, scrutinizing the red men as they would a herd of seals, clinically, objectively, humorlessly. Indians tell riotously comic stories, but the anthropologist does not laugh; he only records, and their humor, flavor, and humanity die in his ethnological graveyards. Naked texts, divorced from living frames, sound rather like gibberish to casual readers. One suspects even the texts when they read like this: "Some time afterward, Manabozho awoke, and, being very hungry, bethought himself to enjoy the fruits of his stratagem." No Indian, or twentieth century white man either, ever talked like that. I heard the story five times, and the tellers simply said Manabozho woke up and wanted to eat his ducks.

As for the Indian stories themselves, their charm and comedy remain largely unknown to an American public fed on Uncle Remus, Grimms' fairy tales, and Paul Bunyan. Yet, given a little sympathy with the Indian world view, they make good listening. The present-day Chippewa handle English prose much more succinctly and efficiently than the stiffly literal or romantically free interpreters who recorded them in the past. Their stories break crisply into dialogue, the plots march directly to their goal, the details are painted in with sure strokes, often with a fine imagery: "When the bear walk, all the ground wave, like when you walk on mud or on soft moss." And the storyteller takes full advantage of his animistic position, keeping you guessing whether his heroine is a deer or a woman at any given time, and sometimes he does not even know himself. All this gives romance an extra fillip of uncertainty.

Before going to the Upper Peninsula I had never met an Indian. My introduction came very quickly. On the ferry crossing the Straits of Mackinac, a cold, windy, preseason trip with only a handful of passengers aboard, I began talking with a short young man shivering on deck without a coat. He was a Dane named Oscar Birge, returning to his camp in the woods near Hessel after three years in the army, and his nearest neighbors and best friends were Chippewa brothers, Mike and John Sogwin (Yellow Feather). He invited me to come up later in the week to

meet them and gave me some pointers about Indians. For instance: if two are in the room, never speak only to one, or the
other will get insulted. Don't press an Indian to talk until he is
in the mood. When he had finished his *do*'s and *don't*'s I trembled
with trepidation at the prospect of meeting these supersensitive
primitives.

Later in the week I drove from St. Ignace to Hessel, a desolate
cluster of half a dozen shacks, and eventually found my way to
Birge's cabin several miles deep in the woods. He drove me over
to the Sogwins' cabin in the middle of the forest and there I met
my first Indian. Mike, the younger brother, was standing in the
rain tinkering with his jalopy, and Oscar said, "Here is the fellow
I told you about who wants to hear Indian stories." Mike's lips
rolled back from his shining white teeth in a slow grin and, standing there in the rain, without asking us inside or indulging in any
of the amenities, he began telling about Nanabush and the flood.
Perhaps the rain suggested the deluge story, and it looked as if
we might drown before he finished. He told half a dozen tales
right there, while I stared in awe at the big, good-looking fellow,
whose crinkled eyes alone betrayed an alien race. He came back
for supper with us, and retold the adventures of Nanabush so I
could write them in my notebook.

But with elder brother John, grayhaired and pensive, and an
even better narrator, the complications arose. Oscar walked me
over to John's shack, explained my purpose, and fenced for an
opening while I waited uneasily. John seemed miffed because we
had called on kid brother first, and Oscar worked hard at placat-
ing him. Finally John threw out a completely irrelevant question.

"Do they have thunder storms in South America?"

"Sure they do," I broke in promptly, happy to enter the conversation on sure ground, for I had once worked up a course in
Latin American history on two weeks notice. "They have terrific
storms. Clouds traveling west can't get over the Andes, and
so . . ."

Oscar interrupted hastily to say that during the entire three years he had been stationed in England he had heard only one feeble thunder clap. I kept arguing, while John Sogwin looked owlish and clammed right up.

On the way back to his camp Oscar explained that I had cut John off short on the point of a real storytelling streak. If John's question had produced the proper flat denial, he would have gone on to say that thunder storms occurred only around the Great Lakes, where the thunder gods had taken the Chippewa under their especial protection. Then he would have given illustrative stories. But I had spiked his guns. I was heartbroken.

Later we had another try at John, inviting him over to a steak dinner and sitting around the table smoking and talking in the proper convivial masculine atmosphere. But every time Oscar or I asked about Nanabush, John resolutely clamped his jaws. Instead he went into a long discourse on Indian child-training, to explain the religious, educational, and psychological background of the Nanabush "stories," which were his Bible but, he feared, my sport.

After my meeting with the Sogwins I made a bee-line for every Indian village I crossed in the Peninsula, and at each one I struck gold. At Brimley, it was sixty-eight year old John Lufkins, star halfback on an 1898 Carlisle football team that had smeared every team on its schedule, including my Harvard alma mater. John's German immigrant father had bequeathed his son heavy Teutonic features that clashed curiously with his burnt skin. (John's wife, a teen-age beauty in her bridal picture, but now a paralyzed and shriveled old woman who pushed herself around on a chair, mixed Scotch, French, Cree, and Chippewa blood in her veins.) At Nahma Mrs. Joseph Feathers, stately in the midst of squalor, described the Windigo and similar monsters. At L'Anse two dignified Sioux, Jake Duggan and Chief Welsh, married to women who had come from their old enemies, the Chippewa, poured forth Dakota legends.

In Watersmeet a few inquiries immediately led me to little old John Pete, living in the forest at Lac Vieux Desert, a depleted pagan village eight miles from the nearest paved road. John Pete spoke no English, but tall, slender George Cadotte spoke and wrote excellent English, and interpreted John Pete's narratives for me. George at one time had had a fine job as a railroad baggage-checker and lived a white man's life. Coming back to Lac Vieux Desert, he relearned Chippewa and when Indian Bureau agents came around collecting data, he interpreted for them at a handsome fee and strode through town gorgeous in a new store suit. A week after the government men left, George lay sodden in the gutter, his suit a muddy rag and not a dime in his pockets.

Finally at Hannahville, where a group of Potawatomi live by themselves on a dead-end gravel road, I met splendid storytellers. Ninety-four year old Mrs. Elizabeth Philemon, a regal matriarch living alone in a bare shack and weaving wicker baskets for food money, presided over the nearby families, who all seemed somehow related to her. One son-in-law, Archie Megenuph, a former baseball pitcher down in Bay City who still wore a baseball cap perched rakishly backwards on his head, interpreted her stories, for she spoke no English. By a lucky chance I gave Archie a hitch on the road to Escanaba, and drove back to the village with him, while he drank beer out of one bottle and wine out of another, in lieu of whisky, which Indians cannot buy, and which I had churlishly refused to buy for him. During the interpreting, jolly, beefy Archie grew increasingly beatific, his eyes and mouth distended childishly, his head sagged, and suddenly Mrs. Philemon stopped talking. Archie explained that she was grieved at his drinking. He contended that he could still translate coherently, but his mother-in-law told no more tales. Archie atoned by leading me to his cousin, Alec Philemon, the outstanding Hannahville narrator and a human treasury of Indian stories. From several visits with Alec and the others I gathered, in a relatively short time, a whole bookful of traditions, many more than can be printed here.

These meetings with the twentieth-century Indians left me with certain strong general impressions which were repeated on each new encounter. They all live in the woods as if the cities of white men never existed, in tumbledown shacks flimsily furnished, with junky autos lying alongside. This squalor does not represent the poverty or tragedy of the city slums, however, for the Indian is not in the struggle for material wealth, and he has temperamental resources that make life satisfying enough. The swollen family unit provides a common strength, and each dwelling houses a pyramiding group, from barefooted kids to surly youths — often ex-GI's — and varicolored females, up through hangers-on and in-laws to the patriarch. Some of the red folk are degenerate and semi-idiotic, like some whites in the adjacent towns, but the community leaders, who are usually also the storytellers, possess a regal serenity and poise. There may be a lineal basis for this air, for the Sogwins claim descent from Pontiac, and Chief Welsh says he is a grandson of Sitting Bull. These outstanding personalities, unlike the rest, feel the stigma of idleness; the Chief stokes a furnace in the Ford mill, Alec Philemon leaves his family all week to cut cordwood for a jobber, and the Sogwins act as guides for sportsmen who visit the Snows to hunt and fish.

Education and literacy, when they exist, do not curb tribal traditions, but rather sustain them, for worldly wisdom helps rationalize the tribal viewpoint. John Sogwin compared dream-learning to book-learning; both produce power knowledge. In describing the popularity of an Indian hero in a fairy tale, Chief Welsh commented, "I read in the paper where a girl took a bunch of flowers to Sinatra on the stage at Chicago, and then fainted. It was the same order." The marvels of science go to prove the second sight of the medicine men. "They used to tell that there would be a bird that would fly through the air, and a wagon that would run by itself without horses pulling it, a man driving it." In the flood story, the basswood bark strung on trees to catch Winabijou is likened to telephone wires.

Exposure to Carlisle or Haskell or the public high school has not changed the Indians from talkers to readers. They possess still the gift for storytelling and story-listening, with the tenacious memories and effective use of words on which oral art depends. Family and social groups today listen as raptly as past generations to the master speakers. This is oral tradition at its purest, and the narrator usually knows exactly where he has heard his tales. "It used to be the custom for the younger people to go to an old lady or man, and give him tobacco, and listen to stories," said aged Mrs. Philemon, adding, "Now the only time we have meetings is when we have a little beer or wine." Her son Alec, who spellbinds his family with legends, learned them that way. "You give those old men some tobacco, and they'll tell you stories all night. And I never forgot them." Parents and grandparents did their quota of entertaining. "I heard those stories in Sioux from my Dad when I was ten years old," remembers Chief Welsh. "He would tell them until I fell asleep, and when my head started to drop he'd say 'Herbert, wake up.' Some stories lasted three or four nights."

The Indians have a keen and gentle sense of humor. They laugh delightedly at the mishaps of Winabijou. Chippewa and Sioux kid each other much as do Yale and Harvard men, and both kidded me for malpractices of whites. "You come tell us you killed your God, and then you blame us for it." They can turn their jests on the arrogant white man.

"Bishop Whipple would come to my reservation and bring suitcases of presents to the Indians, and distribute them around. On one visit Chief Ish-quay-gwon said to him, 'There is a sick woman a long way off. Do you want to see her?' 'Yes, but will the presents be safe in the tepee?' 'Oh sure, there's not a white man around for forty miles!'"

John Lufkins insists that actually happened on his reservation, although the story can be found in jokebooks. But it doesn't matter; he relished the turn of the joke, and enjoyed this next one too.

Some dude hunters from Lower Michigan stopped off at a

reservation on their way to Canada to look at the Indians. One spoke to the chief through an interpreter, and asked the nature expert what the winter would be like. "Going to be long hard winter." "How do you know?" "White people have big wood piles."

Tales persist in Ontonagon about a poker-faced Indian named Charlie Oley who took white men for an awful ride. An agent for William Rockefeller at Cleveland came up to Ontonagon to look over some potential copper and lumber property, and Charlie as a woods-wise Indian was directed to guide him over the prospect. The party passed a dead hemlock, a miserable thing with limbs right down to the ground and no sawlog timber in it at all. The agent asked, "What kind of tree is that?"

"Porc-pine," said Charlie gravely.

"Will it make lumber?"

"If it is cut at the proper season of the year."

"When is that?"

"When it sheds the knots and shakes."

The agent noted this in his memo book and the group moved on. They sat down in a trench to look at an outcrop of copper, and in rising the agent grabbed an overhanging twig to pull himself up. The twig, a very tough specimen, twisted in his hand as he pulled. "What is that?" the agent asked Charlie in surprise.

"Moosewood."

"Is it good for anything?"

"Yes. Peel the bark up, it acts as emetic, peel it down, cathartic."

The agent swallowed hard on this, and Charlie turned to John Hawley (my storyteller, a grand old Irishman of eighty-five) for corroboration. Hawley said, "I've seen that bark often tied up in a bundle behind an old Indian cookstove, drying." He did not say that this basswood bark served for string and thread.

During the night the agent woke up, very ill. The party had camped on the lonely trail from Nonesuch to Besemer where, back in the Eighties, no habitations stood. Charlie stepped into the breech. "I fix." He boiled some bark into tea, and gave it to the patient. The agent got rapidly worse. To the others Charlie apologetically explained that he must have peeled it both ways, for the man was not only vomiting, but he was also showing a strong cathartic reaction.

No tourists have ever heard of Charlie Oley, I am sure.

2

BEARWALKERS

No one would have suspected that the poised lady in the farmhouse talking in cultured tones belonged to the Chippewa community in L'Anse. Her strain of noble French ancestry (les Picardies des Trois Maisons) showed in her features and bearing, but Nancy Picard knew as her birthright the esoteric Indian beliefs. In fact it was she who first told me about bear-walking.

Nancy Picard speaks

• The night my father died, January 14, 1914 — he had heart trouble and couldn't lie down — some member of the family saw a light at the edge of the woods, way back of the house. It came up from the north part of our place, down to the west, in front along the road and disappeared. It looked like a round ball of light. Some of the family went out to see what it was, but chills crept up and down their backs, and they turned back. Of course since our infancy we had heard about this power of evil, and connected it up. My father never had any enemies, that we knew, but everybody has enemies as they pass through life.

I asked what the enemy had done, and what the round light represented.

A learned man at Odanah, Charles Armstrong, part white and a student of the Indians, told me that there must be something in the bad medicine, because he had seen it make fine women low and lose all sense of shame. The whole proceedings is called the bearwalk. A person who has that power to make people evil or sick can take all forms, especially an owl or a bear. The light appears at the same time. Then the one who sees it gets sleepy, gets sick and dies.

Dan Curtis's daughter took very sick, and it was spoken of that way. People watched all day to keep anyone away. Every night they'd see a light hanging in line with the trees; it would dance around like a flame. An old woman, Mrs. Elijah, tried to get in, time and time again, when the body was in the house. Dan borrowed money to go to Odanah, Wisconsin, to contact a person who had power to counteract the evil. He was afraid the whole family would be wiped out. That new medicine was supposed to kill the effect of the original dose.

It was quite a notorious affair. Even the white people in the county were interested.

Little twelve-year-old Fanchon, Miss Picard's niece and a dreamgirl, added timidly, "To get the power you mix the medicine and walk around the fire a certain number of times."

Down at Dan Curtis's shack I inquired of the deaf little old man what Mrs. Elijah had done to his family. Dan had chattered gaily in telling escapades of Winabijou, but now he turned stony and grim.

"Didn't you go to Odanah to get some medicine from the medicine man there?" I persisted.

"When your children get sick, you go look for medicine, you know. If you hear of someone across the bay, you go see him, don't you? Well, I went to Odanah to get some medicine," Dan said defiantly. "My daughter had baby; easy to kill persons at the time when they have baby. Mrs. Elijah make some medicine, get it in the roots, in the trees, kill people with that medicine."

Dan froze up, but his daughter, a plump, Negroid-looking woman, suddenly began speaking.

Dan Curtis's daughter speaks

• She was a witch. She even did things to white people. And when a person is witched, the doctor can't tell what is wrong. You just waste away, get sick and die. Nothing you can do about it. You could almost always tell a person who had that power: eyes all bloodshot, looked at you cross-eyed, could never look you straight in the face.

I nearly got witched once myself, when I was eighteen or nineteen. I grabbed hold of Mrs. Elijah to give her a lift — she was falling down. And it seemed as if my arm was coming right off. Then a couple of weeks later my arm got numb. I couldn't lift anything with it, and it felt so heavy. Then they got that fellow that could cure the witch-medicine, and he made kind of a plaster out of herbs and roots and stuff like that. He'd hold it on my arm for about half an hour, and then he'd take it off. And then feathers, hairs, beads all come out my right arm. It felt tickling like.

My girl friend who had been walking behind me said after, "Did you see them things she had in her hand? They were her little buckskin bags, with the medicine."

That old Mrs. Elijah died an awful death. She got crazy with all that mischief, and used to bother the white people on the lake shore. One time she went down to Tollison's — he had a big poolroom there — and said she wanted to sleep in it that night. He said no, and she said she'd sleep on the pool table. Finally her son-in-law put her in a shack back of Skanee. She went out in the woods, and her guts were dropping out of her and she hung them on a tree and that's how she died. When they found her they buried her right there — no coffin or anything.

There was another witch, an old lady in Odanah, who made a young girl get sick and die. Some men went to her grave on the fourth night. People claim that the witch always comes to the grave four days after to get back the medicine she used. And they seed the fireball coming all around. They all got scared

and fainted away. But one old man didn't faint. (He just died
here at ninety-eight. Old man Star was his name.) And he heard
this t-r-ump, t-r-ump. And he looked up and seed a bear on the
grave, and it was breathing fire. He grabbed hold of the bear
and it wasn't there — it was the old woman. She had buckskin
bags all over her, tied onto her body, and she had the bearskin
hide on her. (Whoever the witches kill, they take a finger or a
toe and put it in the bags. This old woman used to count up all
her fingers at home.)

The old man was going to kill her, but she said, "Don't kill
me and I'll give you my medicine." So of course he wanted that.
And ever after he was lucky at gambling or whatever he did.

Old Dan Curtis cackled. "Lies, like Winabijou!"

More confidential information about bearwalkers came from
Archie Megenuph, the semiprofessional ball player who had
come back to live with the Potawatomi at Hannahville.

Archie Megenuph speaks

• There were five or six bearwalks here from Wisconsin. We
shot them. They can't kill a white man but they can kill Indians,
so we had to get them first. We wait till they come out on the
road and then shoot at their light — they make a big blare of light.
The Chippewas and the Winnebagoes go in for that still —
they're pagans.

If you don't have the right medicine they put you to sleep,
even if you have a gun, and walk right past you to the patient.
It's as if you were paralyzed. They go every fourth night and
on the sixteenth the patient is finished. You can be in the room
with your wife, and you'll fall asleep when the bearwalk comes
in. You can hear him go out; he goes "Koo-rooo." They can take
any shape, fowl or animal. That grasshopper you kick may be it.
On the fourth night after they kill the patient, they go to the
grave, and you can hear the carcass raise right up out of the
casket, and they cut off the fourth or fifth finger and the tongue

tip, and put it with their victim set. [Mrs. Feathers of Nahma told me the eye, finger, or tongue must come from the right side, and that if the bearwalker can't get to the grave, he dies himself after four months.]

You can catch one if you have the right medicine. You chew and sprinkle the medicine on yourself, and wait for the bearwalk. Then you put your arms around it, and it is all naked, except for a string of beads around the neck. Then it asks you to let it go, promises you anything, to suckhole you, to teach you the bearwalk. Then if you let it go, you go and learn from it, like from a professor. They caught one here once that way. I'd like to be a bearwalk [and big Archie shook with little-boy laughter].

If you shoot them, you can't ever catch them. You can't bring them to your premises, they must always go home to die. You don't find anything when you shoot them either, but they die off some distance.

The local bearwalks about Hannahville that Archie referred to had been actually seen by his cousin, Alec Philemon.

Alec Philemon speaks

• When I was a kid, 'bout seventeen, before they built the highway, there was just an old tote road from here to Bark River to Harris. There was three of us, one a couple years older, coming back from Bark River at nighttime. We saw a flash, coming from behind us. The older fellow said, "It's a bearwalk, let's get it. I'll stand on the other side of the road (it was just wagon ruts) and you stand on this side." We stood there and waited. I saw it 'bout fifty feet away from us — close as your car is now. It looked like a bear, but every time he breathe you could see a fire gust. My chum he fall over in a faint. That brave feller on the other side, he faint. When the bear walk, all the ground wave, like when you walk on soft mud or on moss. He was goin' where he was goin'.

Another time when I was thirteen, fourteen, I was going with my mother and sister to visit a sick woman. We left there about eleven o'clock in the evening, and saw the fire right on the main road (which goes to the church now). My mother and sister fell right over. I caught my mother. She said, "That must have been the bearwalk; it was too much for us." Then she said, "You'll live the longest." My sister fell first, and she died first too. They both died in thè flu, in 1918. Those other two fellers, they're dead a long time too. That woman we visited — 'bout half an hour after we got home we heard the bell ring; that woman was dead.

He who withstands the bearwalk outlives those who pass out. Note how the rule holds in the story told by Dan Curtis's daughter, although she held back the secret. As with the *loup-garou*, which the bearwalk closely resembles, all the personal encounters run true to formula. This is no accident, for Chippewa education impresses the young with the concepts of transformation and of "power," malign or benevolent, human or demonic. These concepts underlie the entire Indian mythology, and make sensible the otherwise childish stories of culture heroes, animal husbands, friendly thunders, and malicious serpents. The bearwalker idea fits at once into this dream world — literally a dream world, for Ojibwa children go to school in dreams. Perhaps the best way to explain this educational theory and technique is to let the Indians do it themselves. Here John Sogwin of Hessel tries in earnest words to interpret one civilization to another.

John Sogwin speaks
• The Indians really made use of their religion. It's like your education, the more you work on it the higher you get it. Well, they worked on their dreams.

One day the kid has to go off in the woods. They have a scaffold for him, so a wolf or a wildcat or a snake won't attack him. At first he goes only a little while, then he goes longer and longer, and he has to fast. To begin with he gets a few berries, then only water. "You drink your water when I come for you," the mother would say. If he goes off and eats, and breaks the rules, he won't learn anything.

If he doesn't break the rules, he'll hear something, a sound, a noise, a language that he will understand. Well, where does it come from? Maybe it's a bird, or a squirrel, or a deer, but this time all at once he understands it. In the dream the animal appears as a person, a man or woman. Not till long after do you learn it is a chipmunk or a bear. The person gives him secret words, a password, and whenever the fellow's in trouble he dances or sings and says the password. Now we go to the telephone and talk person to person, but they didn't have any telephone then, so they had to sing or give the secret word.

Next year the fellow gets up to, say, high school. Every year there is some new lesson. The mother will find it out. The first time she comes she asks, "Did you see anything? little birds, little animals?" "A squirrel came and played around." Well that didn't mean anything, but later he'd say, "Something came and talked to me." "What did it look like and sound like?" So he tells her, and that's one lesson he learned that season. Whatever he sees in the dream he makes an image of, an emblem, what you call it — a totem.

It's really hard to explain, this schooling. Some get more power than others, like in your school everybody doesn't get the same marks. Those that really had power became chieftains. My grandfather was a chieftain, but not my father. (Great men are not always born from great men, you know; you are born over and over and sometimes you are born from some doggone fool.) They tested the power in the big powwows they had in the fall and in the spring, like an attorney has to be admitted to the bar.

If they'd never dropped this Indian stuff, what a wonderful thing it would be — if a fellow could still bring rain, for instance. It's too bad they dropped their religion, or whatever you want to call it.

Combine the power of suggestion on the part of the mother (Did you see any little animals or birds?) with the boy's weakened, fasting state, and the business makes some sense. A few further details on dream education (supplied here by Alec Philemon) will bring the bearwalk into focus

• You know, some time ago, just like we send our little ones to school, the Indians have their little ones learn something through their dreams. They give black coal, charcoal, every morning to little boys and girls, and tell them not to eat a couple of days till they dream something. They promise that little one, "If you dream something that's worthwhile, you'll eat tomorrow." And some of these young ones didn't eat for five days. Sometimes they dream nothing, sometimes they dream a man coming. Maybe he got a couple feathers on his head. Well, he commences to talk to this boy and girl. He says, "I'm giving you my power. Tomorrow morning you'll see me." Well, the morning comes, the young fellow wakes up, and he sees a deer standing there, a big buck. Those feathers he dreamed were the horns. Then again somebody else dreams he sees a naked man, striped red, white, and blue — that's the Thunder. The man tells him, "You'll hear me." When the fellow wakes up he hears a thundershower.

Now it's an awful power on that Thunder. Anybody blessed by the Thunder can save a person who's been shot, if he gets there with his medicine before the bleeding has stopped. Or when the Indians want to cross a big bay in their canoes, and it's windy and breathing heavy, this fellow will call on the Thunder to make the wind quiet. Or if it's raining too much, he'll burn some tobacco in the fire and ask the Thunder to stop. Or if it's dry and everything burned up, he'll ask the Thunder to make it rain.

The porcupine, rabbit, beaver, bear, sucker, they all got power if you dream of them, from the fish to the elephant. You can dream even of Christ, even of God, or the Devil (that's how they change the Indian religion you see.) The Devil has more power than anyone else, he wants to own a lot of people. He'll learn you how to steal, gamble, lie, drink, all that bad stuff. There's a hundred and thirty-two people on this reservation; tonight there may be ten, fifteen at the church. Where's the others? It's all the Devil's work. They think it's fun to go to dances and play cards and drink.

Today well educated men use their brains, then they used their dreams. I seen one old feller, he'd take a drink of liquor, fill his pipe with tobacco, smoke, put his head down, maybe go to sleep. After about five minutes he tells you where the lost thing is. If somebody's sick, he'll tell you how long he's got to live.

In the dream they claim the bear is bad stuff. He learns you how to kill somebody. This man in the dream has some part of him like a bear, a little claw, or a tooth, or an ear, or a little bear hair. And you say to it, "I want to be a bear." And he has the power, in his medicine bag, to make you a bear. Then if you got some enemy you want to kill you can do it, see. That's what they call bearwalking.

Another mystery often discussed concerns love magic. So Aunt Jane Goudreau, snappy and positive, gossips with her chum Jenny Belanger, timid and wispy, about bygone love affairs.

Aunt Jane Goudreau speaks

• Indians got all their medicine out of the woods. They would fix up love powders in someone's wine or tea and make the girls chase right after them. Did I try and find out what root they used!

I remember an Indian that used to work for us who married a white woman. He was an odd-looking critter — the LeVakes were all a shiftless, draggy lot. She was an old aunt of ours, Alice Petouche Vallier, and she hated him so she couldn't eat with him. If he was at the table she wouldn't sit down. All the boys made fun of him, but he kept talking about her, and bragged down at the docks, "That's all right, you just wait; I'll have her chasing right after me. All I have to do is go to the woods behind my house and dig up some roots and make some powder." And by God, all of a sudden that old maid turned around and married him! Then he about starved her to death.

I've heard stories like that lots of times. They say that's why so many Indians married white girls.

Jenny Belanger speaks

• I had someone try to do that to me. When Willie was courting me he'd always bring some candy or maple sugar, and once he even brought a bottle of wine. Ma wouldn't let me eat any of it; she gave me some other candy instead. Someone else could eat his candy all right, because the powder only works for the one intended. When he saw I wasn't taking his stuff he stopped coming. His grandmother kept telling my mother, "Oh Willie will have Jennie, Willie will have Jennie." That's how ma knew what Willie was up to.

Some time later I had a great-niece of Aunt Jane in my folk-lore class. She did a little family investigating for me, and identified the love root as the bluebell, to be prepared with this caution: the male plant must be used on women, and the female on men.

During an Indian "social" in L'Anse where stories poured out all night, Chief Welsh got on the subject of love medicine. In fact he had lost his first girl because of the powder, and he related the incident without any reserve before his wife.

Chief Welsh speaks

• When I was at Howe Military School, I used to dance with Emma. But one night Ernest Chapman had a special date with her. I had a car and drove her home, and he followed on his horse in a peeve. After I left he used the medicine on her; she told me so. She said, "Herbert, I can't date you any more, I've been given the powder."

The Chief's father had been an Episcopal minister on a Sioux reservation, and thereby hung another love story.

• Every Sunday I used to go out to the church to play on the organ and help them sing. That was at Fort Totten, North Dakota, in 1929. I met a heavy-set fellow there name of Gray, who wanted to court with this Dora. But she was looking for a slim fellow. He went home, fixed up the medicine, put it in some Ben Hur perfume and sprinkled it on his handkerchief. Then at a church dance at her house, he dropped the handkerchief as he was leaving. Dora noticed that nice, pretty, big blue-red-yellow Western silk handkerchief, and put it on her shoulders to try it. Then she smelled the perfume and held the handkerchief to her face. Two weeks later my father married them.

As if reading my mind, the Chief added, "If you misuse that medicine — say by trying it on a married person — it affects the person who is trying it."

A little later in the evening I saw a handkerchief lying on the floor and picked it up to give to the hostess's daughter, a handsome, peppy girl in WAC uniform. One Indian giggled and said, "Be careful, she's trying to give you the powder," and the whole group laughed pleasantly.

At another village Alec Philemon gave me some more wrinkles on the love chase.

Alec Philemon speaks

• Long time ago, if you like a woman and she doesn't love you, and sasses you, you get some canary root and shave it fine. Sprinkle that root on yourself and next time she says "Go away," just push on her shoulder. Then go away, but after a while she'll say, "I want to see that man." And she'll go after you.

If you rub that root on your hook you can make fish and animals come to you. You know a canary's a nice bird, sings pretty. If you see a canary you'll want to go up and look at it. Well, it's the same way with the deer and the bear, when you use the root.

They'll come up to look at you, you aim your gun, down they go. It's like you were a big canary. I looked all over for that root, never could find it.

Those who think the Indian claims for love powders weird or exaggerated might try objectively reading any current perfume ad.

TRICKSTERS AND THUNDERS

Episodes from the great race battle between the white and red man get wrapped in the Indian imagination and enter their legendary history. Other traditions concern savage intertribal wars.

The infidelity of white agents and commanders has burned deeply in the Indian mind. Mike Sogwin heard his greatgrandmother and greatgrandfather tell how the United States Government kidnapped Chippewas and dumped them on a Kansas reservation. The officials invited the Indians to banquet on shipboard, down in the hold, then closed the hatches and sailed up the Lakes. Since the Indians had nothing with them, the Government men gave them blankets, infected with smallpox germs. When the Indians died off, the agents never reported the deaths, so that they could continue to collect the Congressional allotment of so much per head.

Chief Welsh gives a new slant on Custer's last stand. (His uncle would draw him a picture of it on canvas.) The Sioux used to sit on the embankment and watch the train, a huge novelty to them, pull in to Fort Lincoln where Custer was stationed, out of Bismarck, North Dakota, along the Missouri River. Custer, quite a drunkard, had been trying to stir up trouble, and his soldiers kept approaching the Indian girls. One time they tried to dismount two girls riding ponies with two boys. The girls got away, but one of the boys was battered, and the other was never found. At target practice, on a range near the railroad track, the soldiers would shoot Indian ponies for fun. One day Custer came out to the range a little under the influence, and shot an Indian woman sitting on the bank waiting for the train. She had a baby in her arms, and his bullet went through the baby's heart and killed them both.

In great anger the Mad Bears, the Kanel, and other Sioux tribes from Bismarck to Fort Yates assembled and followed Custer up the Missouri River to Montana. Scouts located him, and the tribes went at the soldiers hot and heavy, with the well-known results.

In more pleasant vein, the Potawatomi matriarch Elizabeth Philemon recounted a "leegend" from colonial times, when an Indian with power aided the Americans against the French. In gratitude the Americans then stamped the eagle, this Indian's protective dream bird, on their coins. Thus the red men record history in their own terms and, naturally, to their own credit.

WHY THE SILVER DOLLAR BEARS AN EAGLE

• A long time ago the Indians decided to find out who was making that big noise and light up in the sky. The medicine man told the chief to dance for two nights steady. At that time the Indians had the power of going places just like spirits, so the chief worked up his power from the dance, and he was able to take the others up over the mountains into the sky. And they found it was a big bird making the lightning. When they came back home the young chief had to go out in the woods ten days fasting. He almost starved to death. At the end of the ten days, the bird formed himself like a human being and came up to the young man. He said, "Unto this day I will give you the power," and he gave him a tomahawk, with a ball on the end to kill people, and a rare little stone to make a fog.

About then the war broke out between the French and the Americans. The big battlefield was down towards New York, toward the ocean. The French were getting victorious, so the Americans called on the Indians to help them. With his stone, the chief brought on a fog, and when the French couldn't see him he killed nearly all of them with his special tomahawk. After they won the war, the American general called on the chief, and asked him where he got his power. "From the eagle." (That's what the Indians called the thunder and lightning birds.) When the white men realized that, they were so thankful they put that eagle on the silver dollar and the half dollar and the quarter, and they put the Indian on the penny.

That chief's name was Neshawsogenebbi. It means eight feathers; he wore them in the war. Oh, he lived a long time, two hundred years. The Potawatomi moved from Chicago to Milwaukee (Manniwok in Indian) during his time. Finally he couldn't lead himself around any more, and he knew he was going to die. One morning he told his household, "Today I'm leaving. I'm going back where I came from." Then he advised his children, "Put a mat woven with grass outside, and also my tobacco and pipe, and my flint too." It was a lovely morning when they prepared him. Then in the afternoon the thunderclouds showed up. He said the birds were coming for him. The thunderclouds dipped low, and after they passed, he died.

My great-grandfather used to tell us that the birds were our friends, and would kill the snakes and the dragons. You remember Jehovah said, "I will send a bird to kill the dragons." So at a certain length of time the clouds pass over a place and you see the fire going into the water. The birds are killing the dragons.

WARS BETWEEN TRIBES

An Indian with power could disperse as well as create a fog. Jake Duggan, a Sioux now happily married to a Chippewa woman in L'Anse, tells how a Sioux chief raised a fog concealing the enemy's camp at Mille Lacs by crying "Vuuuu," his war cry, three times. Then the warriors rushed on the Chippewas and butchered all the women, children, and old men.

The Chippewa had to contend with Iroquois on the east besides the Sioux to the west. At one time the Iroquois pushed as far north as St. Ignace, and quarreled continually with their neighbors below the Straits. A warrior of each tribe met on the ice with a Chippewa girl they were both dating. They argued, and the Iroquois said, "Let's each take half." He chopped the girl in half, and gave one half to his rival. The Chippewas rose up and smote the Iroquois at Bay's Mills, killing even the babies, till Iroquois heads covered half a mile across the sand beach. So says Mike Sogwin.

A white man, old-timer John I. Bellaire of Manistique, preserves this tradition of the Sturgeon War between the Chippewa and the Menomini.

The Menominees used to occupy the Green Bay-Escanaba territory. To get their winter supply of fish they drove stakes across the Menominee River near the mouth, about one-half mile upriver. The water was just knee deep, so the young men could then easily spear the sturgeon, while the women and old men cut them up into chunks, smoked them and packed them.

The Chippewas sent a young boy down to ask if they would let some sturgeon go upriver. The Menominees took a finbone of a sturgeon (ten or twelve inches long, rubbed sharp on a stone and used as a skinning knife), stuck it between his scalp and his hair, and sent him back covered with blood. The Chippewas went on the warpath and killed every Menominee. Now every old Menominee grunts "Ugh" at the mention of Chippewa.

WINABIJOU THE TRICKSTER

You can spot a Chippewa by saying "Winabijou" and seeing his automatic laugh — not a guffaw, not a smirk, but a chuckling grin of recognition, such as Bob Hope's name might bring to the lips of a radio and movie fan. The analogy won't bear much pressure, for Winabijou is a serious culture hero as well as a comedian, endowed with considerable power, and he belongs to a legendary antiquity. He lies at the heart of Ojibwa mythology, and his adventures provide explanations of the world's creation, the traits of animals, the properties of plants, and other facts and forces in nature. On another plane his escapades provide the family with surefire humorous entertainment. Winabijou is a regular rascal, always hungry, scheming, greedy, and an old "letch" to boot, not above seducing his own daughter. The Indians know his character, relish his predicaments, and applaud his come-uppances.

Some of his scrapes are laughable for any audience. In the flood story Winabijou takes refuge on top of a pine tree, and there sits with his face barely above water. I could not quite understand the point of the situation. Dainty Mrs. Holliday finally told me the point, for she had expurgated the story in the first telling. It seems that when she reached that episode she looked around at the others in the group, nodding and winking and tacitly asking, "Shall I tell the professor?" They shook their heads in a strong negative. I had my head buried in my notebook scribbling down her words, and saw none of this. Later in the evening our inhibitions somewhat relaxed, and she added the omission. The flood waters eddying around the treetop kept floating Winabijou's excrement back in his face as he tried to blow it away, while holding desperately on to the submerged branches with his hands. Thus was Winabijou punished for his mischief-making.

All North and South American Indians know the trickster, under varying names. Even with one tribe, like the Ojibwa, the generic name changes slightly in nearly every village. Longfellow spelled it Manabozho, which, accented on the first syllable, sounds much like Winabijou, the form I found most prevalent.

THE FLOOD

Listening to a living tale of the Deluge and Creation gives one a queasy feeling. Here is Genesis before anyone wrote it down. While this myth does not come first chronologically in the Winabijou cycle, it leads in popularity. The plot hinges on Winabijou's search for the killers of his chum, the Wolf, his vengeance, and the reprisal the gods then visit on him. I give here two versions, since the first has details on the killing of the Wolf not in the longer account.

The Wolf is Killed (Mike Sogwin)

• In the early days the Wolf came to live with Winabijou, like a dog, you know. Every day the Wolf would go out with his bow and arrow to bring in the meat, to "bring home the bacon." Maybe he'd get a deer. So the other animals got jealous because the Wolf wasn't doing any work; he'd just bring in the meat and then take it easy while they fixed it up. So they decided to kill him.

Next morning Winabijou wakes them up and the Wolf goes out as usual. (This was some time in the winter.) He sees a pretty spotted white deer. Winabijou says, "Why don't you get it, it would make a nice hide." But when the Wolf gets close, the fawn starts to run away. It stops and turns around to look, and when it sees the Wolf coming it runs some more. (The fawn was in the plot you see.) The deer runs to the lake where the trap was; it was ice covered with snow, but with some watery holes under the snow. The Wolf falls in and gets drowned.

Winabijou is ready for breakfast, and wonders where his chum was. He waits four days, and has no eats. So he gets mad and says he is going to kill all the animals. So they decided to give him back the Wolf — they knew he was dead of course. Winabijou says to the Wolf, "You're just a ghost, you know; you take care of the dead people and I'll take care of the live."

That's why people die now. It's the same thing as Adam and Eve. If the animals hadn't killed Winabijou's chum, people wouldn't die today, and the world would be overcrowded.

Winabijou Looks for the Wolf (John Pete)

• The Wolf was Winabijou's adopted brother, and killed meat for him, always moose. The other animals had to dry it, hang it up, and smoke it, and that displeased their friends the gods. So one day the gods thought they'd get him. They enticed him to take a trail across the river, he fell through a hole in the ice and was swimming near the entrance of their cave down below, and they grabbed ahold of him. They kept him captive quite a while, then killed him.

Next morning Winabijou started out to look for him. The trails of the previous hunts led home, but he finally struck one which led to the hole in the ice. Then he started to cry, and tears fell down his cheeks. Now he wanted revenge, so he wished that the Thunders (the good gods) would send the summer warmth right away, to bring the Serpents (the bad gods) up from their cave. In four days the ice melted and the river began to flow.

Then he started searching the river for likely remains. He looked up and saw a kingfisher sitting on a sharp cliff, looking down at a pool of water. Every once in a while he'd see the fragments of the Wolf and sneak down and get them. Winabijou asked the king-fisher why he was looking so intently. Finally the kingfisher told him that he was eating the Wolf who had been killed by the gods in a cave close by, underneath the ground. Winabijou wanted to know if they ever came out of there to travel around. "Yes, they come out to bask in the sun in a clearing, but they are closely guarded by snakes and birds and turtles, so it is hard to surprise them." Winabijou said he would pay him for that information, and he gave him a necklace of shells which had belonged to the Wolf. That is why the kingfisher has a white band around his neck today.

But Winabijou was angry because the kingfisher had been eat-ing part of his brother. So he asked him to come down and sit beside him, so he could ask some more questions. But Winabijou really wanted to twist his neck. When he grabbed at him the king-fisher flew away, and Winabijou just caught a tuft of hair. So now the kingfisher's head has a tuft sticking up.

Next day Winabijou asked for good hot weather to bring the gods out. He was at the pool way ahead of daylight, and started making a bow and arrow and spears. He wanted the water boiling hot, and sure enough it started to steam. But the gods have many sentinels, and they showed up first — lizards, snakes, crocodiles. They stretched out on the grass: "We'll have a good sleep here." Winabijou turned himself into a charred stump, an old hemlock stump, quite high. Pretty soon the gods came up, in the shape of bears. One was a big brown bear, the other was a white one. The sentinels said to them, "Everything is prepared for you to bask here." Brown bear looked around — "I never noticed that stump before." "Oh yes, that's been there." "Oh no, I'm going over to see." So he walked over there and clawed the charred stump from the top down, scraping the bark off. After the fourth time the bear walked off, saying "No, that's a stump." Winabijou was afraid he couldn't stand that clawing and would scream out. He kept his bow right against his body, so it wouldn't be seen. The sentinels kept arguing back and forth. "That's a stump." "No, it isn't a stump." Finally the big black boa constrictor walked over and wrapped himself around it three or four times, and started to tighten up. Winabijou didn't dare make a move, but he was just about choked up when the snake let go. The boa constrictor said, "That's a stump."

"Well, we're all going to have a sleep." But one little turtle wasn't satisfied, kept looking at the stump to see it move. Finally he went to sleep too. So Winabijou came over and shot the brown bear with the speared arrow, right under the forepaw, in the vitals. The bear went "Poh." Then he shot the white bear, saying "You're the ones that ate my brother up." All the animals jumped into the river, afraid, and dug for their cave. The bears went with them, the arrows still sticking in them; they weren't killed outright.

Winabijou goes off on his wanderings again. He put a reed around his head to disguise himself. An old toad-lady comes along, carrying a lot of basswood bark. She was inquisitive and accused him, "You are Winabijou." "No, I'm not Winabijou," he said in a singsong voice. "Don't you know what would happen to us if I were Winabijou?" He was trying to trick her into answering, he wanted to find out all she knew. She began singing, "Winabijou shot the Ogema (the gods), I'm going to draw the spears out of their sides." He tried to find out more and asked her, "What are you going to do with all that basswood?" She said, "We're going to tie up the earth with it, and string it around the world like telephone wires. When Winabijou touches the strings, the gods will know where he is and ask for water, to flood him out."

She kept suspecting he was Winabijou, and turned to go. So he picked up part of a root, hit her on the head, and killed her. (The blow knocked her swelling down, so the toad is little today; he used to be big like the other animals.) Then he cut the inside out of her and put on her hide and clothes, and went on to the kings' place. They lived in a regular wigwam now, above ground, for the summer. The sentries saw him and thought he was the old toad, and told him the kings were in bad shape, and he should come along right away. Winabijou sang a song like the old woman, "I'm going to draw out the arrows." Then he said, "I'm going to do it different this time. Everybody get out, I'm going to do it all alone. It's getting serious now."

When he was alone with the kings he grabbed the arrows and pushed them further inside, tearing and twisting until he had killed them. "You are the ones who killed my brother!" he said as they lay there dying.

He noticed the Wolf's hide over the door so he took it along with him. When he came out they all knew right away who he was. The flood started. Winabijou kept running on higher land, but the water followed him. He saw a badger and asked him to dig a hole where they could hide, and promised to paint him up nice. (Like with lipstick. The badger has stripes across his face today, you know.) But in the hole the badger made a vile smell, so Winabijou got mad and killed him. Then he had to go on again.

Every time he got to a higher level the water rose some more. Finally he reached the summit of a hill where a big pine tree was standing. He asked it if he could find refuge there, by sitting on the branch. The tree said, "That's what you get for all your wrong-doing. Now the gods are mad at us and we'll all perish." But he let Winabijou climb up the branches to the top. The water rose up to his mouth. He asked the pine tree, "Can't you stretch a little?" The tree stretched four times its own height. "That's all I can do for you." The water rose again till it came up to his mouth, and stayed there. Winabijou sat on a branch holding on to the tree-top with his hands, just able to breathe above water. He had to evacuate, and an evil current floated his stuff back to him, so he had to keep blowing it away as it swirled around the tree. That was part of his punishment for his killing of the gods.

Now the water animals showed up. They had nowhere to go, because the land was all covered with water, and they were tired swimming around. So Winabijou asked the loon to dive down and bring him up some earth. The loon went down and stayed a long while; then his body came up feet first, drowned. Winabijou blew on him to revive him. Next to go down was the otter. He was gone quite a little while, and drowned too. Winabijou brought him to life by breathing on him. Next to go down was the muskrat. He was the longest of any. All he could do was grab with both paws and feet on the bottom, and was lucky enough to hang on to some earth. He floated up drowned, but still had the earth in his paws and feet. Winabijou blew on him too to bring him back. Then Winabijou took the earth, dried it out in the sun, and threw it out over the water. It turned out to be a little island.

All the water animals went there to make their home. In order to reward them he told them what they could eat — the muskrat could eat rushes, the loon could eat muck from the bottom, the otter could eat fish. Then he sent the fox around the island to see how big it was. The first day he came back early in the morning. The second day he came back a little later. After a week or so he didn't come back until late in the afternoon. On the tenth day he didn't come back at all. (That's why you often see a fox trotting alongside the shore today.) Then Winabijou knew the world was ready for living. He called to the gods above and below to come down and live on this earth. That's Christ and the Devil. He wanted them to be in trouble.

The Flood story is the Chippewa classic, which I heard six different times. The main incidents always remain the same, but details vary. George Pine of L'Anse — so old and tottery he can rise to his feet only with a supreme effort — said that when the wolf jumped over the little stream, he landed in the middle of the Pacific Ocean, and the big animals in the ocean killed him. George ends up the history saying, "We're on four lengths of a big pine tree." Rose Holliday ends with Winabijou grinding the sand between his palms until he had a large handful, then throwing it over the water saying, " 'Let there be land.' A bunch of islands grew up. Was it the Apostle Islands or the Thousand Islands?" Mike Sogwin documents the growth of Winabijou's island with his own Hessel shoreline, which has steadily expanded in his lifetime.

The Sogwins localize the serpent shooting in their own neighborhood. Nanabush knelt down on the beach at High Rollway and shot his arrow twenty-seven miles across the Straits to Cross Village (an Indian reservation) in the Lower Peninsula. You can see the prints of his knees in the sand today, in two large hollows. John disagrees with brother Mike, saying they are the marks of his buttocks — which shows how tradition can vary even within one family.

At certain points in the narrative the tellers and listeners always break into laughter. They do so when Winabijou plunges the arrows deeper into the Serpents, while pretending to pull them out, a description accompanied by graphic gestures of twisting and prodding; when the bear claws and the snake squeezes the stump into which Winabijou has changed himself; and of course when Winabijou sits helplessly on top the pine tree puffing at his own excrement. But towards the text *in toto* they are devout and serious fundamentalists.

On the level of entertainment, the adventure of Winabijou that always provokes the most laughs has to do with his attempt to catch and cook some ducks (or geese, or swans). But even in a funny story his actions leave permanent marks on plants and creatures.

The Duck Dinner (Alec Philemon and Rose Holliday)

• One time Winabijou was walking along as usual looking for food, when he sees a lot of geese, ducks, and mudhens swimming around in a lake. "What can I do to get them?" he thinks. So he went up to the woods and made a big shed. Then he walked back to the bay with his packsack, and one of the ducks asked, "Winabijou, what you got in that sack?"

"I got some songs from out West."

"Sing us some songs," the ducks asked.

"Come on up to the shack and I'll sing."

So they all went up to the shack. Winabijou told them, "Shut your eyes or they'll turn red. You'll look good with red eyes!" Then he chased them over to the wall, and he sat by the door. He wanted to get them all. So he took up his drum, and told his friend the stork, "When I start to sing you sing too, and I'll let you go free." Winabijou begain to sing, "Quay-quake-shimoke, quay-quake-shimoke," and the stork copied him. (That's the way the stork sings today.) The birds danced around the shack, and as they came close Winabijou grabbed them and twisted their necks. The stork kept singing and tapping with his long flat feet, to cover any sounds. After a while the mudhen — who looked like the other ducks then — opened one eye just a little. He saw what was going on and yelled out, "By God, Winabijou is killing us!" Half the birds were dead already. Winabijou chased him and kicked him from behind. Now the mudhen has red eyes and a hump in his back.

The rest of the birds flew off, and Winabijou let the stork fly away too, and began to clean the birds. He built a good hot fire on the sand beach so he could roast them, and then buried the birds in the hot sand, with their legs sticking up. While they were baking he thought he'd take a little nap. To make sure nobody would steal the ducks he set a watchman — his rear end. He told it to let him know if anybody came around.

During his nap the Winnebago Indians passed by and saw the smoke. "Hm, Winabijou is roasting something." They went over and dug the birds and took them away, leaving just the legs in the sand. The watchman tried to warn Winabijou but he slapped it and told it to be quiet. "Don't bother me." When he woke up, he was hungry. He couldn't make up his mind which end to start eating from. [Business of walking back and forth.] Finally he pulled one duck up: "Oh it's so well done the feet come right out." He ate them: "Ah, well cooked." He dug in the sand for the rest of the duck, but there wasn't any more. "Oh my, my." He pulled up the other ducks and it was the same thing with all. Winabijou was furious and started to beat his watchman. "I'll fix you for this," he told it. He lit a great big fire, straddled it, and burnt his rear end till it was sizzling.

His rear end hurt so bad he started to run away from it. He ran along the shore with his intestines trailing behind. Every once in a while he'd stop, break them off, and curl them around the tree trunks. "People will eat you now," he said. (That's lungwirth; it's used for cough medicine.) The blood from his rear end colored the willows, so they are red now. "That will be of use, too." (Kinnikinnick is made from the red willow.) Now the Indians eat Winabijou's dirty stuff when they are sick.

Aunt Jane Goudreau explains how some green willows became red — *la hore rouge* — with Winabijou's own words. "One time I was out in the woods and I was 'caught short.' The only branch I could reach was a green willow. I started to wipe myself with it, and it made me bleed. And ever since, the willow turned red."

Mike Sogwin ends with Winabijou wiping his pained rear all over the ground, making the dogwood red and brown. Then Winabijou says, "Let the Indians use that for medicine."

John Lufkins declares that the inside bark of the red willow is a sure cure for diphtheria. "Steep it as strong as you can, and then let the patient gargle it. I told that to one of the best doctors in the Soo."

In his serious role as earth creator and Ojibwa protector, Winabijou commands respect, and Mike Sogwin here tells how he maintains this role up to contemporary times. Although the Western journey to visit the culture hero is a widespread tale, Mike believes the expedition started out from his own home town.

Winabijou Goes West (Mike Sogwin)

• So Winabijou goes West, says he is finished, is going to a rock formation, because the white man is coming. He says he will always be glad to see the younger generation though. About four or five hundred years ago the last bunch went out. He asked them what they wanted. Some asked to live one, two, three, or four hundred years; others asked for medicine and things like that. The old people had told the boys before they went out, "Don't ask any more than four lives — four hundred years." But some of the boys made up their minds they wanted to live the rest of the world. So Winabijou changed them into black granite — the only rock that never changes or rots.

In my mother's time one guy went out and asked for four hundred years. On the way back with the party a grizzly bear tore him all up into pieces. The rest saw that happen and ran away while the bear was destroying their comrade. When they went back they saw him all together again, but scarred up. Winabijou had brought him together again to finish his four hundred years. In the village he never wore any clothes, just a little diaper, so everyone could see the scars. Oh, he was terribly marked. My mother saw him, so it must have been so. That was the last bunch that ever went out from around here.

IKTOMI AND THE FRUITS

At one memorable tournament of storytelling I heard an Ojibwa and a Sioux of the Teton Dakota tribe swap their trickster tales. A few Sioux have intermarried with their erstwhile mortal enemies and come to live in the Upper Peninsula. After Mrs.

Holliday finished with her adventures of Winabijou, Chief Welsh commented, "We have a similar character out West we call Iktomi, the Spider," and launched into his own tribal cycle.

But first he apologized. "I will have to make a private appointment with the professor for the story of Iktomi and the fruits," he told us. We protested and urged him on. When the chief began relating Iktomi's physical discomfitures from overeating, in his gentle, dignified manner, the plot situation was so unexpected, and his underplay delivery so effective, that I collapsed with laughter, and the rest of the group was only a little less restrained.

Chief Welsh speaks

• A story I've heard in the Dakotas is how he ate four or five varieties of fruit. Iktomi starts out from a community and runs short of food. He goes out scouting for something to eat. He comes to some big plants. "Well, brother, what kind of plant are you?" "Wild turnip." "Well, are you good to eat?" "Yes, but if you overdo it, you'll be in trouble." "What kind of trouble?" "Expelling gas." "If it's food, I'll eat it, and I'll be all right."

So Iktomi eats, eats, stretches, feels good, looks for something more to eat. Starts expelling — wanh, wanh, wanh (Oh, oh). He looks back, nobody is behind. He thinks somebody is talking. He goes along, pretty soon another, and another, and it comes out regularly. He can't stand on the ground when the explosion comes. "The turnips were right." Finally he lays himself on the ground, holds onto a stump, holds on with all his might. He thinks, "It's all over" — then another comes.

Finally he walks on, comes to rosebuds. "What's your name?" "Rosebud; if you eat too much you'll get itchy — rectum-piles." "Well, I can eat this, nothing will happen, I'm too tough." He overstuffs himself, so he barely can walk. Gets itchy, starts to scratch. "Well, it's the truth." Walks, stops, scratches, rubs up and down against the tree, no good at all. Finally grabs hold of a tree with rough bark, sharp thorns — a thorn-apple. Gets a branch of that, scratches so hard he pulls out his intestines, his gizzard.

He gets well again, walks along, comes to choke cherries. Sees them hanging on a tree, nice and black. "Brother, what kind of fruit are you?" "Choke cherry, if you eat me and overdo it, you'll be sick." "What kind of sickness?" "Constipation." Wouldn't believe it, so he stuffed himself with cherries. Walks along, wants comfort, tries in one place, can't do it, tries another. "Well, I'll walk along, maybe walk it off."

Comes to pretty red cherries. "Brother what kind of fruit are you?" "Buffalo-berries. If you eat me, you'll have trouble." "I don't believe it, I have had all kinds of trouble." "You'll have loose bowels." Overstuffs himself, walks along. Berries start to work, his bowels moved so much he got awfully weak, could barely walk. "I've had a lot of trouble, guess I'll go home."

Going home, he comes to a little knoll, sits down and rests. A member of the village comes along, and Iktomi asks him what the object is he's sitting on. "Coyotes' manure." That was the end. Iktomi died cold [fainted].

"I've heard that lots and lots of times," the Chief added. "Someone would say, 'Want to hear a funny story about Iktomi?' "

THUNDERS AND SERPENTS

The gods in the sky protect, the monsters underneath harm. That thinking runs through all the Chippewa legends, and the Christian ones too: God power above, devil power below. The aerial spirits are known as the Thunders or Thunderbirds, and are occasionally identified with the eagle, doubtless from American influence; Mrs. Feathers in the following story thinks they are winged Cupids. A term for the land and water monsters presents more difficulty, and they usually are called Serpents or snakes, sometimes lions or tigers, or they retain the Ojibwa name, as do the Mishibiji and Windigo. These monsters are of different sorts, but in common they prey on Indians, who look to their friends above. The Thunders then fight the Serpents, and when the lightning swoops down into the waters of Lake Superior, the battle is in progress.

Windigoes and Cupids (Mrs. Joseph Feathers)

• A man and his wife lived in a wigwam way out in the woods. She was expecting a child. He went out hunting and when he came back a few days later he found part of the wigwam torn down and hairs and pieces of buckskin dress lying on the ground. And he saw great big man tracks. Then he knew his wife was eaten up.

He went out again hunting and when he came back he saw little wee tracks all around by the ashes of his fire, baby feet. Another time when he came back he saw a little wee baby standing under the bunk, and he tried to catch him but he couldn't. He grabbed again, and spoiled him as soon as he touched him, and tamed him down. Then he saw another one and grabbed him too. He tried to feed them with what he ate, meat stuff, but they would only eat broth. They could talk like big people, though.

This man didn't know what to do with the babies. Next time he was going hunting, they said, "You must make us each a bow and arrow so we can hunt with you." He thought they just wanted to play with him inside the wigwam, so he made them some little bows and arrows. When he came home he found them standing on the edge of the hearth, and saw little sticks stuck in the ground with snakes' hearts on them. "Where did you get those hearts?" he asked them.

"Oh, we went down to the big pond and found the snakes there and killed them and took their hearts out."

He said, "You must never go down to the big pond or you'll get killed."

And they said, "Oh no, nothing can kill us." That made him a little scared.

The next time he came back he found them playing around a big heart on the ground by the edge of the ashes. He asked them where they got the heart. "Oh, we went way down a piece, looking for the one who killed our mother, and we went and got his heart."

"How did you do that."

"When we went looking for him, a Windigo must have smelled us. He caught us and took us to the big wigwam where all the Windigoes lived. They threw us in the kettle to make soup out of us, and then went to sleep, waiting for it to get done. When the water was nearly boiling we took our bows and arrows and shot all the Windigoes. Every time we shot a Windigo the arrow bounced back from his body, and we shot it at another. When they were all dead we cut out the heart of the one that killed our mother and brought it back."

The man was kind of scared, looking at that big heart and the little babies, and thinking how they ate snakes and blood, like weasels. So he asked some other Indians to get rid of them or to kill them. But the babies knew what their father was doing, and they shot through the chimney hole in the top of the wigwam when the Indians started coming, and they killed them all, except one to tell the story, I guess. Every time they shot the arrow, it came back.

Then they asked their dad why he told the other Indians to come and kill his little boys. He said, "You're getting too dangerous."

They said, "Well, you'll have to go now. Our mother was killed but we're not going ever to die." (All the guts that the Windigo cleaned out of that woman and threw under the bunk had the babies.) "You're going to hide in the brush, and just come out once in a while looking for something to eat, and then you'll hide again." So their dad flies out like a bluejay. And it's true, you don't hardly ever see a bluejay flying in the open; they're always flitting around the brush.

Before he flew out, the little boys told their father, "You'll hear from us one of these days. We'll be up in the sky, and when you see the lightning streaks, that'll be us." Then the little boys turned around, and they had nice little blue wings on, and they flew up into the sky. The Thunders that you hear are those two little fellows. You never hear of Thunders striking Indians, but they strike white people's homes. There was a man working at the mill in Garden, and he swore at the Thunders, and they struck him. He was just like a rag, no bones at all. Old man Feathers told me that.

I get scared when it thunders. Best thing to do is burn tobacco and say, "That's for you, granddad." They'll protect you. My grandmother told me never to mention the Thunders or say any sassy word at them when you hear them.

I've seen pictures of those little Cupids, with their little bows and arrows and little wings. I bought one. Grandma wouldn't tell me a lie — I don't think — but that's how I know her story is true. How did white folks know about the Cupids to make those pictures?

FAIRY TALES

"Do you know a story about a plant that grows up into the sky?" I asked Alec Philemon, thinking of Jack and the Beanstalk and its worldwide variations. He thought a moment and said, "Sure," but the story he told me was pure Indian, a conflict of power between two men because of a kinship jealousy. And yet it does resemble a European fairy tale; Indian "power" acts much like white "magic"; good triumphs over evil; and there is a skyward-shooting tree, sure enough.

Stink Lake (Alec Philemon)

• An old man and his wife had two daughters, and a young man married the two sisters. One had a girl baby, the other had a boy. The old man didn't like his son-in-law coming into his home, and he thought, "I'm going to kill that fellow."

So he said to him, "Let's go over to Stink Lake to hunt deer." Next day they went over there to the old man's little hunting shack and went to bed; they were going to hunt in the morning. During the night the old man threw the stockings of his son-in-law, which were hung up to dry, into the fire, and his shoes too. He was going to try to freeze him. And a big snow fell.

In the morning the son-in-law said, "I thought I smelled something funny last night."

"That's why they call it Stink Lake," the old man told him. "Well, I guess I'll be going home, there's nothing doing around here with all this snow." And he went along.

The son-in-law rubbed his legs with charcoal and said, "I'll be a deer." He crossed the clear snow where the old man would pass and the old man followed his tracks up to his house. The two daughters were sitting there, one making shoes and one making stockings. When the old man came in, he looked at his son-in-law and said, "Throw him out; if I didn't burn those stockings I'd 'a killed some deer." He said it right out, you see.

Well, the old man kept wondering how to kill his son-in-law. His two grandchildren were growing up quite big already and creeping around. He thought, "I'll fix him, I'll put him some place he won't get out of this time." Out loud he said, "Let's go get some pigeons; I know where there's a nest out a ways. You don't have to take any gun, they can't fly away, but they're big enough to eat now."

The younger woman whispered to her husband, "He's going to try to kill you again." "That's all right," he told her.

The two men walked out into the woods till they came to a little pine tree, and sure enough there was a nest. The old man said, "You can climb up there, reach in and throw them down. Be sure and sit down tight."

So the young man climbed up the tree and sat down solid on the knot of the limb. He looked in the nest and said, "There's only two birds in here."

The old man said, "Up a little bit." And the tree grew up into the sky. By'n by the son-in-law couldn't see the old man down below. "You always wanted Indian to eat, now you can eat that one," said the old man, and the birds heard him.

The young fellow asked one bird his name, and it said "Upward." And the tree grew. Then he asked the other's name, and it said "Downward," and the tree went down. So he told Downward, "Go down." The tree went way downward, to where it was first. "Go down some more." "No, that's as far as I can go. Then the young fellow killed the two birds, took a feather from each one, and went home.

The old man wasn't home yet. The son-in-law took the two feathers and stuck them into the heads of his boy and girl, and told them, "Go see your grandpa when he comes in." So they met him at the door, and grandpa asked them, "Where did you get those feathers?" "Pa gave 'em to us." And he laughed and said, "Oh, he must be all eaten up by this time." Then he saw his son-in-law sitting inside.

Now he was mad. He kept wondering and wondering what he could do to kill the young fellow. So he thought of Stink Lake again. "Let's go back hunting and see if we change our luck." When they got to the lodge the old man fell asleep right away, after they hung up their stockings. The son-in-law got up and changed them round. After a little while he saw the old man get up and throw the stockings he thought were the young fellow's into the fireplace. They sent up an awful smell. "That's why they call it Stink Lake," the old man said.

In the morning when the old man looked for his stockings, the son-in-law said, "Leave those alone, they're mine." He put them on and went out into the deep snow; it had snowed during the night, like before. Then the old man put charcoal on his legs so he could be a deer, but he didn't have the power to be a deer. So he followed his son-in-law barelegged through the snow, but he couldn't stand it. "I'm going to freeze." Then he thought, "I'll be a tamarack stub." He had that power. The son-in-law looked back and saw that stub, and said, "I'm going to burn it." And he burned up his father-in-law.

Why do white man's fairy tales appeal to Indians, who tell them still as they heard them from the French and Spanish in the seventeenth century, when Indian tales cross not at all into white culture? The answer is not hard to seek. Our Indo-European

Märchen with their talking animals and sorcerers and enchant-
ments make sense to the Indian mind, but they have become
archaic in twentieth-century white civilization. Chief Welsh's
story that follows gives a completely Indian locale, down to the
details of Sioux burial customs, yet it really is a well-known European tale, The Bride in Search of her Lost Husband, combined
with a portion of Cinderella. In this version the Indian Tradition
rephrases the European within the context of modern American
society.

The Toad-Son (Herbert Welsh)

• There was a big camp near a village, where a very pretty young
girl lived. The people picked out the best-looking boy to be married to her and become the mayor. When the time came for a
family arrival the medicine man selected the best girls to be
maids for the mother, and the bravest young men to guard the
lodge. Then he set a date for the baby to arrive. After that the
men went out hunting, so they could have a big feast. One got a
buffalo, one got an antelope, others got grouse and prairie chickens. Then they waited for the big day.

The child was due to arrive on Wednesday, so the announcer
got on his horse and rode around announcing that everybody
should gather around the mayor's lodge on Wednesday to help
celebrate the arrival. (In those days the Indians lived in a great
round circle — I've seen it myself — and it took about five days to
go around.) So on the day all the people gathered at the lodge
and waited all day, but the baby didn't arrive and they went
home quite disappointed. They kept the village quiet and listened all night for a sound — nothing. They got up early next
morning, watered their stock, tied them up in different places
while the announcer went around again, and gathered to wait for
the arrival — perhaps two or three thousand people. But the baby
still didn't arrive, and they had to go home disappointed a
second time.

Meanwhile the to-be-mother went out for a little walk; maybe that would help. She walked along a sandy beach by a little river, accompanied by her husband and her maids. Suddenly she saw something bubbling up out of the ground, and told her husband. He said, "Oh, that's nothing, it's only a little spring." "Oh no, it's some animal, I can see his eyes coming out of the ground." She was a little scared. So they went over and found a big toad, coming out to sun himself.

Next day the baby arrived, but it was a toad. It had short legs in front, long legs in back. The people were a little bit disappointed. They had the medicine man perform a ceremony to try to change him back, shaking his rattle while the braves danced in worship to the Great Spirit, Wahtankhep. Nothing doing. But one fortunate thing was that the toad could talk. Finally the medicine man said, "We have a baby and we're going to have our feast." So they celebrated anyway.

The parents made a place for the baby in the corner of the lodge and he stayed there, growing bigger all the time. So years went by and he grew up as a child would, you might say, but the others were afraid of him — different type, you know. One day he told his mother and father he wanted to get married, but no girl would have him. So they told the chief and the medicine man and the braves, who looked around and looked around until at last one girl consented — the toad's folks being the prominent family in the village, you know.

So the day was set for the wedding, and everyone came around for the feast. The prayer-man (Wacekiye Wicasa) married them and tied the knot. Oh, the people were disappointed because the nice-looking girl had to marry the toad. Outside they looked happy, at the celebration, but inside they were disappointed, and felt there was no justice. Well, the family had created an in-law, and she moved over to the chief's lodge.

So days went on, and one morning she wouldn't respond. The maids went in with the mother-in-law and tried to wake her up, but she was dead. The toad was lying in a corner tied up, like a nice little boy. So the announcer announced that the royal family's daughter-in-law had died, and the medicine man told the best braves to go way out to the baddest lands they could find, and there they took four sticks and wove them together with bark, so they could build a scaffold on top of a hill. That was where they would bury the young lady. (The Sioux buried their people above ground on a scaffold, like with the Crucifixion, so they'd go to the spirits. If they were buried below ground, they'd go to hell.) Then they had the funeral procession from the village to the scaffold, and everybody went except the toad; they wouldn't let him go. He sat in the corner looking disappointed as the people passed by and stared at him. At the burial place the medicine man sang a song, and the braves wrapped the girl up in buffalo robes tied with rawhide and carried her up the hill by a secret path. Then the prayer-man gave the prayer and everybody went home feeling sad.

By and by, the toad wanted to get married again. His father said, "Well, we've lost a good girl and if anything should happen this time, we'd probably get ostracized from the tribe." But his mother said, "No, he's my child and if he wants to get married, he will." So they had quite an argument over it, and finally the father gave in and went over to the medicine man and the chief. They looked around and located another beautiful girl. This girl's father didn't want her to marry the toad, but the mother said, "He's the royal family and he has my consent." So the community had another big celebration with maids-of-honor and all, and the royals inherited another daughter-in-law.

Things went along nicely for a while, and this marriage lasted longer than the other. But the mother-in-law began to suspect something, and one night told the wife, "You stay with me to-night." "Oh no, that's all right, he doesn't bother me." The next morning the wife didn't get up, and the mother-in-law rushed in and found her dead. So the maids had to prepare her for another funeral in the same place as before.

By this time the community began to suspect something. So they had a meeting and decided, "Next time we'll have guards all night to see what happens." They thought that maybe the royal family was jealous because the other people wouldn't associate with their son, the toad, and had killed the girl in the night.

Soon the toad wanted to get married again, and after another big argument the mother won out as usual, and sent the father to see the officials. After the third wedding the tribe selected some braves to be bodyguards, and split them up to watch both in the day and at night. Meanwhile, the medicine man was coöperating, shaking his rattle and singing all night to drive away the bad spirits. The first night nothing happened. In the morning the girl got up and did the washing and tended to her business. It went that way for a time.

But one night she decided to stay awake all night. After a while, she heard the old toad jingling, jingling his chains, heard a slap, slap on the floor — the old toad was coming. He gets on her bed. She lay there to see what he would do, ready to give the alarm. He touched her face, and kissed her. She just lay as if half asleep and pretended she didn't know what was going on. The toad kisses her on the neck and makes love to her three or four times. Then he crawls back, falls off the bed, and gets killed.

A little bit later she heard a man whistling in the next room, opening doors, shutting closets, and talking to the guards. And when she saw him he was the best-looking man she'd ever seen — that was her husband. She got up in the morning very happy, and her parents were surprised to see this good-looking young man instead of the toad. So they gave her golden slippers and a golden dress and had a big wedding and gave them a palace — only the Indians called it a lodge.

The toad choked the other wives, you see, because they quarreled with him. But the one who really loved him he made happy. They lived happily for a time. Then one day she got mad. He was so handsome and attractive, and a good singer too, that all the girls stopped to talk to him, and when he stayed late at a conference this day she thought he was up to something. She put the food back in, brought it out, put it in again when he didn't show up, and finally went over to the conference and spoke to him in a harsh tone. "You let them have your meeting and come home and have your dinner." Right in front of everybody. He didn't like that — no way to talk to a prominent man. He excused himself and went home with her, and on the way back she said, "If you' stay out longer you can cook your own dinner." She thought he had a girl friend, you see. But it wasn't true, he was minding his own business. After he came home late once or twice and found no dinner, he decided to pack up and leave. "She's not treating me like a husband." He put her golden slippers in with his stuff, and went away to another village.

Nobody knew where he went. His wife was uncomfortable all night, thinking he was with his girl friend. Next morning she asked his mother and father if they'd seen him: "No." The watch-men said, "Yes, he left after the meeting," but that was the last anybody saw of him. A searching party went into every house in the community, but couldn't find him. They waited a few days, but no report came along. Then they sent some braves to inquire over at the next village, but they came back and reported to the officials that he wasn't there. They tried a couple of more villages, but no luck, no strangers at any of them.

In the meantime this lad thought to himself, "I'll marry the girl who can wear these golden slippers." He fled to a place about four or five villages down the line, and told the council there that he was a stranger who wished to get acquainted, and the young lady who could wear his slippers would be his bride. So the village gathered all the girls from the village and the suburbs into a great big circus tent for the contest. They all fell in love with the young man when they saw him, he was so good-looking. (I read in the paper where a girl took a bunch of flowers to Sinatra on the stage at Chicago and then fainted. It was the same order.) So the girls went to work massaging their feet trying to fit them into the golden slippers. But they were all too large.

By that time the scouts that were traveling from village to village looking for him heard the news about the golden slippers, and they carried the report back that anyone who fit the slippers could marry the stranger and have all the jewelry he inherited from the royals. Pretty soon his wife heard about this and grabbed her shawl — her robe I should say — and took some rations and went to the next village, and the next and the next. She was about giving up hope, thinking it was a false report, when the news came in that this man was just down the line. A fellow from out of town told her, "Yes he was here but he's gone to that other village over there with the slippers. All the girls try them on but some are too big and they slip off and others are too small and can't get in." She said, "That must be my husband."

So she set out the very next day and traveled and traveled till she came to the village. The people told her, "Yes, there's some doings here." She saw some girls walking around with bloody feet, and asked why they were doing that. An old lady said, "There was a nice young man around here with golden slippers and valuable jewelry, and the girls cut their feet with flints to fit the slippers." But no one knew the man and he'd gone on. That was all the information she could get. She didn't say she was his wife.

Then she gathered up her belongings and set out on another long journey. She came to a second great village, and saw some girls walking around with bloody feet crying. They told her about the good-looking young man with the jewelry and gowns. "He just left, went down this road." "Well, how far is it to the next village?" "Oh, about a day." She went off once more and caught up with him at the next village. But she didn't tell him who she was, and asked a family there if they'd put her up for a few days.

In the council ring the chief told the village there was a gentleman come from a distant town, and anyone who could fit the slipper he brought could have the valuable jewelry and gown he'd inherited from the royal family. So the girls all tried to fit the slipper, and carved up their feet, with no luck. This went on for two days. On the third day the wife disguised herself with some red and white paint, put on her shawl, and said, "Well I'll try this time, and get in the row." All the girls sitting on the bench kept trying on the slipper, till the last one. Finally she said, "Oh, those are my slippers, I've been looking for them for two days." And she put them on and stood up. He was surprised and said, "All right, here's a girl from a far distance who has fit the slippers, so we'll have a ceremony." Then they got the chief and the medicine man and the prayer-man and had a big doing. And the chief gave them a lodge to stay in. She took off her war paint, and he saw that it was his wife who had followed him all that distance.

And they went back to their own village, where all the people welcomed them and gave them a celebration. But now he told them, "I'm going back to my place where I came from, and when I return you won't be here. So dig a big hole in the ground and make it solid with braces, within two days, because a big storm is coming, and that's when I'll go."

Some didn't believe him, but the chief did, because this was a strange man. The braves built a good solid hole, and the man said, "Now I'm going to that land over there, and leave you here on earth, and when I get over there I'll disappear. You'll see houses and people and trees flying in the air — that's a sign of destruction. But don't mind about me." And he told his mother and father and wife to get in the hole. Then he sat down like a toad. A big storm came up like he said, and all the houses of the people who hadn't believed him flew around while his folks were safe in the hole. When the storm was over, he was gone.

And as a result of that, after a storm the toad comes up out of the ground. I've seen that out in the Dakotas; after a certain kind of rain and sun the toads come up. People think they fall with the rain — you know how those big drops of rain splash — but they don't. My father and mother told me, "After this rain, you'll see the toads." And I did.

PART II
THE EUROPEAN TRADITION

4

CANADIENS

THE first white men to enter the Great Lakes were French, and three hundred years later French folk still live on their shores. St. Ignace was visited by the fur trader Jean Nicolet four years after Puritans landed in Boston. Only St. Augustine and Jamestown precede Sault Ste. Marie as America's oldest communities. But the French families one meets in the Peninsula today scarcely reflect the seigneurs, Jesuits, and voyageurs who founded seventeenth-century forts, missions, and trading posts. They are Canadiens from Quebec province, lured to Michigan by the lumber boom of the 1880's and 1890's that promised them familiar work in pine forests. The boom is long over, the crossings have stopped, and today St. Ignace, Sault Ste. Marie, and Marquette are French more in name than in fact. But the color of the Canadiens has dyed the land, for there is no such thing as a drab "peasouper." At least I never met one.

For one thing, all Canadiens brim over with fearful superstitions, of *loup-garou* transformations, black Bibles, visits of the Devil, evil omens of death. These are old beliefs, brought over to Canada by Norman peasants from the France of Louis XIV, and since then sharpened by the terrors of the wilderness, the matching myths of the Indians, and the cultural poverty of Canadian life. Your Canadien tells them with devout sincerity, in nasal rhythmic tones that provide a funereal acampaniment to his macabre scenes. You do not laugh at his phantasms, and I am not sure that you completely disbelieve in *loup-garous, lutins,* and *la chasse galerie* when time after time you hear them solemnly described. I did not laugh when Aunt Jane Goudreau and her buddies appalled each other with accounts of people who turned into bears, pigs, and owls; or when young Herm Manette told the boarding-house audience he saw the ghost of Mrs. Shilling flutter past him on the street while she lay dying in bed; or when Bert Damour fixed me with bug eyes in a saloon booth and explained how the bonesetter cured his stiff neck with mumbled words and a pinch of salt thrown into boiling water.

This richly embroidered superstition of the Canadien mind is balanced by a volatile humor and an unwitting comedy. A Frenchman gesticulates, grimaces, mimics, chatters in a flurry of excitement, which no one understands better than he himself. Burt Mayotte at the Soo, a wiry, dark-haired Alsace Lorrainer, who makes a specialty of reciting French-Canadian dialect stories to local groups, portrays his kin with genius. When he chants his lengthy yarns, his eyes dance and flicker, his head bobs and weaves, his hands dart about in a constant agony of emotion. Burt is enacting an excitable character who commits all sorts of gaucheries in his hopeless ignorance of American life. Paree at the carnival (actually Burt himself in his youth) has never seen "popnuts" or "peacorn" or "hasscrim"; he longs to go on the "hup-go-wheel" and to eat a "hot puppay all squeeze in a swim suit," but he lacks the necessary five cents. When he hears a barker offering twenty-five dollars to anyone who will stay with the carnival wrestler for ten minutes, he jumps at the chance, but Tiger ties him up in painful knots. Paree is ready to quit the match, when he sees an opening; he bites a big red behind — but alas, Paree has bitten his own behind.

Around these comical Frenchmen — Joe Bedore of St. Clair Flats, Fred Felteau of Gratiot Lake, Joe LeMay of Escanaba, and a dozen others — whole cycles of apocryphal anecdotes form, and the folktype behind them becomes American property. Even if the Peninsula Canadiens are thinning out, it takes only one anywhere to start a legend. There is, as I say, no such thing as a colorless Canadien.

LEGENDS

THE LOUP-GAROU

When you ask a Canadien about the *loup-garou*, he will throw back his head and laugh or look startled. If he (or she) does not react in some such way, you may be sure you are not speaking to a Quebecker. Quebec families raised their children on the *loup-garou*, terrifying them with stories of its appearances, and instructing them how to handle the danger. In the French communities of Lake Linden and Flat Rock, at the northern and southern ends of the Peninsula, folks know all about this monstrosity. Courtly, well-educated Henry Roberts of Flat Rock explained precisely how a man becomes a *loup-garou*.

Henry Roberts speaks

• In order to run the *loup-garou*, one must engage oneself to the Devil. You must have forgotten your religion for seven years, not approached the sacraments, not gone to communion, not confessed.

In former times things were very hard, money was very scarce. There were many people who said, "I am going to engage myself to the Devil."

They waited for him from nine o'clock in the evening right up until two o'clock in the morning. They cursed, the Devil came, they said, "I come to engage myself to you." He gave them a certain amount of money, forty piasses, for example, for as many months as they pledged themselves for the *loup-garou* — let us say six months. Then they turned into a wolf, a dog, an ox, or a bear. At the end of the stated time, they must be delivered at the same hour, unless the Devil took possession of them. In order for them to be delivered, someone must strike them and draw their blood. Then they turned into a man. That is why, when one encountered a *loup-garou* at this moment, he did not let you pass, he blocked your legs, so that someone would strike him in some manner or dart him with a knife. Then the skin of the wolf falls to the earth, and a man all naked comes out.

The queen of *loup-garou* conteurs, and a fabulous personality in her own right, is Aunt Jane Goudreau at St. Ignace. Probably better than anyone else alive she knows this bleak Straits of Mackinac country, the oldest corner of the Northwest, which still carries the look of wilderness. One of her grandfathers came down from Quebec to homestead on St. Ignace, the gateway to the Upper Peninsula; the other crossed over from France, built fishing boats for the struggling colony of French, Irish, and Indians, and married a full-blooded Chippewa. Aunt Jane spent most of her life in the half-breed fishing villages stretching along the Lake Michigan shore from St. Ignace west to Seul Choix and Naubinway, where long winters meant a diet of blackstrap molasses and brown bread, and to compensate, the relating of marvelous tales. She tells them still to her old cronies when they stop by for an evening's gossip. At eighty-one, she lives alone in a house on a hill overlooking the straits, and takes in summer roomers since her husband died, Captain Louis Goudreau, who piloted the Arnold line steamers to and from Mackinac Island; "My Captain," she calls him.

Brisk, sharp-tongued, and gifted with talk despite her years, Aunt Jane seldom wants for company. Her kinsfolk, who stretch from the Soo to Escanaba, her many friends, and the merely curious troop through her house to hear her witty comments and see her upstairs "museum" of relics, curios, and gifts. There the visitor may spy the reed handbag in which Mrs. Bouriseau carried her baby seven miles to town, the day after she bore it in the woods while picking cranberries; or a blood-spattered timber Aunt Jane lifted from the bunk of the much-shot-up King Strang, who ruled the Mormon colony at Beaver Island from 1848 to 1856.

The stories about Aunt Jane rival those that she spins. One time a tourist admiring the view of Mackinac Island from her kitchen window saw her pick up a .22 shotgun from the corner and march toward him; he backed against the wall and elevated his hands, but she, fully savoring the situation, walked past him to the window and peppered a dog that was smelling her fishpond. "They never come back once I shoot them," she says matter-of-factly. The framed "Prayer for the Day" in her bathroom greets her roomers first thing in the morning with this pious admonition: "Oh Lord please help me to keep my damn nose out of other people's business." Today, as she tends her house completely unaided, Aunt Jane defies time and mocks the age with a pioneer stoicism and vigor. "People don't walk any more," she observes scornfully. "I used to walk from the ship when my captain docked, with a gallon crock on my shoulder, three miles to the cottage in the snow, and go fishing through the ice. And they never put a knife in me yet."

My first day in the Upper Peninsula I called on Aunt Jane, whose name had already reached me, and asked for a room. She peered at me suspiciously at first — an erect, handsomely wrinkled old lady with a throaty voice, glittering earrings, and a royal manner. Finally she agreed to take me in for a couple of days until she started her spring cleaning; that evening when she casually mentioned that her previous roomer had brought home ice cream in the evening, I rushed out and bought a quart of vanilla cream, and established our friendship. All that week we ate ice cream in the living room in the evenings, Aunt Jane lit her pipe, and launched off into her old tales. She overflows with wild superstitions of both Canadiens and Chippewa which blend with startling pioneer experiences in her repertory of dying local legends.

Like so many of the Canadian French, she has seen and heard warnings of death.

Aunt Jane Goudreau speaks

• The French believe a dog howling is a bad warning. Before the Captain died a dog howled by his bed. I didn't count the howls, but it meant he had so many days, weeks, or months to live.

I picked up an old clock from my grandfather; I always had a mania for picking up things. It didn't run any more. One night it gave three clangs — DENG, DENG, DENG — so loud, in the room right outside my door. I was never so scared in my life. The next day one of the kids came from up the hill to say Grandfather Goudreau was very sick. He died on the third day.

Grandfather Derusha was coming along home, and my mother went outside and said, "Your grandfather looks drunk, he is staggering along and holding on to the fence." (Our house was all fenced in with an old-fashioned fence.) He came in and said, "I'm awfully sick." He looked terribly pale, and kept asking, "What time is it, what time is it? So many hours more." And he kept saying the prayer. He said he had a warning, just as he was coming up the hill to the fence. "I had an awful, awful feeling," he said. He died inside a month.

You are notified thirty days before you die — in a vision. You say the prayer and are supposed to show it to one of your family; it's a secret. I didn't want him to tell my aunt — I don't want to know the hour I'm going to die — we all have to go soon enough.

But Aunt Jane's choicest mysteries are reserved for the *roup-garou* (the St. Ignace corruption of *loup-garou*). "Seventy-five years ago," she recalls, "if the people see a man look into the house and disappear, they lock all doors and shut up the windows, and even stuff up the cracks. He might be a *roup-garou* who would throw some medicine into the house. We never hear anything of that any more; all those *roup-garou* people are dead."

As if to belie her words, her younger brother, Frank Derusha, a squat pop-eyed man of seventy-odd, and an old friend, shy and frail Jenny Belanger, paid Aunt Jane a call one night during my stay, and fell to reminiscing with her about the old community and its *roup-garou* wizards. They corroborated her tales, chimed in with expressions of horror at the climaxes, and added further mischiefs. Aunt Jane's voice rose almost to frenzy as she told again about the grudge that Mrs. Lozon had openly expressed for Mrs. Champain, and the strange malady that afflicted Sarah Champain shortly after.

• Old Sarah was very sick all the time, she was choking. Every night she took ill and had to go to bed, when a great big *ghibou* came and perched on her clothes line. It came the same hour every night. It is unusual, you know, to see an owl right in the city. Mrs. Champain got the doctor and the priest but they couldn't tell her what was wrong.

The clothes line ran right out under the window — she was in an upstairs apartment — right next to my aunt's house. The door of my aunt's room was open in the summer, and she would see the owl when she went to take the clothes in. She told her nephew to kill the *ghibou* because he would get the chickens. So he takes a shotgun and shoots the *ghibou*. He sees it flop over, puts the gun away, and goes to pick up the *ghibou*, to cut it up for a feather duster. But he can't find it. He goes round the house to the highway, down to the trail — the building was set up on the hill — and sees old Mrs. Lozon, lame, trying to crawl up the hill. She'd been perfectly all right the day before, but now she could hardly walk. Charlie Lottie picked her up in a rig and took her over to one of her sisters. She never got over it — she stayed there till she died.

The man, Jimmy Vallier, ran back, all excited and numb, crying, "That was no *ghibou*, that was a *roup-garou!*" Jim said he was afraid to follow after Mrs. Lozon because she might do something to him, to keep her secret. My aunt laughed and said, "That was only a *ghibou*; I saw it right out the door." My aunt changed her mind later, though.

And do you know, when Mrs. Lozon died, old Sarah got better right away.

Jenny Belanger clucked in sympathetic horror, and Frank Derusha said aggressively, "You *had* to believe it — it was true." He recalled how a black dog got between his legs one time when he was coming home, which he suspected was Antoine Truck, one of the men who worked for his father. Truck would get up in the night and take long walks across the beach. "He'd come back just before work and lay down before pa'd call him. He must have done something — turned himself into some damn thing."

"Yes, and you were afraid to kick it," said Aunt Jane.

Frank felt no shame in fearing *roup-garou* power. He told of an occasion when he worked unloading wood from a schooner at Pointe La Barbe in a gang of fifteen men who, at nightfall, sought shelter in a deserted house. During the night they heard a chain dragging overhead, but the party that went upstairs found nothing. When they heard it the second time all fifteen men left the house and went in the woods to sleep. "The *roup-garou!*" said Frank, and laughed without any humor; I can still see the gleam of awe in his eyes.

Aunt Jane then recalled another favorite gossip item about two local half-breeds. "You remember what a stink there was at the church when Mésois shot Bennois? That must be over twenty-five, thirty years ago — that would be the last thing the people would remember. Bennois told that other Indian he'd get him. Mésois was coming back from the marsh with a load of hay, and a bear stopped his horse. Mésois shot the bear and it turned into Bennois. The people found Bennois sitting on the edge of the road, and brought him home; he walked all bent over. He wouldn't show the wound or let the doctor see it. I wouldn't go to see him, but I saw him through the window early in the morning fixing himself in the guts, in his nightclothes, when he thought nobody could see him."

"That damn Indian was a bear when he shot him!" screamed Frank.

"When he died," said Aunt Jane, highly excited, "all the Catholics went to church to see if something terrible would happen.

Old Pat Chambers said, 'I expected to see the ceiling drop down.' The Irish believe that can happen, you know. They went to the priest about it, to stop the mass, but he said you couldn't prove nothing."

I asked Aunt Jane if Bennois might not simply have covered himself with a bearskin. She thought a minute over that, for she had earlier told me of an Indian witch who draped herself in turkey feathers and gobbled like a turkey. Then she said, "But they never found any bearskin."

Now she thought of still another case that decisively proved the fact of transformation.

• An uncle of mine once delivered a pig. Tom Vallier was telling me that he never believed in any of those terrible things the half-breeds used to talk about, until this happened to him. He used to go on a toot, and one night when he was drunk he told me; he was pale as a ghost. He said he'd been on a drinking party, quarreling and all, up at the Martins. That old Frank Martin was there, drinking with the bunch. Tom started to come home on a trail behind the old Cadillac hotel, which is burned down now. Between the barn and the back of the house was a big pile of manure where people used to go and get manure.

As Tom got there, a little white pig ran back and forth in the path and around him, just like a dog, and finally got close to his legs so he couldn't walk. He thought it was kinda funny, and he gave it a kick and it flew right on top of that manure pile. He walked on a ways, and began to think how hard he kicked it and that he must have killed it. So he went back to see, and there was that old man Frank Martin lying on the manure pile with his arms behind his neck. And Tom said, "What are you doing here?" And he said, "It's you that put me here." And Tom saw that he had his neck all cut around here [Aunt Jane indicated with a gesture]. He was so scared the hairs stood up on his head. A week later he saw Frank on the street, and his throat was all bandaged up, right where he kicked him.

Tom told me, "You can see for yourself." I went and looked at old Frank in a store one time, and walked all around him, and I saw that mark on his chin. But I didn't let on. You can't tell a *roup-garou* you know what he is, or they'll get you.

I asked Aunt Jane if she knew who had put the spell on Frank Martin and why.

"Old Mrs. Louie Pond, that Indian — everybody was scared of her. She used to go into the woods and get roots, and probably he got in trouble with her. Old Frank used to hang around a lot with the Indians.

"I couldn't sleep for three nights thinking about it. Who would have thought that Frank Martin would turn into a *roup-garou!*"

LUTINS

Canadiens fear the *loup-garou*, but they are rather amused by the *lutins*. They all know about the little men who ride farmers' horses at night, and return them with heaving flanks and knotted manes in the morning. No one I met had seen the midget riders, but plenty of people have seen the tangled manes that defy combing. Some afflicted farmers place brass rings in the hair of the mane at night, to prevent knots forming.

Sometimes, conversely, the *lutin* cares for and grooms a favorite horse. Adelore King of Rapid River testifies to that from his own experience. "Years ago in the lumber camps here, a *lutin* would take a fancy to one of the horses, tend to him and braid his mane, give him oats and hay and feed him up nice and slick. He didn't do any harm, except to rob the oat-bag to feed his horse, and the others wouldn't get any. The *lutin* would stay maybe a month. In the morning the teamster would find one of the horses all trimmed up, and he'd say, 'That *lutin* was in last night.' Some claim they seen him — a little man with whiskers, the same height as a monkey. There must be something to it to get it a-going."

Once a daring attempt was made to catch a *lutin*. George Cota of Crystal Falls, an encyclopedia of northwoods anecdotes, tells about this near-miss.

George Cota speaks

• This horse used to be taken out every night and ridden by the *lutin*. As a rule the horse was spirited and full of life. In the morning this one was all worn out, and he had little loops in his mane where the *lutin's* paws had grabbed him. The *lutin* was intelligent; he could open the door and take the horse out. A *lutin* is the spirit of a horseman doing penance, you know.

So the people decided to catch him. They hung around the barn at night until they saw a glim inside the stable — the *lutin* must have had a candle. They dug a hole in the manure pile outside, and formed two rows from it to the stable. The old grandfather held the sack over the hole in the manure; he was the only one who had the nerve. Another man opened the stable door and rattled it. The *lutin* ran out between the men and through the manure hole into the sack. The grandfather closed the sack and let it struggle inside. (The *lutin* is very wiry; "*c'est lutin*" is a common expression to describe a wiry person.)

They stayed up all night holding it. They would not dare open it at night. When daylight came they opened the sack. The *lutin* jumped out of a window through a hole where the cat went in and out, so fast they never saw it. All they saw was a black powder in the snow.

BLACK MAGIC

Flat Rock lies on a scrubby plain twenty miles north of Escanaba, a tiny French pocket of half-hearted farmers. My Parisienne friend Ariane and I drove there without leads, and knocked at farmhouse doors. Strange people opened them; an ogrish hairy fellow in his shirtsleeves; a dried up heavy-lidded witch of a woman; but none knew or would vouchsafe tales until our last call on courteous, fine-looking Henry Roberts. Born the son of a

woodcutter in Ste. Adele, Quebec in 1868, he had helped his
father clear the woods in 1890, where we now talked. He had
gone to school and even a year and a half to college. This education had not erased his Canadien beliefs, and through a long
evening, with his family closely attentive, he told us some esoteric and truly diabolical business.

La Chasse Galerie

• The Chasse Galerie, it is a bunch of people, of men who have
forgotten the good God completely.

In the winter of 1862, at Catineau, not far from our home,
there were at least fifty men in the camps, in the forest. Now
there was one of them who was exceptional; he stayed all alone,
all by himself, without saying anything to anyone. When someone
spoke to him, he would only reply yes or no. He had a little smile
from time to time. He listened to the others working. They said,
"What would I give to see my father, or my mother, or my
daughter! Ah, if I could only see my sweetheart right now!"

They were a thousand leagues from Ottawa. They had been
there six or eight months and they had not yet returned.

Then this man who was so serious and always alone in his
corner went to them with a smiling air: "If you will listen to me
and do for me what I will tell you to do, I will lead you home."

He was a man who never partook of the sacraments, who had
no religion. He said, "We will set out from here at eleven o'clock.
I will have a boat at the camp, on the roof of the bunkhouse. I
will have some oars."

And these men listening, asked this man, "Are you telling us a
joke or the truth?"

He said, "If you will do what I am telling you to do, you will
arrive at your home without even knowing it."

And all those men were so anxious to see their sweethearts they
said, "Yes, let us go there! Let us go there!"

"Very well," he said, "go get on a ladder, climb over the yard,
and you will see the boat."

"But how can you get the boat in the air?"

"You don't need to know my secret. You will get home. Do what I say."

They said, "We promise to do everything that you say."

They climbed into the boat. Everyone had an oar.

He said to them, "Do not think of the good God. Think of your wives, of your sweethearts. Do not pray to the good God."

Some of these men said they felt a shiver pass over their bodies.

They climbed into the boat. They all shouted the same thing, at the same time, "Home! Home! We wish to return home." They began to row. The boat set out. While they rowed, they sang:

> *The oars which take us, which take us,*
> *The oars which take us in the air.*

It split the air. It passed like a minute. They arrived at their homes like a dream. People below heard the noise of the oars, above in the air, and the voices which sang:

> *The oars which take us, which take us,*
> *The oars which take us in the air.*

My grandfather said to me, "I have heard the Chasse Galerie; they are bad spirits who pass above in the air, like an aeroplane. One can still hear the noise of the oars and the song:

> *The oars which take us, which take us,*
> *The oars which take us in the air.*

Selling the Black Hen

• To sell the black hen, it is necessary to possess no religion, no faith, to say no prayers and not to think of the good God. To have a black hen takes nine years. You take a black hen today, in your hennery. You cover it. You wait for a chicken. The following year you cover this black hen, and for nine years you do the same. It is the ninth generation of a black hen that you can sell and then, after the ninth black hen, you set out with it; then you go into a large field, near a green wood, about eleven o'clock, midnight (it must be after nine o'clock in the evening), you put it on a sort of elevation, on a large rock or a large stump. You call the Devil, "Come buy my black hen."

In an instant the Devil will appear. Then it is a question of the sale. He says, "I can accomplish your purpose. You have a black hen to sell. How much do you want for it?"

He who has the hen asks three hundred, four hundred, five hundred dollars. He has much cash for this black hen.

The Red Dragon

• The "Red Dragon" is a powerful book. You can do everything that you wish with it. It is in nine volumes. It is only the priests who can have the ninth, no one else. An extraordinary secret! With it you can put out the fire a hundred miles away. It is a book which possesses the Devil.

Fifty-four years ago, the proprietor of a hotel in Escanaba was a man who made no practice of religion, who owned this book. One day I went up into his room, I saw this book there. It was written in red, as if with blood. It was stamped, "printed in London." In that city are published many indiscreet books, books the most secret. It is forbidden to read that book. It gave me a fright. I started to read the book; I could not make it out! "Black magic" is something that you cannot understand.

This man died twenty years ago. If he would return here, he would say, "Ariane, look in your pockets." You would have seen, on your lap, a dozen little chickens, all alive.

A MIRACLE

Power for evil must always yield to power for good: the Devil will be humbled by God, the sorcerer by the saint, the witch by the priest. And the priest, being most accessible, best served the Canadien. Priests could cure diseases, break up black magic, and perform miracles. Never strike a priest; if you do, your arm will shrivel up and never strike again.

In Lake Linden the Canadiens all revere the memory of Father

Menard, who once saved their church from burning. Bert Damour told me his recollection of the event at our first meeting.

Sitting in Ermart's cafe in L'Anse, a wild and scenic town on Lake Superior with the usual Upper Michigan polyglot population, I heard a stranger beside me chanting, "The father, the son, and the holy ghost." I begged his pardon, and he began amicably to explain to me the perditious state of the world. He was a short, chunky, ragged, and unshaven man with large, almost hypnotic eyes, and he was a little intoxicated. His name was Albert Damour; he had been born in Champion sixty-five years before of a European-French father and a Canadian-French mother; most of his thirteen brothers and sisters had been born in Canada. His trade was carpentering, but he was not working now because he could get no materials, and he was broke. The Damours had spent most of their family life in Lake Linden.

I asked him about the Lake Linden fire.

Albert Damour speaks

• I remember dat fire. I was t'ree, going on four. We were living right next to de Protestant church on de turn going into town from Hubbell, but we moved from dere couple day before de fire to a liddle log shack two mile from town. If we'd stayed we'd have been burned up.

De day of de fire my sisters came back from town crying — deir clothes was all burned. Dey used to work as hired girls for seven, eight dollars a mont', and wore a four-dollaire dress. I can just remember de smoke and de hexcitement — causes a kid to be a liddle more bright, you know. Den my mudder used to tell me about it.

De fire made just one line going nort', toward de head of de lake. It burned de brewery, and beer flowed t'rough de streets and into de sewer. Dere was foam on de lake a foot high for one quarter mile. De firemen from Houghton pumped beer back into de fire.

Den de fire stopped and turned up de hill, just when it got

alongside de h'old Cat'olic church. It was a wooden frame building and it wasn't more dan two hundred feet from de danger.
Everybody t'ought it was a miracle. De Protestant church burned
to de ground.

According to what dey used to say, de nuns was praying in de
convent, and de priest, Fadder Menard, went into de street wid
a cross. He t'rew some blessed medals in de fire, and said, "De
fire will not burn my church." And his prayer make de wind
change.

Bert told me a great deal more, about healings and haunts and
visions, as his memory unfolded and the old beliefs came throng-
ing through his mind. I left him with real regret. He had run into
bad luck, and lost all his savings in the depression; when I met
him he had less than a dollar in his pockets, besides owing room
rent. He was so hungry he ate handfuls of sugar from the sugar
bowl. Yet he talked well, and thought clearly, and spoke his
words from his heart.

SIGNS

The advent of death, the committing of a sacrilege, the utter-
ance of a blasphemy — these dread things brought awful signs
from *le bon Dieu*. Bert Damour knew such warnings.

• You know, on Good Friday and Saints' days you're supposed
to pray, fast, take it quiet. But one farmer who didn't believe in
notting, an unbeliever, hitched up his horses to de plough on
Good Friday. He seen a streak of blood behin' his plough. Like
if I trow a pail of water into any hinstrument dat turns up de
groun'.

In dem days you would go and see de pries', for anyting like
dat. So de farmer tol' him, "I was workin' and I seen blood in de
gutter of de plough."

And de pries' said, "You were workin' on Good Friday! On de
day when de Lord had his passion! When he was drawin' his last
blood, you were still draggin' his blood into de eart'. You were

notify and you were prove dat you were draggin' de blood into
de lan'."

And de fellow nearly went crazee.

Bert said this slowly and somberly. Then he went on to analyze
the occurrence.

• Dere wasn't any education den, or any books, and tings
wouldn't stay in de memory. Dere had to be something like dat
to bring civilization. De people needed a sign. In dose days you
were punished in de act. De poor fellow probably didn't even
know it was Good Friday.

Of course it was mentioned to me by some old heads, like I
mention it to you now.

George Cota had heard of a most strange apparition.

George Cota speaks

• This happened in Canada, close to Rivière du Loup. This man
Calevette was coming home from a christening; at christenings
the people take more gin than they should. He was riding down a
lane, when a little animal ran around his horse. He stopped to see
what it was; the animal turned south, and got as big as a sheep; it
turned north, and got as big as a yearling calf; it turned east, and
got as big as a steer. He took his whip and hit it three or four
cracks; it just shook its head. He stepped out of the rig to hit it
with the butt, and heard a voice from the outside tell him not to
strike. He got back in and drove away to beat the band.

Then George thought of a curious spell he had heard described
many times by a seamstress in Three Rivers, Canada.

• A father cursed a baby because it couldn't keep its nakedness
covered. When it grew up, the boy could never keep his pants
on; he was all right when you looked at him, and then they would
suddenly fall off. They painted his hands to see if any print
showed up on them; his hands touched nothing. The family even
took him to Boston to see the doctors there, but they couldn't
help. He had to work in the field with just a shirt on.

Of course George knew about the *fi-follet*, an illusion feared by all devout Canadiens.

• I heard a French Canadian say he saw the *fi-follet*. The *fi-follet* is a kind of vision that appears to you if you are a bad man: if you go out without permission of your parents or your religion. It looks like a man in flame; coming home you see it all around, on the fence or in the house or in some dark corner.

It was following this man, out in the farming country. He made for the first door he came to and shut it, bang! When he opened the door, there was a knife stuck in it, half full of blood.

Herm Manette told his boarding-house listeners how he had seen a death sign, when he was a boy right there in Munising.

Herm Manette speaks
• Dad had a lot and a shack at the west end of town, a flat-roofed shack with a little window, when I was maybe four years old. Dad's sister in Montreal was ill at the time. We were all abed, and the kerosene lamp had been turned down low for the night. Both mother and dad heard a zing through the window, as if something had broke the glass. Dad got up and found the lamp chimney broken, and the rocking chair going. He was kind of scared, and right away said something must have happened.

Next day a letter came, edged in black. His sister had died.

Dad told me that lots of times.

The questions flew at Herm from the listeners. Hadn't someone thrown a stone through the window and broken the lamp globe?

No, Herm explained methodically, because the glass in the window was not broken, and the window had been closed tight.

No one could break Herm's story, and the group turned to another marvel.

BEGGARS
In Quebec the French who had land lived by farming, and those who had none lived by begging. The farmers treated the

beggars with care, for they had powers — for good, for ill. A grateful beggar brought fortune to the family of Bert Damour.

Albert Damour speaks

• My mudder tells about dis feller came into her place. (She had a farm on de main road, at Saint-Jean-Port-Joli, a liddle port in Canada, below Quebec.) He was supposed to be a beggar for eats. Dere were beggars going t'rough every day, and dey'd want something to take along wid dem, a piece of pork or bread. Dat's de way dey used to make deir living. You couldn't get any money cause dere wasn't any, fi' cents was de mos' you could get. De farmers would never turn down a man for a meal, cause dey had plenty of food on de location.

After de meal dis feller started to tell stories. And he said, "You're very poor, I'm going to do somet'ing for you," and he spit up money on de floor, vomited it up, sous and dollars and half-a-dollars. Dere wasn't much silver money den eider. Yes, he just said, "Now I gotta pay you," and he made some kind of a motion and de money come outa his mout'.

Mother t'ought he was dealing wid de devil to do dat, and didn't want to have him around. But father didn't care as long as dere was notting done.

On the porch of the old-timers' cabin at Lake Linden, spare, solemn Wilfred Marcotte remembered about a malicious beggar.

Wilfred Marcotte speaks

• Some people in Canada go around begging, to get somet'ing to eat. One farmer said he wasn't very rich and couldn't give dis man notting. So de beggar wished dat his calf would get full of lice.

De farmer roasted de calf, and burned de lice. De beggar come running back, and asked him "What for you do dat?"

De farmer said, "I t'ought you make my calf suffer, I make you suffer."

De beggar didn't wish him no more lice.

ONE VERY STRONG MAN

There are marvels that rise from natural as well as from super-natural powers. Lake Linden Frenchmen talk much about George Garmache, who resisted a team of horses with each hand, and of "soople" Joe Montferrand who, as every Canadien knows, kicked his footprint on a tavern ceiling.* But they were as babies beside Maxine Duhaim of Three Rivers, Canada, although Maxine has not their fame.

At the edge of Lake Linden, seventy-nine-year old Joe Racine stood bareheaded in the rain beside his woodpile and recited feats of Max Duhaim. He knew him well, for Max had chopped wood for his father.

Joe Racine speaks

• Duhaim was second cousin to my father, and worked for him when Dad had a contract. They start to cut in the morning before they begin to skid. Max was a man who didn't like to work steady. He says to my dad, "Joe, if you don' min', I'll take de wood all myself. You don' have to use a team. It'll go quicker like dat."

So instead of the team skidding out the logs, he'd pick them up and throw them out on the road. It only took him a minute to throw out a thirty-inch log, but it took time to cut the trees down.

He cut a pole out of ironwood — bois dur — to make a pry, four to five inches thick, six to seven feet long. An ordinary pry was two inches thick. My dad said Max's pry was strong enough to hold two teams if they were hitched to it. But when he raised a log up with it, you could see the pry bend. It would be a load for us just to carry it.

If there was a windfall lying in the road, he'd make holes on both sides, put the pry under it, one end on his shoulder and the other end under the log, and clear the road by himself.

The threshing machine was in the barn — they'd been thresh-ing peas — and there was thirty-six bushels of peas on the sled.

* Garmache is corrupted from Grenache. Montferrand is pronounced Moufron.

The sled was on a plank floor, and it was difficult to pull because there was no snow on the floor. My uncle said, "I'll give you a bottle of whisky if you pull that out." So Max pulled it out by himself. It would take a horse to do that.

He never worked steady, but did little jobs around. He never had a penny. When the farmers used to have a bee, to make a barn out of square timbers, he'd do all the heavy work. He'd pick up a whole timber by himself. When he was cutting wood, and the snow was three or four feet high in the forest, he pulled the sleigh himself to the main road. "I am afraid my horse cannot pull it," he said.

One time a passer-by asked him where Duhaim lived. That was him of course. He unhooked the whiffle-tree and picked up the plough with one hand and pointed: "Dat's his house." [They tell this also on Joe Montferrand and George Louisier.]

My uncle had a kicking horse of which he was complaining. He had a New Year's Eve party, and got a little drunk, and was talking about the horse. Duhaim said, "Show me the horse." They went out to the barn, and the horse started to kick. Duhaim put one arm around the post, and when the horse kicked he put his other arm around his legs and held him.

"He's not such a cross horse," he said. The horse never kicked after that.

• Joe Montferrand was the strongest fighting man in Quebec. He had fists like a horse. But one time he met his match.

When Maxine was seventeen, he went to the dock at Quebec to get a job. The boat was going from Quebec to Montreal on the Ottawa River; it was loaded with all kinds of stuff from England. Joe Montferrand was boss to unload the boat, and he met Duhaim on the dock. He asked him if he wanted to help unload, and then he went back on the boat.

Duhaim told the other two fellows, "Just bring up them barrels, and I'll throw them over on to the dock." The barrels were from two hundred to five hundred pounds — pork and whiskey.

The two fellows had been throwing them over the railing together. One fellow went back and told Joe Montferrand.

So Montferrand come over. He was two hundred and forty, fifty pounds, a dry-bone man, six foot six or seven. He put his hand on Duhaim's shoulder and said, "If you watch yourself you're going to make a pretty good man."

Duhaim said, "I think I'm as good as any other man around here." He did not know who he was talking to.

"You don't know me, I'm Joe Montferrand."

Duhaim lifted him up by the arms and shook him up and down on the boat. Joe Montferrand didn't say no more after that.

• The strongest man from France came over to put on a show — Garmache. He put the show on at St. Ursule, on the outside of Three Rivers in Maskinongé county. There was a big yard back of the store, and he set up the show there.

Duhaim didn't go over. So a man named Lessard went over to get him, and he still wouldn't go. But my father went over, and Maxine said, "I'll go for you because I work for you." So he went over and shook hands with Garmache. Garmache fell down to the ground, and when he got up he had tears in his eyes.

"Excuse me, I didn't squeeze so very hard," Duhaim told him.

Garmache started to open up the show. He picked up an iron ball about fifty pounds, and threw it up in the air and caught it with one hand. He coaxed Duhaim to try that. "You come try that." Duhaim picked it up, and threw it up in the air two, three times, and laughed. "Dat's a kid game you play, notting for a man. If I couldn't do better dan dat, I wouldn't show up."

Duhaim was sleeping in a hotel in Three Rivers and sixteen men beat him up, cut his face all up. It was an election, and they were jealous of him. The parties used to travel around together then — the Red and the Blue.

The next day on the platform he was speaking and he said, "Today you caught me sleeping last night, but dis morning I no sleep. De first one who opens his mout' I'll get him." Nobody said nothing.

I seed the man. I was seven or eight year when he die.

CONTES

On the main street of Marquette, the largest city in the Peninsula, two aged *conteurs* sit on a porch and chat through the hours. No one suspects their gift, but this superannuated pair can reel off the entertaining *contes* and *cantes-fables* that in past centuries enchanted Breton and Norman peasants, and now have withered away before pulp magazines, soap operas, and movie thrillers.

For several months I had tried to locate such *conteurs*, hoping against hope they still could be found. The president of the French-Canadian Society in Marquette had said positively, "You'll have to go back to Canada for that kind of story. We're all too educated here. The only stories we know are those in books."

She should know if anyone did, and I left disconsolately, thumbing through the remaining names on my list of prospects. I headed for the post office to pick up my mail, and remembered that a newspaper friend had suggested, not very hopefully, an old fellow who lived just a block away from the post office building. "He probably doesn't know anything," the friend had said, "but he lives right on Washington Street and he's always home, so you might as well stop by." And by that merest reference I was led to a champion fabulist, Trefflé Largenesse. Furthermore, he had a pal, Charles Rivard, who also had *contes* in his craw.

Partly senile at seventy-nine, Trefflé maundered in his tales every so often, and his big face lit up with a toothless grin and an idiotic leer. Perhaps not so idiotic, for he aimed his leers at pert little Ariane de Félice from Paris, who was helping me with the French collecting, and leaned toward her as if he would gobble her headfirst. But a question or a reminder, and he was back on the story, tracing the adventures of heroic Tit Jean with

dragons and witches in faultless style. Trefflé's family and neigh-
bourhood see him as a shambling shell of a man, powerful of
body, weak of mind, spinning his life out on the porch steps. His
daughter who keeps his house listened to tales on his knee, but
little suspects their art or age.

Trefflé had heard and told stories all his life, stories in the pure
oral tradition, for he was illiterate. His father had recited *contes*
to him in Joliet, up in Quebec, before Trefflé came to Marquette
as a youth of seventeen. Then in the Peninsula lumbercamps he
heard more, on Saturday evenings in the candle-lit bunkhouse,
where Finns, Poles, Scotch, Irish and French gathered around
their particular raconteurs. "The Irishmen told lies; you cannot
beat an Irishman," he said admiringly.

But Trefflé is hard to beat himself, even at his most factual.
His biblical tales make strange gospel.

Trefflé Largenesse speaks

• Adam was de first man on de eart'. It was all covered wit' wood.
Adam said to God, "I want a woman, make me a woman." He
could talk real good, you know. So God made him an Indian
squaw, a goddamn squaw. And he said, "I don't want her." Then
God made a Chinese woman — eyes like dis [and Trefflé pulled
his lids apart]. And he didn't want her. And he made all kinds of
people. And finally he made a French girl. And Adam said, "I
want her." Her name was Eve.

The Tower of Babel episode also stuck in his mind.

• Lot of gypsies ['Gyptians] was building a tour in de sky, so
anybody gets tired of being here dey could go to heaven. Den
God knew dey was crazy and he change de language. After dat
dey all spoke different languages, Italian, French, English, like
now. So dey couldn't understand each odder. "Bring me de stone,
de mortar, a hammer," one say, and dey bring anudder ting. So
dey quit.

Dey got up to de top by steps all around de outside, like an
auger. Samson, he was a young man about twenty-two, twenty-

three, gave it a push and it fell down. A lot of gypsies got killed. Nobody try any more to climb to heaven.

Trefflé tells contes in the simple, rhythmic, repetitive prose that marks the true conteur, and embellishes his words with dramatic gestures and thunderous belly laughs. An American flavor has crept into the Old World tales, whose Canadien patois Trefflé strews with Yankee colloquialisms like "by gosh," "plug horse," and "buggy." (He can tell the contes in English too.) For his American auditors he must insert explanations of "king" and "fairies" and "dragons." The currency of his fairy-tale universe has become dollars, and France now is "on the other seashore" and Canada close by, so evidently Tit Jean and the giant are contesting in the United States. Strangest of all, the age-old formula of the hero's escape from the dragon by blocking his path with magic objects which grow to mountainous size, has taken a twentieth-century hue. In place of the traditional twig and stone, or bamboo shoot and rice paddy, or whatever the local vegetation, we now find a bar of soap and a rusty razor.

The Dragon and the Razor
• There was a little boy who set out to search for the blood of a dragon to carry to a princess for her cure. Now this dragon was in a great forest. You understand, dragons are bad; when one is angry, it runs after a man, and devours him. He is strong, a dragon!

The little boy went to seek the dragon's blood to cure the princess's daughter; he would be well paid if he brought it back.

He set out. He went into the woods, he walked, he walked. He came to a little cabin. An old fairy lived in the little cabin there. You understand, the fairies are like the gypsies. The gypsy, he tells lies to the devil.

The old fairy said, "Where are you going like that, my little boy?"

"I am going to seek dragon's blood to cure the princess."

"But how are you going to get dragon's blood?"

"Well, I will have to bleed him."

"But you have not the power to bleed him. This dragon stays a hundred miles from here. If he is awakened, you cannot even approach him. In any case, if you get to see him, I am going to give you something; I am going to give you a bar of soap, then a bottle of water, then a razor, an old razor. If the dragon runs after you, throw these behind you."

It happens that the little boy takes the soap, the razor and the water, and goes to meet the dragon. Now the dragon was not sleeping, and the little boy, he had to come back right away, with the dragon running after him. He ran, he ran, my friend. The dragon was on the point of catching him, the little boy throws his bottle. . . . a great lake, my friend! This bottle formed a great lake. The dragon was in the water, by gosh! The dragon was in the water, he swam, he swam; then he made a dive. He comes across to the end; he is strong, a dragon, you know! He kept gaining, gaining. When the little boy saw that the dragon was close to grabbing him, he threw his bar of soap. There was a great mountain of soap . . . . ah, he was buried in the soap, the dragon! The foam blew everywhere; he had it in the eyes, in the throat. He beat it strongly. He rolled out of it. He finishes crossing the mountain of soap. He gained, he gained, he had almost rejoined the little boy. When he saw that the dragon was close to catching him, he threw his razor, the little boy. . . . By gosh! a mountain of razors. The dragon, he cut his paws. There were razors everywhere. They cut here, there, everywhere, they cut especially the neck. The dragon, he was feeble. He fell on his back, he bled, he bled.

The little boy came back when he saw the dragon was on his side bleeding. The blood gushed, by gosh! He filled his bottle. He went away.

It took six days for him to return to the king. He arrived there: "Here," he said, "your majesty, here is the blood of the dragon."

"Blood of the dragon! It is not possible."

"Certainly. Yes. If you had seen how the dragon bled!"

"Good," said the king, "It is all very well. I will give it to my daughter. It will restore her." (It was a remedy, that.)

He gave it to his daughter; she is become beautiful, beautiful, she is married right away.

Then the king gave a hundred dollars to the little boy.

It is all! It is enough!

Roclor and the Giant

• Well, Roclor, he had made a chum of a giant. Now the giant stayed with his mother, an old witch. The giant had much money, you understand. Roclor, he had no money at all. He reflected; he thought to himself how he could get the giant's money.

He said to his mother, "I am going to see the giant."

"Oh, don't go there! Don't go there! He will swallow you up."

"He won't swallow me up," he said, "Good-bye, mother, I'm going."

"Take care of yourself."

He walked, walked, walked, through the woods, you know. The giant lived in a great forest, he had a little cabin, a log cabin.

The little boy said, "Good morning, great giant."

"Good morning, little boy. How come you're here?"

"I've come to make a wager with you."

"A wager? What do you want to wager?"

"I want to wager that I am stronger than you."

"Oh, you are not stronger than I. You are too little, you."

"But I am able." (He was small, Roclor, but he was clever.)

The giant asked, "Where do you come from? From far away?"

"Yes, from far away. I have been walking three days. Give me something to eat."

The old mother of the big giant made them some porridge. The giant was also hungry. Roclor said, "Here, I'll bet you that I can eat more porridge than you."

"Good," he said, "all right."

They bet five dollars.

The big giant, he ate, ate, ate. Never had he eaten so much

porridge in his life. Roclor, he had opened the collar of his shirt and all the time while he was eating the porridge, he threw it in his shirt. He was filled with porridge! Then he said, "To see who has eaten the most, we must cut open our stomachs." He cut open his shirt and the porridge poured out.

The giant said, "I am not going to cut myself open. If I cut myself open, I would die." He gave the five dollars to Roclor so he would not have to cut himself open.

The great giant, he had a bar, a large iron bar. He said to Roclor, "Let's go into the forest. I am going to throw the bar. If you throw it farther than I," he said, "I'll give you five dollars."

Roclor said, "I will have it."

They went into the forest. The great giant grabbed the iron bar: it was a thick bar, like that [gesture]. There was a little clearing there.

He said, "It is here that we will bet."

Roclor said, "That's fine."

"Look," he said, "I'm going to throw it. Now," he said, "it's going to fall back here. Better pay attention. Go under the tree so that it won't fall down on your head" (because it was heavy, you understand).

He threw the bar a good two hundred feet in the air. "Now," he said, "Roclor, throw it, you, to see if you can send it further than me."

Roclor was too small. Roclor, he said, "Hey, you'll see." He grasped the bar with both hands. He cried out, "MY BROTHERS IN CANADA, ATTENTION YOU ALL, I'M GOING TO THROW YOU A BAR."

The big giant said, "I have some brothers in Canada myself. Don't throw it."

"Well, I'll throw it to the other shore of the sea, down there in France. MY BROTHERS ON THE OTHER SEASHORE, ATTENTION ALL OF YOU, I AM GOING TO THROW A BAR."

"No, no, don't throw it there. I have some brothers there also."

"Here's your bar, I won't throw it."

The great giant said, "No, don't throw it. I'll give you the five dollars."

"All right."

He takes the five dollars, he puts them in his pocket.

The great giant said, "We must wager again. Let us see who can strike a blow of the fist the harder, who can flog the other the harder."

Roclor said, "When do you want to begin the wager?"

"Immediately, if you wish. Wait, I am going to show you how I strike with my fist!"

Roclor said, "I can strike myself also." He said, "Let's go to dinner and then come back after dinner and do the striking."

They went to the cabin, the great giant and Roclor. What did they have for dinner? Porridge! [Laughs]. Roclor said, "There is nothing except porridge here!"

The old woman gave him a kettleful of porridge. Roclor could not eat his porridge, he had eaten too much of it the evening before!

The great giant had a kettleful also, he ate it clean. And then Roclor, he said, "Listen now, great giant," he said, "do you have a drill?"

"Yes," he said, "I have an old drill. What do you want with it?"

"Oh, it is to see how it is made. I hear often speak of that, a drill. I do not know how it is made. I would like to learn."

"Here it is. Listen," he said, "do not go to strike the blow of the fist on the tree — not today. Tomorrow we shall strike. The one who enters his fist the farthest will have five dollars."

The great giant wanted to "scheme" Roclor like a Jew, to get back the money which he had lost; he had given ten dollars to Roclor. In the night, Roclor got up and went into the wood with the drill, and made some holes in the tree. In the morning, the great giant, having rested, having slept, then ate his porridge. They went to strike the tree. Now the great giant, he strikes on one side. He drove his fist in almost up to here [Trefflé indicated on his arm]. Another. blow drives his fist in again. Roclor made a hole immediately right through the tree. Ah, it was greater than the giant's, that! The giant, he winds up, pis paf! on the tree. But Roclor, he draws back, he enters his fist right up to the elbow through the tree [gesture].

"There, great giant," he said, "strike like that, strike like mine, great giant!"

Ah, he did nothing to his fist, Roclor, the hole was pierced, you see! [Laughs]. The great giant gave the five dollars to Roclor.

Then he said, "Let's carry some water for my mother. Let's see how much water you can carry. If you carry more water than me," he said, "I'll give you five dollars."

The next morning, the great giant, he had two great jars you know, well filled, two great jars which he was bringing to his mother. Roclor could not carry these great jars. He went to the well, now, he began to put a handle on the well. The giant was in the house, he turns round and sees that Roclor was about to put a handle on his well.

"What are you doing, Roclor," he asked, "putting a handle on my well?"

"Do you think that I am going to carry these jars of water?" he asked. "I am not going to carry water. I am going to take the well to the house."

"Ah, you are crazy," he said, "do not put a handle on my well. Leave it there. Do not carry any water. If you have to put a handle on my well, here is the five dollars."

He gave the five dollars to Roclor so that he would not put a handle on his well, you see!

Then the great giant said, "Roclor, go to your home. I am not going to have anything more to do with you. You win the wagers every time."

Roclor went home with all his money. His old mother was very happy.

Me, I was there to see if Roclor had arrived, indeed; he arrived; now the story is finished.

DIALECT STORIES

While the legends and contes of the Canadien belong to a European past, his comic dialect anecdotes spring strictly from native American humor. Like the perennially stupid Jean Sot in the fairy tales, he commits all manner of idiocies in the strange world of Yankee slang and baseball games and power machines. His weird English talk gets repeated, his woeful stunts get talked about, and he emerges as a full-fledged folk character in his own right.

Some of his mis-sayings become proverbial. At Marquette a Frenchman loading supplies down at the mercantile docks found himself in a jam. Trying to maneuver his team into position, he ordered the horses to back up, which they did, but then he could not think how to make them stop. He implored and entreated a halt, all in vain, and saw his team back over the towering dock into Lake Superior. "Well, I hope you got your damn satisfy," he cried in rage, and Marquetters still use his phrase to express pique. A Frenchman selecting a horse for a prospective rider said to him, "Take dis one here, she's de mos' wore out." He meant that the horse was the best broken in, but folks around Escanaba stick to his original phrasing.

Especially in the lumber camps, to which they streamed in numbers from Quebec, the miscues of Canadiens grew into fable. Adelore Blanc, cutting cedar poles on a piece-work basis, finished his job, received his pay, and walked from camp nine miles to the railroad tracks. There he met an educated Frenchman, Big Joe, who could read.

"Let me look at your slip, I'll tell you what you got," said Big Joe. "Hm, you got two six-inch thirty-five foot cedaire poles."

"Dat must be wrong," said Adelore, "I know I cut elevenne." He walked back the nine miles to camp and told the boss, "You know you made a mistake, you. I cut elevenne and you only pay me for two."

"That's right," said the boss, "I marked down eleven."

"Can't *be*, you only got two marks!"

After getting his camp pay Joe Deronseau once went to Green Bay, the big Wisconsin town south of Menominee, and ordered a meal at a hotel. The waiter gave him a written menu. He pointed to the first three lines and was brought three kinds of soup. Then he tried the last line and the waiter gave him a toothpick.

A French cook was busily stirring a big batch of batter in the cookhouse. A jack standing by asked him what he was making. "I don' know," he said. "I drop pieces in de wataire. If dey float dey're doughnuts. If dey sink dey're dropcakes."

"Strange as it seems, this story is pretty true," began Ranger Bernard McTiver in his isolated headquarters home in Lake Superior State Forest.

Bernard McTiver speaks

• It happened in my father's camp at the Sucker River, when they were hauling pine and hemlock to Perry's Landing on Lake Superior. In those days we had a bucking board (today they call it a bulletin board) in the office to get the various teamsters to compete with one another to see who could haul the most logs. The names of each of the twelve teamsters were written on the board, and every night a scaler placed alongside them the number of board feet hauled that day. At the end of the week he added up and wrote down the total hauled by all the teamsters, as the record of the camp that week. The idea was to give the teamster who hauled the most logs for the month a mackinaw, worth about fifteen or twenty dollars, and of course to get the camp to boost its weekly record.

"Among these teamsters was Pete Sherette, a Canadian Frenchman who could barely read or write. He came in every night, looked at the board, hauled his logs with great energy the next day, came in and studied the board again, and kept doing that all month till his horses got so poor you could count their hip bones and ribs. The last day of the month when he went into the office he looked at the board for about an hour. Finally the foreman, seeing him there, said "Pete, you've done pretty well, haven't you?"

"Yessie, by Chris', I have," said Peter. "But show me dat goddamn man Total."

As the Frenchmen loved the woods, so they despised the mines, and never consented to work underground. At the most the Canadien would take a surface job with the mining company, but that was enough for him to create mining legends too.

A Frenchman named Genoss had been trained to drive a new electric locomotive that pushed an ore-laden tramcar to the ore pile, where it dumped its load. On the baptismal trip the surface crew all turned out to watch. Genoss started his engine successfully, but he kept on going right past the caution signal and over the bumping block. Ore-car, engine, and Genoss landed on top of the ore pile. The superintendent was the first to reach Genoss — a big man, but he made speed that day.

"Are you hurt?" he asked Genoss as soon as he got his breath.

"No, I'm not veree much hurt."

"Why in hell didn't you stop then?"

"Jee Chris', Mr. Super, I say 'Whoa' feefty times but she never stop."

Some Frenchmen lingering on beyond the boom days have become fixtures in the folklore of decaying towns. For the most part old shackers and saloonkeepers who have retired from heavy woods work, they still cling to the gutted forests, and still perform the follies that distinguish all peasoupers. Your northwoods raconteur with the mimic gift can tell you any number of yarns about such celebrated characters. In fact, Walter Gries from Negaunee recites these yarns to laughing audiences all over the state. Mr. Gries is a mining company executive, a German, and a well-spoken man, but he can talk Cornish and Canadien dialect like a streak, after hearing it around him all his life. His favorite story concerns Fred Felteau.

Walter Gries speaks

• Fred Felteau was a great big fellow who weighed about two hundred and fifty pounds. He ran away from Canada and came to the Upper Peninsula as a boy of fourteen or fifteen, where he worked in the woods till he was fifty and got rheumatiz. Then he "retired" to a shack on Gratiot Lake in Keweenaw County, a little cabin with the hind seat of an old automobile for a front porch.

Electioneering was the big time for Fred. He'd go to town with the rest of the boys, who gathered round the store to talk things over and see who was going to run for office. A township caucus is still held to nominate officers, at Eagle Harbor, and there are just enough year-round residents so everybody can serve on the school or county board. Well, this year the boys tanked up at the bar, took their free chew of tobacco from the poorbox that went with each drink, and after settling things moved down street to the schoolhouse for the caucus.

Fred, the leader, his mouth full of tobacco, got up on the little rostrum. "Well, I guess we better start de mee*ting*." He switched the chew from the left to the right side of his mouth. "First ting we gotta have is nomeenation for superwisor. I'm de best man so I'll be dat." He switched his chew back. "Next ting we gotta have is nomeenation for townsheep clerk." Somebody got up and said, "I nomeenate Camille Rielle for townsheep clerk." Fred replied, "Well Camille he can't read and he can't write, but he can make hees cross, and we ain't got very much beezness anyway, so I tink Camille be all right for dat." He switched his chew back again, looked around for a place to spit, and said, "By gar, I tink de nex' ting we gotta have is cuspeedor." A French-Canadian friend got up and said, "I nomeenate Joe Bellack for cuspeedor."

5

COUSIN JACKS

To the Peninsula people, every Cornishman is a character. In a land that abounds with salty characters, this makes high tribute. The Cousin Jack (a nickname supposed to derive from Jack's habit of cussin') differs markedly from the exotic Finn and the explosive Frenchman. His spice is a comical gravity. He twists sense with a wise and solemn air. He mangles pronouns, scrambles words, and misplaces h's with a pundit's assurance.

"There is nothing so ignorant as an ignorant Cousin Jack," says the son of a Jack. "He is comical and he don't know it. It's the dry unconcerned way he brings it out." And a toastmaster known for his dialect stories adds, "They really coin words for their own use. They sound like the action they are trying to describe."

These observers speak soundly. All the aging Cousin Jacks I saw belonged to the same unmistakable genus: many shapes and sizes, but one in their unconscious drollery, giving an effect of little boys play-acting like men. And in a sense they are, for Cornish lads left school at nine or ten to hold drills for their dads in the mines, and spent the rest of their lives underground.

Cornishmen began crossing the ocean in the 1850's to work the Peninsula mines. The world's best miners, trained over the centuries in the deep tin mines of Cornwall, they fanned out all over the world, to dig gold in South Africa, copper in Spain, iron in Cuba. Inevitably the iron and copper strikes in Michigan demanded and attracted their skill. The Cousin Jacks became the mining captains and taught their craft to other stocks and cheaper labor, the Finns, Swedes, Poles, Italians. (In Iron Mountain they say the great Captain Martin Goldsworthy of the Chapin mine would tell the job-hunting I-talians, "Go away, and when you can say Bodmin Land come back and I'll give you a job." Martin came from Bodmin Land, and the worst jail in Cornwall was Bodmin Jail.)

The big mines are played out now, and the mining wizards from Cornwall have long ceased their transatlantic trek. "When I came here fifty years ago from Cornwall," Herb Beard told me in Iron Mountain, "there was 90 per cent Cornish here. Now Cousin Jacks are scarce."

All the more because their numbers decline, the Cornishmen are cherished as lads with undoubted mettle and a special flavor. This flavor has permeated the north country, whose peoples eat their pasties, listen to their carols, watch their upright wrestling bouts, and remember their callithumpian parades on the Fourth of July. Each mining location in the horse and wagon days of Keweenaw put on its callithump. On the wagon festooned with evergreen boughs a Cousin Jack in a brown fur cutter robe played bear in the forest, dancing to the tune of a mouth organ, rolling over, climbing trees, and performing similar ursine antics. On another, a band screeched and thumped merrily with music from tin whistles and mouth organs, while miners in colored dresses made coy faces at the spectators and the horses jingled red, white, and blue bone rings and dangled red tassels from their bridles. In place of fireworks, the English folk — admonished in the Old Country to celebrate the Independence Day or be deported — concentrated on picnics with barrels of lemonade, baseball games between fathers and sons, and foot-races for beribboned youngsters in white suits and dresses. In their frolics and their foods, their songs and their speech, the Cornish families brought to the Peninsula distinctive folkways, for no Cousin Jack or Jenny forgets his Cornish culture.

Take singing. Every Cornishman as a matter of course sings hymns and carols and lyrics with true, clear pitch. He will enter into song in the midst of a conversation without the slightest self-consciousness. Stubby Herb Beard at Iron Mountain, sitting in a swing in his little garden and turning the ragged pages of a Cornwall guidebook, broke off in his plods to sing me "The Sweet Little Woodmouse."

> *A sweet little woodmouse once made a snug nest*
> *In a cornfiel' belongin' to good Farmer West*
> *Where everything grew that was pleasant to eat*
> *From beans, oats, and barley, and beautiful wheat.*
> *At the door of 'is 'ousehold a carpet of green*
> *The woodmouse oft sat and surveyed a fair scene.*
> *"This is truly a very fine cornfiel'," said he,*
> *"And doubtless was planted on purpose for me."*
>
> *He nibbled the corn as it lay on the ground*
> *So sweet as a lark and so soft it was found*
> *So safe in its nest far from turmoil and noise*
> *Not worried by dogs nor molested by boys.*
> *Farmer West was the man that saw him day after day*
> *But he never attempted to drive him away,*
> *For, said he, "Since we've plenty and God gave it all*
> *A little we'll spare for a creature so small."*

In Crystal Falls I tried to pump a story from deaf old Joe Keast, who had drilled ore in a dozen mines in the Peninsula and, according to report, had once strapped his captain to his waist and taken him down a condemned shaft. They both came up alive, but the captain spent the rest of his days in the state insane asylum at Newberry. Mild little Joe scarcely looked the part, especially when his wife Mary Jane clamped him up most savagely when I introduced the subject. Joe would talk no more, but out of the blue he sang a song of his own composing, dedicated to safety on the highway. I can see him this minute, swaying back and forth on knotty legs, eyes closed, a coal shovel in his hand, chanting sweetly the virtues of the pedestrian who looks before he crosses.

At Ishpeming it was Dave Spencer, a russet-hued rascal with madly flailing arms and an Elizabethan ribaldry, who sang off-color verses with the sweet Cornish voice. When Dave spewed out schoolboy jokes and rhymes, his wife ran from the kitchen and boxed his ears and shut him up tight, the way Mary Jane had stoppered Joe Keast. But this time I had a better break, for author John Voelker came with me on a repeat visit and carefully decoyed the Cussin' Jack into a downtown saloon, where Dave could drink and talk and sing with uninhibited grace. He praised whiskey:

> *When I'm dead and in my grave*
> *No more whiskey shall I crave,*
> *And on my tombstone let this be wrote,*
> *Ten thousand gallons run down my throat.*

And the money that bought it:

> *O Almighty dollar, thy shining face*
> *That speaks thy mighty power*
> *In my pocket find a resting place*
> *For I need thee every hour.*
>   *Amen.*

and sang a ballad he had picked up in Nova Scotia in 1887, where the miners engaged in song contests, and a fellow named Bill Chisholm had thought up "Steve O'Donnell's Wake."

> *Steve O'Donnell was a gintleman,*
>   *That everybody said,*
> *He was liked by all the rich and all the poor*
> *And they all felt so sorry when they heard*
>   *That Steve was dead.*

They tied a knot of crepe upon his door,
They sent for the barber to cut the spindles from his throat,
They cut his hair a la la pompadour.
Red necktie and buttonhole, bouquet was in his coat,
And a bunch of shamrock in his hand he bore.

O meself and Annie Fielding helped to lay the rascal out.
There were lots of flowers sent for friendship's sake.
O Steve me boy, why did you die? the weeping widow cried,
And we all got drunk at Steve O'Donnell's wake.

O they were fighters, and biters, bums, and dynamiters,
Ale, wine, and whiskey, there were cake,
There were men of high position,
There were Irish politician,
And we all got floored at Steve O'Donnell's wake.

Or take food. The pasty is already legend, that crust-covered meat and vegetable pie which is driving hot dogs out of the Peninsula. Conventional pasties contain round steak, potatoes, turnips, rutabaga, suet, and onions, but some exciting recipes employ seedless raisins supported with rice and butter, or kidneys with bacon strips and shaved potato chips, or dates or berries or eggs or liver — but never beans. A Chinese cook once made that mistake in a Colorado silver mining camp, and the Cousin Jacks bounced him gently from the peak of Silver Mountain to the valley below.

Cornish folk have other sacred food loves: their scroll pilchard, saffron buns, and scalded cream. Herb Beard brought water to my mouth with his recipe for scalded cream.

Herb Beard speaks

• Milk a cow, strain the fresh milk in a pan, put it on the cold granite stone floor till next morning. Then boil it on the stove; the cream goes to the top. Put it back on the floor to cool. Put a skimmer under the dish, take the cream off, and pour it into glasses. It is so stiff it can hold up weight; I've seen it hold up a pound. Cousin Jinnys make it over here. Scald cream put on treacle on bread and butter is called thunder and lightning.

Even shriveled old Lydia Pearce of Crystal Falls, her wits half gone, had enough left to describe the preparing of scroll pilchard.

Lydia Pearce speaks

• Lay the fish on the roof for several hours in the sun, split open and lying flat like your hand. Then cook it right on the coals, sizzling in its own fat — pilchards alone in the fish world come from the sea wrapped in their own cooking grease. Or thrust a thick stick through the bones and hang the fish on a tree until the sun forms a film on the skin. Then take it down for roasting.

Cornishmen in America still savor their other standbys, but pilchard they must sorrowfully forego, for the fish does not appear in American waters.

The men from Cornwall exchanged one peninsula for another. Cornwall is fastened on to England by a chain, the ferry across the river Tamur, and the saying goes that one leaves, or enters, England when he crosses the Tamur. From Redruth and Penzance and St. Ives came a true country folk, economically wedded to the hake, sprat, and pilchards of the sea, the crops of the field, and the tin ore of the earth, and like all people of the soil, drenched in traditions. They brought to America a fair cargo of their luxuriant folkway, and in addition droll personalities to inspire new lore. One Cornish American has faithfully narrated, in a long rhymed autobiography, *Cornwall and the "Cousin Jack"* (printed of course by a Cornish press), an archetypal history of the crossing.

At seventeen T. J. Nicholas left Cornwall and eight pounds wages a month for the Michigan Peninsula, after nearly signing up for Africa. He carried his belongings in a carpet sack, spent much of his little hoard to buy a mattress, tin cup, plate, knife, fork, and spoon on the boat, huddled miserably in his steerage bunk while the ship heaved, landed at New York with two dollars and sixty-five cents, survived the railroad trip on bread and water, borrowed money for clothes at the mine town, worked ten hours a day, repaid his passage money in five months, and sent five dollars home to his mother. Nicholas fared well in the new land because he could read and write. He rose to be a shift boss and mining captain. He has lived fifty-seven years in the Peninsula, enduring the fire hazards of the stinking dry-houses and the caving threats of hastily built shafts, watching the slow struggle of the unions to lift the miners above penury and criticizing with equal bitterness the profiteering owners and stingy coöps. Three times he returned to his birthland to renew his traditions, and in between subscribed faithfully to the *Cornish Post*. Today he holds a high county office in his second homeland. Captain Nicholas is American by law and by career, but he is irrevocably Cornish, too, saturated in the folk history and folk culture of his people. He can name you a dozen kinds of pasty, recite a hundred archaic Cornish words, recount the plods and sainted wells and myriad superstitions that cover the duchy from the Tamur to Land's End. In all this he exemplifies the true spirit of a Cousin Jack.

TRADITIONS

Should you pass through the little town of Palmer in the hinterland of Marquette County, one house beside the highroad is sure to catch your eye. It has a cobblestone chimney, an enclosed porch, and a flower garden adorned with hundreds of large green bottles. Most particularly, a little arbor stands in one corner of the garden, on whose roof can be seen a triangular concrete slab, painted black with gold trim, and bearing fifteen yellow rocks and the device, "One for all and all for one." The triangle represents the Cornish coat-of-arms, which in turn symbolizes a tradition that not even Cornishmen always know.

Captain T. J. Nicholas knows it, though, and has erected this symbol of his Cornish faith in the county he now serves as Chairman of the Board of Supervisors. A tall, brown-faced man, with raven black hair and eyes deep set in their sockets, resonant and orotund in speech, Mr. Nicholas likes the idea of exchanging a mine shaft for a writing desk and giving information to professors who call on him.

The Fifteen Gold Bezants (Captain T. J. Nicholas)

• During the crusades the head nobleman of Cornwall was taken prisoner and sent to Turkey. A ransom of fifteen golden bezants was then demanded for his release. In order to raise this money a collection was made throughout the county, each person giving what he could afford. This no doubt explains the words of the Cornish motto, "One And All," because the money was collected from one and all.

In 1337 the new title of Duke was created by King Edward III, to confer on his son in place of the earldom then in abeyance. So the famous Black Prince became not only the first Duke of Cornwall, but the first Duke of England. The fifteen bezants with the motto "One and All" was then adopted for the arms of the new Duchy of Cornwall.

It is an interesting point that an heir to the throne of England is invested with the honors of Prince of Wales and Earl of Chester if and when the sovereign thinks fit, but he becomes Duke of Cornwall automatically.

And Captain Nicholas gazed fondly at the gleaming gold balls on the shield, quite oblivious of the surrounding Michigan wilderness.

FLOGGING THE HAKE

That hake were actually flogged by fishermen of St. Ives, most Cousin Jacks agree, but on the why and the how, they argue.

Captain Nicholas asserts that a single hake was flogged through the streets by irate fishermen who caught him in the ocean with pilchards in his throat. They then set him free as a lesson to his fellows never to eat the prized pilchard. The men of St. Ives valued the pilchards because the profits on their sale maintained their numerous cats and wives, and further, they delighted the palates of Cornishmen, when properly prepared, of course. Too well did the hake learn their lesson, for none ever came again to St. Ives.

Little, wizened Art Caddy of Ironwood, a husk of a man at seventy-nine, but once the lightweight Cornish-style wrestling champion of Michigan, tells a varying tale.

• They used to have so much fish come into Newquay that one year the people used them for manure on the farms, instead of giving to the poor. Bigger pilchards used to come into Newquay than anywhere else, nearly as big as mackerels; they came in in squalls, or schools. But after that year the fish didn't come any more to Newquay.

John Chappell, Bill Palmatier, and Ralph Wolfe give three more interpretations.

• 'Flogging the hake' is a fighting expression to any man from St. Ives. At one time so many hake were caught, the fishermen flogged them in the boats. The hake never came again.

• The Cousin Jack caught the hake, and had never seen one before, so he tried to make him talk. He wouldn't talk, so the Cousin Jack dragged him through the streets and horsewhipped him.

• There lived a man in St. Ives by the name of Hake who was a lawyer. He cheated a number of his clients in their transactions with him. When each found out that the others had been cheated too, they formed a party, tied Hake to a cart, and followed him through the streets flogging him with whips and switches. This is what is meant by 'Flogging the Hake.' There is a fish called the hake, but this expression has nothing to do with a fish.

COO-COO TIME

In Laurium town, the home of the great Calumet and Hecla shaft in the heart of the Copper Country, the veteran Cornish miners who first opened up the range can still be found, perhaps sitting around the Old-Timers Lodge next to the fire station. ("Tell them in that book," said one gnome to me, "that they didn't eat nor drink nawthin.") But they are an aged, dying stock.

Captain Arthur Williams died within the year I met him. Captain Arthur had retired from a life in the mines, but he still sang Methodist hymns in the choir and bounded around town with furious energy. In repose he presented a striking figure, tall and athletic, with clean chiseled features, whose high ruddy color nicely balanced his steel-gray head. Captain Arthur could easily have sat for a "Man of Distinction" advertisement, posed with a tall tumbler of whiskey in his right hand and an executive look. But when he opened his mouth, the image changed abruptly. Captain Arthur became galvanized, as if his nervous system had suddenly been switched on to a high voltage circuit; he batted the air savagely, swayed and danced, darted and cocked his head about, in a spasm of expression. Soon I saw the reason of the matter; Captain Arthur's meager vocabulary sadly lagged behind his pulsing thoughts, and he must needs pound out his meaning and enrich his scanty monosyllables with flailing gestures. Even at that I found the going rough, and a friend had to interpret his sense a time or two.

Captain Arthur, in the course of punching out his remarks, happened to light on the subject of unusual reflexes in men he had known.

Captain Arthur Williams speaks

• There was a Frenchman — he was in the National Guard during the 1913 strike — anybody holler, "drop it," he'd have to drop whatever he was carrying. He dropped a whole tray of dishes one time. Another fellow, George Labby at Allouez, French too, would kick if anybody touch him — couldn't stop that foot — just touch him in the ribs, up fly his boot.

'Spose a man just go round say his own name, they say he's coo-coo. That's what the coo-coo does. This Hungarian — laborer in the Wolverine mine — would say "Coo-coo" at coo-coo time, in March-April-May-June, if anybody tickled him and said "Say Coo-coo."

I didn't follow this at all, and asked Captain Arthur what he meant by "coo-coo time.' He then recited to me, with his own interpolations, a rhyme about the cuckoo I subsequently found known to every Cousin Jack in the Peninsula, for the cuckoo abounds in Cornwall.

In March it sits on its perch (don't sing nor nawthin')
In April month it sounds its bell (just sings one note)
In May he sings night and day (you can hear him anytime)
In June he alters his tune (gook-koo, gook-koo, gook-koo three
     times)
In July away he fly.

His feathers change in July — don't know for sure where he goes to. The teeter lark always flies around with the coo-coo. Then when the coo-coo goes away, the lark makes a nest and sits on the coo-coo eggs.

This miner, he just say his own name, except in the coo-coo months. Then when anybody tickled him he'd say "Coo-coo" three or four times — couldn't stop. He was coo-coo.

BELIEFS

The old Cousin Jacks and Cousin Jennies in the Peninsula believe still in witchcraft and omens.

• I've talked with witches in the Old Country. It would branch out that some woman in the village had mysterious powers, and we were afraid she would ill-wish us. Margaret M. in Cambourne was such a one; she had no trouble keeping us away from her garden, and she had nice red gooseberries. [Captain Nicholas would not divulge her last name.]

• There was an old fellow in St. Day, in the Old Country, they said could ill-wish [Herb Beard declared]. I knew him well, he went to the same school I did. He always wore his hair under his hat in a red handkerchief. There were four brothers named Kinsman, all stone masons, who mocked him. He knelt down and wished they would die before they were forty. And they all died right off, of t.b., and their sister too. People say the old bugger should of been hanged.

• The tapping of a bird's beak on the window means death of a loved one [warned Captain Nicholas]. Eighteen years ago, Mrs. Kendall came running up the hill to my house and said, "There's a bird at home tapping at the window pane, and somebody in the family will surely die." Her husband died a week after, from phthisis he got while working in a South African mine.

• If a person dies and his hands are soft and warm, somebody follows him to death. [A bystander hearing me chat with a friend about Cornish beliefs in a telegraph office in Calumet burst out with this. She was Bertha Muggelberg, and both her parents had come from Cornwall.] When mother died, I told my sister, "May, I don't like it, Mother's hands are soft." Undertaker Thomas tried to tell us that often happened with older people, but when any of our relatives died their hands were cold and hard as ice. Before Christmas that year (1944) my niece's little baby died. That was the third death in the family, because another niece had lost her husband overseas just before mother died. Deaths come in threes, you know.

• Glass cracking in a picture-frame is a sign of trouble in the family. Dad had a picture made of himself in 1907 — that one there on the wall [and Mary Burgan of Lake Linden, a fragile Cousin Jenny in her eighties, pointed to a large elliptical portrait sheathed in heavy convex glass, showing an unhealthy-looking face with white hair and a white beard, above a black bow tie and a dress jacket]. Dad died that same year; he had pernicious anemia. When we were at his funeral the glass cracked; we saw it when we came home. Later we found out that his sister died just about the same time. She still lived in Redruth, Cornwall, and she was always afraid he would die before her and she would be left alone, the last of the family. They never knew of each other's death — the letters crossed.

Many still current Cornish beliefs about good and bad luck have crystallized into proverbs and customs.

• A rooster crowing at midnight is the sign of death of a relative. (Many roosters have had their heads cut off in the morning for this reason.)

If a gamecock crows too early in the morning, the owner will be injured in any mine he enters. (The miner's wife would implore him to stay home that day.)

Wherever you see a little light jumping all around one spot — an open place, or near furze bushes — there's rich mineral near. They claim that's what makes those lights — Jack O'Lanterns they're called — dance around. If you sink a shaft there you'll find ore.

A green Christmas makes a fat graveyard. (No one here likes to see a green Christmas. If snow is late in coming, everyone gets worried.)

In a number of homes no one is allowed to sweep the floor after the fire is lit. It sweeps out the good luck.

Do not wash blankets in May month — you wash your friends away.

If you wear green you will wear black. (This Cousin Jenny said she would never buy another green dress as this proved to be true.)

Never return borrowed salt. (Many housewives do borrow salt, and are usually told not to return it. One lady always refused to lend any, and carried on whenever she was asked to, explaining that she could not get the salt back.)

If you draw a slice of the bride's cake through the wedding ring, and put it under your pillow, you will dream of your future wife or husband. (This is still done, but more for the fun of it, now.)

It is unlucky for the church clock to strike during the performance of a marriage ceremony. (Most churches have installed electric clocks.)

If the youngest daughter should be married before her older sisters, they must all dance at her wedding in their stocking feet, if they wish to have husbands.

Horseshoes bring good luck. Outside a number of English homes one will notice a horseshoe on the door, occasionally upside down. This is kept there for good fortune, and may be taken down and turned around as long as it does not touch the ground. The Cornish miners would take a horseshoe down with them when sinking a winze in the mine and nail it to the supporting timber. Upon starting their shaft, each miner would touch the horseshoe four times, for luck throughout the day.

Faith in the home remedies of the Old Country continues yet, or at least is still remembered. Bessie Phillips of Eagle River, once a populous settlement of Cornish families, recalls these treatments.

Bessie Phillips speaks

• Years ago children and grown-ups were subject to sties on their eyelids. The mother would apply a poultice of tea-leaves until the gathering would break. Another cure was passing the tail of a black cat nine times over the eyes; for double efficiency the tail should belong to a tomcat.

In the early days all children wore around their neck a small bag of flannel containing a piece of camphor, as a protection against mumps, chicken pox, and measles. The older folks would wear a piece of red yarn tied around their wrists or a narrow strip of red flannel wound about their waists, to help their rheumatism.

In some homes the Good Friday bun was hung on a string and left to dry up until the next Good Friday came around. A fresh bun was then hung out, and the old one grated and used to cure such diseases as members of the family might contract. Bread made on Good Friday never gets mouldy, as long as the loaf is not placed on the table upside down.

Instead of wearing glasses, the old-time Cornish wore earrings, which were believed to strengthen the eyesight. The menfolk heated a darning needle, held a cork tightly behind the ear, and pierced the lobe with the needle so that it entered the cork. After the bleeding had stopped, a silk thread was pulled through the hole in the ear to keep it open, and the earrings inserted when the wound had healed. Today it is women who clip on earrings simply for ornament.

To treat childern's hiccups when they last a long time, wet the right forefinger with spittle, then cross the front of the left shoe three times at midnight beside the child's bed, while repeating the Lord's prayer backward three times. (This has often been done with good results.)

Many older folks still eat an apple before going to bed, especially if they have insomnia. Not only does "An apple a day keep the doctor away," but "An apple in the morning is the doctor's warning;" "The roasted apple at night starved the doctor outright;" "Eat an apple going to bed, knock the doctor on the head." Apples will keep you in good spirits as well as good health; "Without an apple in your eye, you'll see no good in earth or sky."

PLODS

Many jests or "plods" that the Cousin Jacks tell on themselves center about the Cornishman's love for his pasty. The pasty originated, says tradition, because the arsenic in the mines rusted the lunch pails, so the wives protected the lunch with a covering of flour and water. Then someone thought of making the cover good enough to eat. One hears further that the miner did not carry his lunch in a pail, but under his shirt, so that the hot pasty would take the chill off his chest in the morning, and when noon arrived his body was warm and sweated from working, so that it kept the pasty nice and hot.

One plod testifies to the durable quality of the pasty crust. A newly wed Cousin Jack found to his chagrin that his bride lacked the finer art of pasty making. He complained sorrowfully, "Damme, when I got down the shaft the pasty was all busted up in the pail. Damme, mother make a pasty you could 'eave it down the shaft, and 'it a 'undred feet down, and it wouldn't bust."

In the Upper Peninsula the pasty plods acquired some new twists. A Dane tells of the Cousin Jack who died, went to heaven, and knocked on St. Peter's door. "What do you want?" asked St. Peter. "I want to come in," said Jan. St. Peter looked through his books, pondered, and replied, "You're a Cousin Jack, you'd better go back. We can't afford to cook pasties for one man."

A Cousin Jack met a Swede in a Hurley bar and swapped drinks with him. He left Axel to make a trip to the outhouse, and rushed back excitedly. "My jacket's dropped hin, my good worsted jacket," he explained. "Will you 'elp me fish 'er out, Haxel?" Axel went to the outhouse and tried to reach it with his longer arm, but couldn't make it. Jan kept moaning about his jacket, so Axel cut a long pole and tried again, with no luck. Finally he threw the pole down in disgust and asked Jan, "Vy the hell you vant to get a rotten smelling yacket ut of the uthouse?" "Hit's not the jacket so much," said Jan, "but there's a bloody good pasty in the pocket."

In Cornwall the cuckoo bird enjoys a special fame because for one thing he lives there in numbers, and perhaps again because the Cousin Jack senses an affinity with the maligned creature. Instead of saying "April Fool," the Cornishman says, "Fool the coo-coo." A well-known plod has two Cousin Jacks building a hedge out of turf to catch the cuckoos in flight. A cuckoo came along, flying low, and just cleared the hedge. "Damme, Dick," said disconsolate Jan, "One more turf and we'd a had'n." Hence the saying, when someone makes a silly mistake, "Coo-coo, one more turf."

The Cousin Jack's ignorance glares out in his wonder at new-fangled inventions. In the early days everybody had two-wheeled carts. The first time a four-wheel buggy was seen in Redruth, the people all ran alongside the front wheels and yelled, "Go along little feller, you're 'head, keep 'head." Up at St. Ives the waves washed ashore a big anchor. Nobody had ever seen anything like it. So Uncle Jan was fetched, the oldest man in town. He was too lame to walk, so they trundled him in a wheelbarrow. He looked closely at the anchor, and said, "Wheel I round." So they wheeled him around it. He studied it some more, and said, "Wheel I round again." They did, and he looked it up and down. Suddenly he cried out, "O damme, he's the father of all the picks, run for your lives!" Everybody ran away and left old Jan in his wheelbarrow.

American humor seized delightedly on the Cousin Jack, mimicked his idiom, burlesqued his ways, and replaced his Old-Country plods with fresh-minted dialect stories. Sometimes actual mishaps and malapropisms gave rise to stories, and again old chestnuts worked into the Cousin Jack cycle. Native humorists may be of Cornish stock, but they may equally well be Swedes or Finns or Yankees. The Peninsula's favorite dialectician, Walter Gries, happens to be German. In the throes of recitation his stocky frame becomes animated, his voice ascends to a shrill and jerky pitch, his eyes brighten and his head tilts knowingly; he is Cousin Jack himself.

A weird grammar flavors these anecdotes, and even becomes the butt of the joke. Harry Soady complains to an old Cornish friend about his use of language. "I dearly love to visit with the Cornish people. I love them because they are quaint people and good people. But there's one thing about them that has always bothered me."

"What is it, 'Arry?"

"It's the way you Cornish use your pronouns and verbs. You don't seem to have any rhyme or reasons, any rules or regulations for the way you use them."

Jimmer said, "I tell 'ee 'Arry, 'ere's 'ow it is about they pronouns; we got a rule for they."

"You have!"

"Yes we 'ave. We do call everything she excepting a tomcat, and we call 'er 'e."

Remembering this basic grammar rule helped one Cousin Jack solve a vocabulary problem. Puzzled by a strange word in the newspaper, "category," Jim asked his pal Dick what it meant. Dick had been attending a free night school to polish up his English.

"Let me look upon it a minute," said Dick. He mused a bit and then said, "Naow, my teacher do say when you 'ave a new word like that you must h'analyze it, and so h'I'll h'analyze it for 'ee. Cat — anybody knaw what a bloody cat is. 'E — that's a 'e cat. Gory — that do mean bloody. Why, it's a bloody tomcat, that what 'e is!"

Misplaced h's always betray the Cornish speaker. Thus one Cousin Jack miner says to another, "Bet you can't guess what I 'ave in my dinner pail; it begins with an H too. "Horanges?" "Naw." "Happles?" "Naw." Honions?" "That's right."

The Cornish manner of expression produced some gems. A Cousin Jack passed a fruit store where some especially large oranges were on display. "Damme," he said to his companion admiringly, "It wouldn't take many of they to make a dozen." Or he tells about going down town. "I was goin' up the bloody street and I seen father. And father looked down the bloody street and he seen me. But damme, when we got up to each other 'twasn't naither one of us."

Apart from word play, the simple naiveté of the Cousin Jacks makes fine story stuff. Here are samples as told by Walter Gries.

Walter Gries speaks

• A Cousin Jack named William Jan was terribly worried in the slack days of the depression because he had no job. He said to his wife one day after he started to spend savings, "Mary Jane, I'm h'awfully wearied."

"My love, what are you wearied for?"

"Well, 'ere we are with our children, I aren't workin', and naw-thin' is comin' in."

Mary Jane reassured him. "There ain't nawthin' to be wearied for at all. With our little 'ouse and farm 'ere, we'll get along grand."

"Well anyhow I'm wearied, for if we 'ad another child I couldn't take care of it."

In the fall another son was born, and William Jan reproached himself bitterly, saying, "Mary Jane, I'm so wearied about our children and this 'ere new son that I'm feared I'm going to 'ang myself."

"O my 'andsome, dostn't thee do nawthin' like that."

However in his chagrin William Jan went out in the barn, put the noose of a rope around his neck, and threw the rope up over the rafter. He stood on a box, got ready to jump off, and then hesi-tated. " 'Old fast 'ere pardner," he said to himself, "maybe thee art 'angin' of a h'innocent man."

• The iron miners formerly used lard-oil lamps in the mines, which provided a big flame in the wick. If the lamp went out, they believed that trouble was brewing, and it was best to get out in a hurry. Alfred Penpraze's lamp went out, so he climbed up to the surface and went home. He noticed a light in the bedroom, peeked in the window, and saw that his wife had company — the captain of the mine.

Alfred turned around and scooted back to the mine. Going down the shaft and resuming work, he reported to the boys, "Well, I fooled Captain Dick tonight. He doesn't knaw that I saw 'im 'ome there with my missus."

• Jimmer came into the mine one morning in great excitement and told his partner, "We 'ad a great thing at the 'ouse last night."

"Well, what was it 'en?"

"We 'ad driblets."

His partner asked, "Driblets? What sort of thing is driblets?"

"Well, we had three babies come at once."

"I can't believe it — I don't believe 'tis possible."

The proud father said, "Well, we ab en at our house, and 'gens we finish our shift, I'll take ye over to my 'ouse an' I'll show them to ye."

After the shift they went to Jimmer's home, where he showed his partner the three bouncing babies. Dick said, "'Edn't that grand, my son, I never seed nawthin' like it before." Then pointing to the middle one he added, "Damme pardner, if it was me, I'd keep this one 'ere."

Still another element of Cornish humor comes from tall-tale puffery. There is for instance the tale of the talented canaries.

• Two Cornishmen out hunting rabbits in Keweenaw County spied some wild canaries. Sammy said, "See there pardner, see the pretty birds, wild canaries they are. My mother got one they birds 'ome, and my mother's bird is a grand singer. 'E does sing ' 'Ome Sweet 'Ome' so bloody natural you'd think you were sitting 'ome on the front porch in Cornwall."

Whereupon Harry said, "My mother got one they birds 'ome too."

"Do 'e sing?"

" 'Ess, my mother's bird is a powerful singer. 'E do sing *The Village Blacksmith*, and 'e do sing it so bloody natural that thees can see the sparks flying outa his hinder."

6

FINNS

The coming of the Finn has rocked the northwoods country. He is today what the red man was two centuries ago, the exotic stranger from another world. In many ways the popular myths surrounding the Indian and the Finn run parallel. Both derive from a shadowy Mongolian stock — "just look at their raised cheek-bones and slanting eyes." Both live intimately with the fields and woods. Both possess supernatural stamina, strength, and tenacity. Both drink feverishly and fight barbarously. Both practice shamanistic magic and ritual, drawn from a deep well of folk belief. Both are secretive, clannish, inscrutable, and steadfast in their own peculiar social code. Even the Finnish and Indian epics are supposedly kin, for did not Longfellow model "The Song of Hiawatha" on the form of the *Kalevala*?

But where the Indians lost, the Finns have won the Peninsula. Streaming into America after the Civil War, Finns today live in every northern state from Massachusetts to Oregon, but cluster most thickly in Michigan and Minnesota. Michigan has more Finns than any other state, 63,671,* and four-fifths of them live in the Upper Peninsula. In eleven of its fourteen counties they form the largest foreign-born group. Many settlements are almost entirely Finnish: Toivola, Nisula, Mass City, Winona, Tapiola, Forest Lake, Rock, Kiva. Finns sprinkle every village and are

* Census of 1940.

lumped in every large town. Bullied by Russia and ground by feudal landlords in their homeland, they now own and till most of the private land in the Peninsula.

A whole folklore has grown around the Finn. One hears it spoken, in hot and excited tones, when natives swap tales in the boardinghouse parlor or around the kitchen table.

• A Finn is stronger than an ordinary man. I've seen a couple of Finlanders down by the railroad tracks, fooling around with some car wheels. Finally, one takes the axle in his hands and lifts it up over his head.

Finns always fight with knives. They hold a knife in their fist and scratch you up and down with the blade, just breaking the skin, not digging in deep. There was a Finn found lying on a lot outside the church when the people came out of Sunday service, lying like dead with his chest all crisscrossed and bloody with knife cuts. They sent for a doctor because he was too weak to move. The doctor took a look at the chest, and poured some turpentine over the cuts. You could see smoke come out of his flesh. He sat up and screamed "Satana." Then he got to his feet and walked away.

You can't believe what a Finn can stand. I saw a fight between two Finlanders at Calumet during the Copper Country strike in 1913. A little fellow who was on the union side came into the store and slapped a big company-man Finlander standing there so hard he knocked his hat off. The big one, John Lonzo, pulled out a gun and shot a bullet right through the little one's hip. We set little Aljo up on a grocery shelf, and wanted to fix him up. But he just laughed, and said the bullet had come out, so he'd walk home and be down again in the morning. He was dead in the morning. They got the big guy later though — the Finns don't forget. The company protected him then, but after the strike he got a job with a construction gang in Lion Mountain, New York, and some of the workers pushed him off the side of the road and dumped wheelbarrows full of gravel over him.

Maybe they got tough from taking those steam baths. I've seen them in their saunas, those wooden bath-houses, pouring water on the hot rocks until the steam is so thick you can't see. Then they beat each other with birch branches to whip up the blood. Men and women go in there together. After they get hot enough, they run out naked and jump in the snow to cool off, or chop holes in the ice and go swimming in Lake Superior. Is that why so many Finns have t.b.?

Speaking of those steam baths, did you hear that story they tell of the Finnish G.I. who was captured by some cannibals in the Philippines? They put him in a big pot to boil and left him there about six hours. Then the cannibal chief lifts up the cover, and the Finn sticks out his head and says, "What blace is de switches and towel?"

Shoveling sand is the hardest kind of work. Only one man in ten can do it — it's in the way you grab hold of the low end of the shovel. We had a Finn working for us, by God how he could shovel! He'd come in so drunk he couldn't stand up — we'd lift him up, he'd fall again — finally the third time he stayed up. In twenty minutes he was covered with water. There would be two men on the other side of him and he'd fill his half of the truck even with them.

The Finns always stick together. They have a peculiar last-ditch loyalty and defend each other right or wrong. If one's done a murder, it's almost impossible to convict him, because they won't talk to an outsider, no matter how much they fight among themselves. Besides they have their own way of settling a matter. There was an old Finn in Ontonagon County who used to play around with his own daughter. He had a child by her, and the fellow she was engaged to found out. He told the other Finns, and a group took the old man out in the woods and strapped him down to a stump. They piled pine boughs around the stump in a circle, leaving a little alleyway, and set them on fire. The girl's fiancé walked down the alley, and gave the old man a straight razor. The old fellow could do three things. He could stay there and burn. He could slit his throat. Or he could cut himself loose from the stump by cleaning out his crotch. That's what he did.

SOCIAL TALES

A half-blind old Finn living by himself in a lonely tar-paper shack turned out to be a human anthology of Finnish folk tales. I met Frank Valin by the sheerest good luck.

The last week of my trip I turned back to Marquette and hunted up a new friend, Aili Johnson, a young American-born Finn whose enthusiasm for her people's lore had already aided me greatly. I told Aili that, although I now had a fairly good bag of Finnish stories, the prize game, the most elusive quarry, still disappointed me: the fairy tales, which the Grimm brothers had discovered so abundantly in Europe, but which very few collectors have found in twentieth-century, mechanized America.

Aili had a hunch; she knew some friends in Forest Lake who might help. We drove to Forest Lake, a few farmhouses in a wilderness. Three browned Finnish farmers stood by a gate and gossiped. Aili descended on them with a torrent of Finnish and friendly handclasps, fanning some childhood acquaintance; they were beaming; we were in the little house, and they were talking limpid Finnish while I followed their faces eagerly for signs of a strike. But the talk dried too soon, save for a story or two about wizards, and we rose to go. I walked to the door with our host, Viking-built Charles Niemi, and asked him, more by way of conversation than with any serious hope, did he know any teller of Old-Country stories.

Like a shot he answered, "Sure, Frank Valin at Rumeley."

"Who is he?"

"He is an old man who used to work in the lumber camps, and lived with us between seasons. He would often tell us long stories in the evenings. I heard them many times."

"How can I find him?"

"Oh, he is usually at home. He doesn't work any more. Why don't you bring him back with you for the evening? We have not seen him in a long time."

And now the men knotted around me and began to discuss the prospect of fetching Valin and having a party with some enthusiasm. Niemi turned to Aili and said in Finnish:

"Night after night he would sit by the box stove in the lumber camp and tell stories. Night after night, year after year, we always listened as if it were the first time. He knew songs, fairy tales, jokes, romances; he was a true word-smith."

We agreed that Aili and I would drive to Rumeley, and try to find Frank and return with him. Off we went in some excitement, although of course this might be another false alarm, like so many before; we might not find Frank, he might not talk, perhaps he knew only stories from books, perhaps he had forgotten what he knew.

Rumeley proved to be a handful of empty dwellings, without even a postoffice. Nowhere did we see any sign of life. We drove slowly up the highway looking for Frank Valin's shack. That must be it, that tiny structure pinpointed in the open fields.

We knocked on the door. A frail old man opened it and peered out. He was dressed in rags, wore thick-lensed glasses, and showed only a few stumps of teeth when he opened his mouth. A pathetic, wispy man of seventy-six, speaking no English, separated by an ocean from his family, walking six miles a day to get his wants.

"We hear that you are a true word-smith," Aili began, and he smiled with pleasure. "We have been told that you charm your listeners with stories and romances. Your friends at Forest Lake wish to see you, and to hear again your stories."

Yes, Frank would come as soon as he had fixed up a bit. He put on his good serge suit.

At the Niemi home that night no one would have thought that a black forest lay outside the door. Frank, the center of the stage, sat on a sofa and spun his romances to the three husky farmers sitting across from him, who listened all attention, occasionally

chuckling, eyes shining with interest. Niemi's daughter, a para-
lytic, wheeled about the kitchen and prepared the coffee and
cakes Finns always serve their visitors. The house stirred with a
cheerful spirit of reunion, and a sense of pride because faraway
guests had called. In the back country, a visit is a major occasion.

His friends had not underestimated Frank Valin. He knew genuine fairy tales in the oral tradition — tales replete with kings and
princesses, dragons and trolls, wizards and heroes. And he knew
other kinds of stories, about *noita* magicians and peasant heroes.
On the way home he suddenly burst into a plaintive folk song.
He was thanking *us* for the evening.

Valin told us he was born in the province of Pori, Finland, in
1870, and came to Sault Ste. Marie in 1904, without his family.
He writes to his sons, one of whom was injured in the recent
Russo-Finnish war, but they steadfastly refuse to leave Finland.
Actually Valin would appear to be the last person to strike out
on his own in adventurous fashion. "As a boy, I was not like
other children," he says simply. "I was always undersized, a weak,
spindling coward. The sight of blood was horrible to me, and I
suffered greatly when my father made me hold the sheep at
slaughtering time."

After a term of compulsory army service, Valin returned to farm
work as a "trenki" or hired man to the large landowners. Although he attended the "Kansakoulu," the public school, for one
year, and was praised by the schoolmaster, he never followed up
his education. "If I had not been so meek or shy," he says, "I
would have become a scholar, or at least a clerk." In this country
he has worked as a road laborer, and as teamster and blacksmith's helper in lumber camps. In this last occupation he nearly
lost his sight when sparks flew in his eyes, and has since lived by
himself on an old-age pension.

Valin came to America to escape the bitter serfdom of the
crofter's life, and his memory burns still at its rigors. "The share-
cropper's life was very hard. Until 1906, when the reform came in,
the laborer worked from four in the morning until eight, when he

was given breakfast, from nine until one, and from two till eight in the evening, or later when some task made it necessary. After the reform, the working hours were shortened to from six in the morning to six at night. The food was always miserable; sour milk thinned with water, potatoes and herring, day in and day out, while the tables of the landowners groaned with stews of beef, lamb and pork, and carrots and onions. The lakes were full of fish but we could not fish in them; neither could we hunt game, except by stealth, for the land was owned by our 'betters.' Is it a wonder that we left Finland to come here?"

Then Frank Valin told with relish a cycle of tales about Jussi the workman, who always discomfited the landlords.

Jussi the Workman (Frank Valin)

• Jussi went about from landowner to landowner, hiring himself out as a workman for a year at a time, as was the custom. Jussi was a strong, robust rogue, but a good workman when it suited him to work. He never spent more than a year at one house, but all the crofters and servants knew that where Jussi went, the food grew better.

Once Jussi was at a farm called "Kesti." The landowner was a stingy man and drove his men from early morning until late at night without stopping.

The story goes that Jussi had been having trouble with his stomach. This day he had been ploughing, but cramps had driven him to the edge of the woods once or twice for relief. The master saw the horses standing idle, and called loudly from the other end of the field, "What are you doing, loafing out there in the woods? Get to work."

Jussi returned meekly enough, but the next day when he came to work he was wearing only his shirt, with its long tails tied up about his waist. He chose the side of the field next to the public road, and all day long he walked up and down the furrows behind the plow, fertilizing the field as he went.

Someone stopped him and asked, "Why do you do this?"

"Our master is a busy man; we can't take time out for anything."

At another house the servants were given potatoes floating in water for their noon meal, always potatoes and water and nothing else.

"I like this place," Jussi said, in the hearing of the housewife.

"How is that?" asked the fat dame, flattered with praise.

"In the last house they were not very clean; they kept messing up the stew with meat and carrots and turnips and such — it made it thick and dirty. Here the soup is so nice and clean — so clear — and the potatoes are so white."

Suddenly he leaped up and began tearing off his shirt.

"What is wrong?" asked the frightened housewife.

"I saw a bean floating in my soup; I'm going to swim for it."

One spring day Jussi saw the master getting his lines together for some fishing. Jussi watched him take out the boat.

"What is that?" he asked.

"A pig trough — for pigs like you," said the master.

"I'll not go in that on the water," said Jussi, and went back to his farm work.

Later in the summer, noting what fine catches the master brought home for his own household, Jussi asked him, "Why can't I go fishing?"

"Why didn't you go last spring?"

"I wasn't feeling so good." (He had been insulted.)

"Well, fishing is the sport of the gentry, but you can take the basket and lines and get us some bream."

Jussi went out in the boat, and caught a fine lot of bream. He went back to the shore, cut off the heads and tails of the fish and put them in the basket. The middle parts of the fish he put in a weir and hid in a stump. Then he went back to the fishhouse of the landowner, where his master was cleaning fish with his wife.

"This is a heavy basket," said the master.

"A good catch," said Jussi, and walked off. He had not gone far when he heard his master calling, "Jussi, come here."

Jussi came back slowly.

"Where are the middle parts of these fish?"

"Oh, do you take those home, too?" asked Jussi innocently.

"You idiot, of course we do."

"Jas soo," said Jussi. "Up to this time I have never seen anything but the heads and tails of fish; how was I to know the middle parts are fit for food?"

NOITA TALES

The peasant Finns had not only their own landlords at home to dread, but also the Russian monster at their gates. Their sons had to serve time with the Russian army, greatly against their will. "When I was of age to be conscripted, I entered without resisting," Frank Valin told us. "But many young men who were braver than I cut off their fingers or their feet so they would not have to serve Russia."

Against the Russian bully the peasants had in the past called on their *noitas* for succor. The *noita*, varously described as a religious magician, a wizard, or a healer, played a prominent role in village life. He cured the sick, with or without herbs, charmed and cursed evildoers, and on special occasions used his powers to defend his people from the enemy and so became a national folkhero. Such a one is Kalami of Varpus, whom Frank Valin celebrates.

Kalami of Varpus (Frank Valin)

• At the time of the Great Hatred, about 1808, when Russia was invading the Finnish people, there appeared a *noita* called Kalami of Varpus. In Ikali people still talk about his power; a man called Kusta of Isavalta told me these things and he said they were true. The Russians were afraid of Kalami, let me tell you! He had the power of turning men's eyes, so they saw things other than they were.

Once Kalami was surrounded by Cossacks. They could see him standing alone from where they were hidden. But when they rushed on him, he disappeared into a thin wisp of smoke. Another time he turned into a gray stump before the very eyes of the Cossack troops.

A third time they were sure they had him circled; he was standing in a meadow with his black horse beside him. They pressed closer, and all at once he was gone, seemingly into the horse's mouth. The soldiers killed the black stallion, but of course they found nothing of Kalami.

Kalami was a kind man in many ways, and loved by the poor people who worked the rich farms for the landowners.

One Saturday night he went out to the hayfields where there were sixty crofters working to gather the hay to take it to the lofts. Evening was near and the rain clouds were hanging low.

"It's time to quit work, boys," said Kalami. "The sauna is waiting."

"We can't stop now," the men said. "There is too much hay left on the field."

"I'll take care of that," said Kalami. He took a bundle of hay under each arm and walked to the loft. Whoosh! At once all the hay from the field was in the loft.

"Be on your way. I shall meet you at the sauna," said Kalami. Then he said to a lame man who was left behind the others, "You see that mattock? You sit on one end, I'll sit on the other."

The lame man did so, and whoosh! At once they were at the sauna, long before the others came.

Another time Kalami killed a Russian who was carrying mail and money from Finland to Moscow. He took his money from him, of course. No one paid any attention to this misdeed except the Russians. (This was at the time of the Great Hatred, as I told you.)

This money he stole from the rich Russians, Kalami gave to the poor. There were many crofters in the land who could not pay the heavy taxes, and it would have gone badly with them without Kalami.

Kalami went to the Russian sheriff who was sitting with eight of his men about a table. "Here is money for the taxes of this province," he said, throwing down his heavy money bags.

The Russian sheriff gave him the proper receipts.

"Is the debt paid?" asked Kalami.

"It is, indeed," answered the sheriff, who counted the money into a box before the eyes of his eight men.

The next morning the sheriff went to count the money again to make sure it was right, and what do you think he found? A drawer full of birch leaves.

Following Frank Valin's tales of the legendary Kalami, his friends began to gossip about *noitas* they had known personally. "*Noitas* were burned in Finland," said Michael Seppi, "and sometimes hanged for their witchcraft. The hanging law is discontinued, however, because it was found that the weakest of the *noitas* could be strung up, and hang there rattling for a week or two, and then walk off when he was cut down. He'd twist his neck about a bit, and say, 'This is good training for the neck muscles.'"

"Even in my time there were several people in the Old Country who had *noita* knowledge," Charles Niemi said. "I remember one man who liked to trade horses, and would play tricks on the buyers in the marketplace. The biters, kickers, and most mischievous of horses appeared docile and well tamed when he was with them. He would sell one of these horses, and a few hours later it would kick up a fury, break away from its new owner, and return to the *noita*."

"Did you ever hear of the *noita* called Tilli of Kuru?" asked Seppi. "He had the power to open church doors and to heal the ill. He would set the person to be healed in the cemetery, instructing him not to take any hand that might be proffered. Then in the middle of the night he would call the headless folk, and they would come and walk about the man, calling to him and reaching out their hands. But if he did not grasp their hands, his sickness would go with them."

"In this country, too, are people with *noita* powers," Niemi said a little fearfully. "When a man won't let anyone enter his barn, you can be sure he has some *noita* tricks. There was August Sunnell, who lived in Munising about thirty years ago, and could escape from any kind of chains or boxes or from any jail. He became a rich man, and his pride was a flower garden with an iron fence around it that cost five hundred dollars. Suddenly he left Munising, overnight. That was not strange, but what made everyone wonder most was that his flowers disappeared with him, and in the morning when people went past his iron fence they saw only sand inside."

FAIRY TALES

These strapping sunburned farmers believed beyond question in the feats of *noitas*. But when Frank Valin began telling them about a *noita* shoemaker who eloped with a princess, they knew this was a fiction, a fairy tale, and sat back to enjoy it.

Contrary to general belief, fairy tales are not syrupy fantasies for children. Your genuine *Märchen* bristles with violence and death, and displays earthy touches fit only for adult ears. Grown men tell and listen to *Märchen*, like these Finnish farmers who sat fascinatedly listening to the stories they had often heard Frank Valin tell, laughing heartily when the giant burst after plugging up his behind with a stick, or the peasant hero literally skinned the intriguing generals. A Marxist could read a good deal into the social tensions revealed by his tales. The princess won't marry her successful suitor when he appears in rags, but acknowledges his claim as soon as he dresses up; hatred of the military class crops up plainly in one story where a swineherd ridicules the king's generals.

Valin's peasant tales show Finnish local coloring, with frequent references to the sauna and to *noita* magicians. His flight-from-the-dragon story uses an older form than the one Trefflé Largeness gave, with the conventional rock and twig as the magic obstacles rather than a razor and bar of soap; but his version of Cinderella has a modern prize which the suitors strive for, not gold and silver apples, but a photograph of the coveted princess. Like Hollywood movies, the tales run to standard box office types and plots, with characters all black or all white, romance triumphing over class obstacles and gangster-villains, and enough topical allusions to fit the particular audience.

The Shoemaker and the Princess (Frank Valin)

• There was once a king who needed a shoemaker, so the best shoemaker in the land went to live in the king's castle. He had been there for some time when he noticed that the king's daughter was never seen to go outside the castle; she always remained indoors.

"That is bad for the young princess," said the shoemaker.

"The young woman is enchanted; if she goes outside some evil will come to her," answered the king.

"I shall protect her," said the brave shoemaker, but nevertheless, when he and the princess went to walk in the courtyard, a large thunder cloud came, swooped low, and carried off the princess.

Then the shoemaker, who knew some *noita* tricks, was sure that an evil giant had taken her. At once he set out flying like a bird, and soon reached the house of the giant.

There the shoemaker changed himself into an ant, and crawled in between the crack of the door, into the house, and into the room where the princess was hidden. He resumed his man's shape and spoke to the princess.

"I cannot escape," said the princess. "The house is made of bricks and there is no way out."

"Wait a bit. Then say what I say when the right time comes, and we shall escape," said the shoemaker, changing himself once again into an ant.

The giant's wife was sweeping the floor when the giant walked in. "Who has been here?" he roared. "I smell Christian blood."

Together they began to search, but they could not find the shoemaker, who was hiding in a sand box as an ant.

"I must go away; I shall be gone for two weeks," said the giant and started off again.

Again the shoemaker crawled into the room of the princess as an ant, and changed back into a man. Then the princess showed him three charms which she had found in the room in which she had been hidden: a drop of water, a twig, and a rock.

"It is now time for us to go," said the shoemaker, "and I know the use of these charms." Thereupon the shoemaker spoke the magic words "Mikkel myyra," and became an ant.

At once the princess repeated, "Mikkel myyra," and she too became an ant. Together they hurried out through the crack in the door. When they were outside the shoemaker said, "Foken falk," and became a bird. The princess repeated, "Foken falk," and set out flying with him.

But the wily old giant had lied; he had returned, and finding the princess gone, at once came as a thunder cloud after them.

The princess looked back and saw the giant thunder cloud.

"Drop the rock," said the shoemaker. At once the rock became a mountain that towered so high that the cloud could not pass over it. The giant had to stop, then hurry back to his home for a hammer to break down the mountain.

After a while the princess looked over her shoulder and again saw the thunder cloud, whereupon the shoemaker said, "Drop the twig." She did so, and the twig grew into a great forest, so high that the cloud could not pass over it. Thus the giant had to return to his home for his axe, and it was a long time before he was able to cut his way through the giant thicket.

Once again the princess saw the giant coming. "Throw down the drop of water," said the shoemaker, and at once the water became a great lake.

The giant at first began to try to fill the lake with sand, which he picked up in great mouthfuls and spat into the water. Then he began to drink the lake dry, but to no avail, for the water ran out his other end.

"Put a stick in your behind for a tap," sang a small bird. And when the giant did this, and began to drink, he swelled larger and larger until at last he burst in two.

The shoemaker carried his princess home and there was a wedding, as you may well believe. There were sixteen hundred men gathering corks at the drinking bouts; this is too much feasting for a sober man, so I soon left.

Cinders (Frank Valin)

• There was once a king who made a glass mountain; he placed his daughter on the top, with her photograph. Whoever could ride to the top of the mountain and receive the photograph could get the girl for a wife.

A nearby smith had three sons; the two eldest were anxious to win the king's daughter and worked at forging shoes that would carry them to the top. The youngest son was Tuhkimo, "Cinders," a bashful boy who stayed at home tending the fire, and who slept on the hearth so that he was grimy with ashes.

"Can I go to see my brothers ride?" Cinders asked his mother the first day of the trial.

"Go, but return before the others," said the mother.

That evening when the eldest sons returned, Cinders asked, "How did the riding go?"

"Stay behind the hearth and don't ask what doesn't concern you," answered the brothers.

Now I forgot to tell you that each night an old man would come to Cinders and talk to him in his place behind the hearth. "Go now to a place in the forest and I will give you soldier's clothes and a horse with silver shoes," said the old man.

The boy did this, and the next day he appeared at the trials in fine clothes and riding a horse with silver shoes.

"Would Herr Lieutenant like to try?" asked the king. The boy tried to climb the glass mountain, but the silver shoes were slippery and he did not succeed.

The next day the boy appeared again at the trials, wearing fine clothes, and riding a horse that had golden shoes, and the king asked, "Would Herr Captain like to try?"

The boy tried again, but the gold shoes were too soft, and wore away, so that he did not succeed. Again, as on the night before when he went home in his rags and asked his brothers, "How did the trials go?" the answer was, "Go to your hearth, and don't ask what doesn't concern you."

The third day of the trials the boy appeared in finer clothes than before, riding a horse shod with diamond shoes. "Would Herr General like to try?" the king asked.

The boy rode quickly, so that crumbs of glass flew right and left, crunch, crunch, to the top of the glass mountain. Here the king's daughter gave him her photograph. Instead of riding back the way he had come, the boy clattered down the other side of the mountain, and back to the forest to change his clothes.

Again he asked his brothers, "How did the riding go?"

"It doesn't matter to you. Get behind your hearthstone."

Then the king sent out his soldiers to seek the man who had won the trials — two in each direction.

Two soldiers came to the home of the smith. "Are all the men at hand?" asked the soldiers.

"Here we are," said the two brothers.

"Did you try to ride the glass mountain?"

"We tried, but we failed."

"Are you all here?"

"There is the youngest, behind the hearth, but he never goes anywhere."

The young Cinders was fetched, and as the soldiers began to search him, the photograph fell out of his *miekko*. (The *miekko* is a kind of long shirt, that field workers used to wear. "A smock?" "Yes, that's it.")

In all his rags, Cinders was taken to the king. "Here is the man with the photograph," the soldiers said.

There was great laughter, and the king's daughter said, "I don't want to marry that ragged dirty fellow."

"Can I go outside? I shall soon return, but I must take the photograph with me," begged Cinders.

Out he went, and to the forest, where he changed his clothes again, and took his horse with the diamond shoes. Then he returned to the king's house where guards met him at the gate.

"You cannot enter," they said, "You have no permission."

"Here is the passport," said Cinders, showing them the photograph.

And now he was truly welcomed. "Hevonen talliin, mies selliin." "The horse to the stable, the man to the table" as the old saying goes, and the wedding was held, and they may all be there yet.

SEER TALES

"Seers and second-sighters command great respect from the Finns," my friend Aili told me. "Some say a child can become a seer if his face and eyes are washed in water in which a dead person has been bathed."

From her grandma she heard much about a famous Old Country seer, John Katajamaki of the province of Oulu. Sitting in a Finnish *tupa* he would say, when nothing could be seen in the distance, "I see a horse-drawn sleigh coming. It's old Heikki with his wife and children." And half an hour later Heikki would arrive. On one occasion Katajamaki attended a wedding, when the bridegroom was suddenly stricken ill and could not stand.

"There's evil at work here," said Katajamaki, and asked the bridegroom to remove his coat. From the lining he drew out nine rows of pins laid in sets of nine.

"I'm sorry that I couldn't avert the evil entirely," he said and buried the pins. The ceremony was continued, but nine months later the husband died. His jealous rival had applied to an old witch who had employed a charm to prevent the wedding.

"Are there seers in this country?" I asked Aili.

"There was one in Marquette County who died not long ago. All the Finns here still talk about him. He lived for a while in the house of Herman Maki, who is Dad's best friend, and a locally famous humorist; we'll drive over and see him tonight. He has built a typically Finnish home out in the woods."

We drove off into the forest, and came eventually to a cleared spot, a piece of Finland tucked away in the wilds of Michigan. In the middle of the clearing stood a red and white log house with a broad porch facing an islet set in a little lake, reached by a toy red and white bridge. On the porch stood Herman Maki, round and twinkling, but with the pointed features of the witty Savolainen. Behind him huddled Mrs. Maki, timid and withdrawn like the Old Country wives, one eye on the stove where the coffeepot perpetually simmered, symbol of Finnish hospitality. The group fell to chatting genially in Finnish, and as I looked at them all in that setting, Aili with her high, slanting cheekbones and her husky father, Theodore Kohlemainen, bronzed and furrowed with the outdoors, I thought myself in a foreign country.

At the first break in the chatter, Aili asked the men, "What do you remember about Emmanuel Salminen, the mystic?"

Maki's twinkle died down, and Kolehmainen's pleasant features grew grave.

"He was heavy, dark, and tall," said Herman. "He was like a tree; he had his roots in the ground, but tore them loose from Mother Earth."

"I saw that man, the far-sighted one, when he came from the East and stayed in Negaunee and Palmer," said Theodore Kolehmainen. "The first time I met him I said, 'I understand you know something about the future.' I didn't really believe it, but I wanted to try him out.

"'Not much, but something,' he said.

"I asked him where I came from, without telling him my name

or anything. He told me, 'You come from the south and are going north a few miles to get something, but you will have to go back empty.'

"I said, 'No, I guess not. I'm going to the Consolidated Lumber Company with my truck and catch some lumber.'

"I left him and went on up to Negaunee, but I found that a large truck was taking lumber back to Gwinn that day, and the company wouldn't load my small truck. So I had to go back south to Gwinn empty, and his prediction came true."

The two men (both hardheaded storekeepers, incidentally) fell to comparing the prophecies and visions with which Salminen had amazed the Finns of the area. People often visited him to see what their relatives in the Old Country were doing. The mystic would close his eyes, place his hands over them, and get his second thoughts. He could see the dead even better than the living, if one wished to know of the dead. The hardest to communicate with among the living were those whose spirit was "away," because they drank, were immoral, or behaved in similar ways which they wished to keep secret from their families.

Salminen once made Herman Maki a map of Herman's home in Finland — which the seer had never seen — perfect down to the last rowan tree. The house, barns, trees, the distance from the main road, were all indicated in exact detail, even to the color of the neighbor's house, yellow. But here Herman objected, saying the color was red. Salminen reconsidered, and then said, "You'd better think." Maki thought. Suddenly he remembered the house had been painted yellow the year before he left for America.

Salminen forecast his own death. Because he was sick and cold, Mr. Maki brought him to his house. The seer said, "On the fifteenth of March I will know whether I will live or whether I will die." The evening of that day Mr. Maki found him downcast in his room.

"My days are up," Salminen said. He asked that he might die in the bed in which he was lying. Maki promised, but during the night the seer took a turn for the worse, so Herman decided to send for a doctor to take him to a hospital.

In the morning Maki and the doctor entered the seer's room, and Salminen said, "I know what you want to do, but you should have kept your promise. Go ahead, but the doctor won't help."

The doctor marveled that Salminen could read his unuttered thoughts. He had Salminen taken to the Twin City Hospital at Negaunee, where the nurses all feared him because he could read their minds. In three months he died of cancer.

Herman Maki had known another mystic intimately. "When I lived in Mass," he said, "the Finns of Ontonagon County marveled at John Bjorklund, who left Iso Kyro as a young man to come to Michigan. Even as a child he knew events beforehand, although he could not distinguish the past from the future until he reached maturity. People would laugh at him, and call him crazy, but in time his prophecies and eccentric ways won him respect. He traveled widely about the United States, usually on foot, and prospected for gold in Alaska and California.

"Once he came to Lukkarila's, having just returned from out west, wearing six or seven pairs of trousers and several shirts. Whenever he traveled he wore all his worldly possessions, and it gave him a queer and laughable appearance. To begin with, he was thin and shaggy-haired, and had odd blue eyes.

"In California he lived on a mountain with a rattlesnake as his only companion. In Michigan his neighbors noticed that no animal ever feared him. We tested him often with angry dogs, and no dog, however angry, would growl in his kindly presence. Anyone who was near him could feel his power over living things."

Many skeptics became convinced of Bjorklund's esoteric powers. Maki remembers well the first time Bjorklund impressed him as a seer. Herman was walking along the streets of Mass with two other men to a coöp meeting, when they encountered Bjorklund looking sad and dazed. "I saw a strange happening," he said. "Within three days a man will cut his throat on a high hillside of stumps."

Neither Herman nor his companions, Jack Luoma and William Store, felt any surprise when a fellow called John Maki cut his throat on a high hillside of stumps in the next three days. But John Bjorklund declared himself much surprised, saying, "I could have sworn it was John Kermu who would do this. I could see the happening very clearly, but not the men. I suppose I mistook Kermu for Maki because they are both thick-necked men."

And on occasions such as this he would say sadly, "The gift of sight is not always a happy one."

TALL TALES

The talk of second sight had sobered the group, and my friends now asked Herman Maki to brighten up the atmosphere with some of his famous comic stories. He rattled off a string, Aili translating them for me, and I was startled to hear "American" tall tales coming out from the Finnish.

How Herman Maki Met the Devil or One of His Little Cousins

• When I was a boy of thirteen, living in Merikarvi in the province of Pori, I went out walking one Sunday morning. I had just received a new double-barreled shotgun from America, and I was very proud of it. Because I worked hard every day of the week, I thought I would try the new fowling piece on Sunday. I had worked already for many years as a hired man on farms, tending cows, ducks, and geese.

As I was hunting birds in the woods, I saw a rather odd-looking man coming through the woods. I turned, sat down on a stump and waited for him to approach. I noticed two very short horns on his forehead. When he perceived I saw them he drew his cap down over his eyes. Then I noticed that while one foot was like any other man's, the other was shaggy with a horse's hoof. Next I spied his long black tail switching from behind his coat. He hastily tucked it under.

You understand, I'd never seen the Devil.

Then he spoke to me, "Why are you always in the woods on Sunday morning, young man?"

"I have no other day to come out into the woods and I come out to get fresh air."

"What is that thing you have in your lap?" he asked. (The gun was on my lap.)

"That's my pipe," I answered.

Then he said, "Let me taste it to see what kind of tobacco you smoke."

So I put the double barrel in his mouth and let her blast with both barrels. (I had fine shot in one barrel and buck shot in the other.)

"That's mighty strong tobacco for a young one," he said, spitting out the fine shot and the buck shot.

Now you understand I've never met the Devil, but that might have been one of his little cousins.

How We caught the Silver Fox in Finland

• We do not wish to kill the silver fox, nor to tear his pelt with a bullet. So we put a nail in our guns, wait until the fox stands by a large tree, and fire the gun, nailing the fox to the tree through his tail.

Then we draw a cross on the fox's nose with a knife, splitting the hide. Finally, we whip the fox with a little switch until in its fury it runs out of its skin.

After two years the same fox would have grown himself a new coat, and would be ready to be skinned again.

Hunting the Bear in Finland

• A long pole was peeled and tapered down toward one end. The opposite end of the pole was fastened to a stand and bolted, at about the height of a bear from the ground. In the small end of the pole a hole was bored, and a crosspiece made that could be taken off when it was needed.

The pole was smeared with syrup. When the bear came around, smelling sweets, he licked the pole. He kept on licking it, and the pole went further and further into his mouth, down his gullet, and at last came out the other end. A man holding the crosspiece was watching, and at this moment he slapped it on the pole, and thus we had our bear, captured alive without a bullet wasted.

A Clever Hunting Dog

• My dog can tell by my gun what I am going to hunt. When I pick up my shotgun, he starts out to hunt birds. When I pick up my rifle, he knows I'm going to hunt game. I even try fooling him by picking up the gun, clicking the hammer twice, and then putting it away quickly. Musti is already out in the woods. So I pick up my fish rod instead. And what do you think Musti is doing? He is under a pine tree digging worms. When I get there, he has dug a big pile, and he looks up at me and winks as if to say, "You can't fool me."

Shooting Partridge in Michigan

• I am an old hunter who has long traveled the woods, and folks often ask me for a tip on good hunting. It reminds me of the time the deacon asked me to go partridge shooting. "You ought to know a pretty good place," he said.

"You bet. I know a fine place, but it takes two shots to get a partridge."

"That can't be much of a place. How do you figure it takes two shots for one bird?"

"Come with me, and I'll show you," I promised him.

Soon we were in the woods and as we came near the partridge, they set off flying from a small thicket. There were so many of them that the beating of their wings sent off great clouds of feathers, so that the sky seemed dark, and not a single bird could be seen.

I shot a hole through the cloud of feathers, and through this hole we aimed at the partridge, and brought down a fine catch. We filled our knapsacks, and could have broken all conservation laws on partridge catches . . . but it was Sunday, and the deacon was there. Besides, it's good to leave a few birds for another day.

An Unhappy Bear Hunt

• We get a lot of lower Michigan fellows up here to hunt. A year ago four men came up and rented a camp not far from here. They set out the first morning all bright and cheerful in their nice red jackets and red caps, carrying shiny new guns. By ten o'clock every one of them was back in camp, all hot and tired and disgruntled because no one had seen even a porcupine.

One of the fellows said, "The rest of you stay here and cook up that ham we brought. I'll go out for one more try."

He hadn't gotten very far out from camp along an old logging trail when he ran onto a large bear. He lifted his gun to shoot, but the bear leaped toward him so quickly that the man got nervous and dropped his gun. Then he started back on a run towards the camp, with the bear behind him. He got as far as the camp door, where he fell on the door-sill, having strength left only to grab the door open. The bear behind him ran with such speed he jumped over the man, scraping his mackinaw with his claws as he went. The terrified hunter quickly shut the door and fastened the outer latch, leaving the bear and his three companions inside. "Skin this one!" he yelled to his friends, "I'm going off after another one!"

He got back to Palmer where he told the folks what had happened. After three days some of the men got up enough nerve to go out and see what had happened, and took along a few conservation officers. When they opened the door a crack and peered in, they saw the bear sleeping happily under a woolen blanket in a bunk in the corner. On the floor could be seen nothing but a pair of shoelaces and two underpants buttons.

A sign "Do Not Disturb" was hung on the door, and the next spring the bear was given a medal for heroism. I think it may be this same bear that can be seen on so many of the conservation department posters.

SAVOLAINEN JOKES

The Finnish sense of humor is salty and sharp. In sly rural anecdotes and spoofing tall tales it betrays a surprising kinship with what is called native American humor.

One favorite species of the Finnish story is the Savolainen joke, so styled because the wits in the stories come from the region of Savo in central Finland, and are nationally known for their agile retorts. This humor compares with the Attic salt of the Greeks, representing shrewd psychological insights distilled over the centuries. So Martti Nisonen told me, professor of music at Suomi College at Hancock, and himself a fine-looking Savolainen, with pointed features and a clever tongue. The jokes are deceptively simple in appearance, but all neatly puncture conceit, pomposity, and arrogance. I have heard Savolainen jokes from many Finns, from saloonkeeper Gus Ilminen to President Nikander of Suomi College.

When I called at this Finnish college in the Copper Country, young, studious Dr. Nikander greeted me politely, but could offer no suggestions. The idea of recording Finnish traditions had never crossed his mind. He called in Professor Nisonen, who had no help to give either, but relieved the tension with a Finnish joke. The president countered with another, and suddenly the two educators were discharging Savolainen jokes as fast as they could talk.

• A man from Savo was working on a construction job, and fell off the fourth floor. Everybody was quite shocked, including himself. When he picked himself up, the people crowded around and asked, "Did that fall hurt you very much?"

"It wasn't the fall so much," he answered, "but the sudden stop."

• Kuopio in the province of Savo has a railway station two and a half kilometers outside the town. One day an important salesman from a big city, after making the long walk, complained to a man in Kuopio, "Why did they build the station so far from town?"

The Savolainen answered, "They must have wanted it by the railroad."

• A Savolainen riding on a train took a bottle of whiskey from his pocket and drank from it. A minister passing by said to him, "Don't you know that is a slowly killing poison?"

"I'm in no hurry," said the Savolainen.

• A Savolainen went to Helsinki with an old white horse. A city slicker sneered to him, "How much do you want for your lime-boat?"

The Savolainen lifted the horse's tail saying, "You go down and ask the captain."

• The hired man was taking a high-toned lady out in the sleigh. The snow was deep, and she kept complaining about losing the way. He went out to look at the road sign, picked it up and brought it back to her.

"I don't know how to read, so I brought it over to you."

Lapatossu, which means "shoe pack," was a knavish railway worker about whom many jests are told.

• Lapatossu kept moving about from place to place as a laborer and did not keep himself very clean. One time when he was traveling on a boat, the captain saw him scratch himself several times; he had some "renters" on his person.

The captain said to him, "I will give you a new coat, shirt, and pair of pants if you will lie still on the deck of the boat for five minutes."

Lapatossu, who badly needed new clothes, lay down at once, but the creatures made him wriggle and he couldn't lie still.

"Captain," he yelled out suddenly, "when you give me that coat, will you put a button here" (and he pinched the skin hard to show the place) "and here — and here — and here."

So Lapatossu won the suit of clothes, with a coat of many buttons.

• Lapatossu asked the conductor, "How far is it from Tampere to Helsinki?" He was told, and then asked, "How far is it from Helsinki to Tampere?"

"Well, you numskull, don't you know it's the same distance?"

"No, it doesn't always work that way," replied Lapatossu. From Christmas to New Year's is one week, but from New Year's to Christmas is a long way."

• Lapatossu went to the drugstore so often the druggist told him, "Don't open your mouth when you come in the store." (Druggists were just like dictators then; they thought they were learned professors.)

Lapatossu came in and stood on the floor and said nothing. Finally the druggist snapped at him, "What are you looking for?"

Lapatossu answered, "I'm looking for what you have to sell."

"Only donkeyheads, dumbbell, don't you see!"

"By gosh, you must have a good business then, because there is only one left behind the counter."

• Lapatossu went to the druggist and tried to explain his wife's ailment. "I don't know what is the matter with her," he said, "but she is wriggling, shimmying, swaying, and squealing, like this." And he demonstrated.

The druggist could understand from the actions what the trouble was so he got peeved and slapped Lapatossu twice. Lapatossu walked home without a word and hit his wife once across the face. Her toothache stopped hurting at once, and she stopped wriggling.

Lapatossu walked back to the drugstore and slapped the druggist, saying "I only needed one of your pills, here is the other one back."

7

BLOODSTOPPERS

O<small>NE</small> evening I sat in a cafe in Munising, a paper and sawmill town that boasts the largest liquor consumption per capita of any American city, and listened to two slow-speaking Slovenian boys. They were relating local stories of violence and dread, and one youth described a knife fight in the nearby village of Shingleton, between little Mike Bobic and six-footer George White. On a certain winter's night they had gotten violently drunk, and a year's grudge flared out.

Said George, "We're going to fight when we get done drinking this beer."

Bobic went into the next room, which was partially blocked at the doorway by curtains. When White tried to follow, stooping to brush aside the curtains and enter, Bobic slashed him across the chest with a knife. Bleeding badly, White staggered half a block through the snow to Dolaski's tavern. He crumpled at the door, and hollered "Help," feebly.

"He had blood all over him — I seen him. We drug him inside and set him against the bar. The stream of blood had splotched all over the snow. They sent for a doctor in Munising, eight miles away, but they figgered he'd bleed to death before the doctor could come. An Indian, Archie Clark, who lives in Van Meer, happened to be there. He uttered a prayer and stopped the bleeding."

"How did he do that?" I asked. "Did he apply some herbs to the cuts?"

"No, he never touched White. He just used the prayer. The prayer is passed from man to man in a family, unless a woman intercepts. You can ask anyone in Shingleton if it didn't happen that way."

The next day I drove out to Shingleton, a bleak collection of shacks which had grown around a now silent shingle mill. Emmet Clement, a tough-looking bruiser who owned the local gas station and had lived nearly fifty years in the village, sneered when I asked about two haunt tales the boys had told me. But he was more guarded on the White-Bobic fight with its climax of bloodstopping. He had heard it of course, and would not dispute the common report.

"You can stop blood with wasps' nests," he said. "Or touch a horse's wound with a wooden wedge, then drive it into the stump to stop the blood."

Across from the gas station a sign read "Dolaski's Tavern," and I wandered in. The place was empty except for a little wrinkled old man behind the bar. He turned out to be the proprietor, Dolaski, also a Slovenian, and he remembered the White affair well.

"Yes," he said, "I saw Archie Clark stop the blood. White was lying on the floor right here, with a pillow under his head. The Indian just touched the wound, and mumbled a few words, and the bleeding stopped. It wasn't so wide, but it was bleeding a lot. When the doctor came, he asked how the bleeding stopped, and when they told him he said, 'Oh, I see.'"

I didn't see at all. Dolaski tried to explain the matter. White being unconscious, he couldn't resist the Indian's power of suggestion. "There are two minds, the objective and the subconscious or subjective. You're still living in your sleep, but your objective mind is at rest. If you could develop your subjective mind, you would have much more information. You don't learn from the outside — that's only what you see. All you know is inside. I knew a woman in Cleveland, Ohio, who could tell you what you had in your pockets when she was fifteen feet away from you blind-fold. She'd studied the subconscious for twelve years."

This psychic analysis by a backwoods saloonkeeper was the only attempt at a rational explanation of bloodstopping I was to receive.

Next I stopped at the tarpaper shack of Cal Wright, a three-hundred-pound old-timer of the woods, who sat in the doorway completely blocking the entrance with his bulging body. He dismissed the boy's haunt legends as mere childhood scare stories. But the bloodstopping was another matter.

"I've heard Archie Clark say that a man could tell a woman the prayer, or a woman could tell a man, but that one man couldn't tell another." He pointed to a house across the way. "White went from that high-shingled house there to the beer tavern, and just as he got to it he fell. There were perhaps twelve or fifteen people inside. They went for the doctor and the State Police and when Dr. Shutz came he said, 'He ain't a-bleeding.' With all them wounds he would have bled to death, you know. He had them stabbed right through."

"What finally happened to White?"

"They took him to a hospital, where he stayed six months. After that he went in the army, got married, and now lives in Pontiac."

Cal then began to tell me other instances of bloodstopping he knew, from his own family experience. "I had a brother lived at Percy, four miles from here, Roy Wright. He had a tooth pulled and the bleeding wouldn't stop — he had to hold his head over a bucket. They fetched him down to my brother-in-law's here. There was a dance at Shingleton, and they went and asked this fellow Medley to come up; they knew he was one of those fellows could stop bleeding. He stopped a minute and looked at them and said, 'All right, I'll go, but it won't be bleeding when I get there.' And when he got there the bleeding had stopped, and it never started again. So there must be something to it some'eres."

"How long ago did this happen?" I asked Cal.

"About fourteen years ago; Roy was around twenty-two or three at the time. I remember it like yesterday. He was so weak he could hardly move his fingers. You couldn't make my brother believe no other way but that Medley stopped that blood."

As Cal's memory stirred, further illustrations came to his mind. "The first time I heard about stopping blood was in Carr Settlement, Lake County, Michigan," he recollected. "I and my cousin were threshing wheat, and the bandcutter cut his hand. (They have self-feeders now, but used hand feeders then.) When he reached for the bundle, the bandcutter caught him with the knife, right across the back of the hand. We took him up to the house, tore up some sheets, and bound them to his hand, but we couldn't stop the bleeding. I started up the team to go for the doctor, and on the way I met an old feller named George MacDonald — the same name as George here (and Cal pointed to his neighbor who had meanwhile joined us). George had been helping thresh about there, and seen what happened, so he asked, 'How is he?'

"I said, 'He's bleeding to death.'

"He said, 'He ain't a-bleedin' at all.'

"That kinda made me mad, so I said, 'Don't tell me that, I just come from there.'

"We went back, and Del was white as a sheet, but he wasn't bleeding at all. It was seven miles to the doctor, and I was sure he would bleed to death."

Visitor George MacDonald, a very old, petrified-looking man, a veteran of the Alberta lumberwoods, now spoke up in a barely audible voice.

"I know two girls come to Drummond Island from Canerdy, claimed their father could do that. A man can learn a woman and a woman can learn a man. They do it with words that are learned out of the Bible. This fellow Bill Johnson shoved a cork into a pop bottle, the gas burst the bottle, and the glass cut the artery of his hand. I went and got one of the girls and she passed her hand over the cut and the bleeding stopped. Then in the night it started again, and she came and did the same thing, and it never bled again. Back in '88 that was."

Cal came back with another instance. His George MacDonald had a neighbor whose horses cut themselves to pieces on a barbed-wire fence. The neighbor, Dan Trumbauer, ran to George, who said, "You go back, I'll be there in a few minutes as soon as I get dressed. They ain't a-bleedin' at all." When Dan got back not a drop of blood was flowing from the horses' cuts. "George was a genuine Christian, too," added Cal. "He could stop blood or the toothache. My folk always claimed that anyone had that power was born with a veil over his face."

I drove back to Munising, mulling over these stories, and had supper at the Victoria Hotel where I was staying. After the meal, boardinghouse fashion, the diners took seats in the little room adjoining the dining room which served as the hotel office and general gossip parlor. Only natives stayed at the Victoria, which catered to long-term boarders rather than transients, and in the oblong room I saw all the unmistakable Peninsula types, dark solemn Canadiens, red-faced lumberjacks, angular Swedes and a puzzling exotic or two, maybe a Slovenian or a Croat or even a Luxemburger. Some I had talked with before, and I now timidly mentioned my afternoon's findings.

No one laughed or even smiled. A youngish Canadian Frenchman with dark curly hair and a serious manner, Herm Manette, spoke up at once.

"I've seen this stopping the blood. Bill Dory's dad in town here could do it. He used to work in the printing office. One time he stopped the blood on a horse that went down and cut his front knee — old man Looshie's [Lucia's]. He told Looshie, 'If ever you're hurt, think of me.' We'd eat candy and get the toothache and go to him, and he'd say, 'Go on, you haven't got the toothache.' And it would go away. You're not supposed to thank him or anything. If it acts too quickly some people die from the shock. The gift is handed down from man to woman and woman to man."

Alec Belfry, the hotel's proprietor, a small grave Canadien who habitually leaned over the cigar and candy stand sadly viewing the talkers, declared that his father-in-law had had the power. "One eighteenth of May I cut my ankle. I remember I had on a brand new pair of boots. My father-in-law was skidding logs, and I said to him 'Jesus, I put the whole bit of the axe into my boot.' He asked, 'Can you walk?' I said 'No.' He said, 'I'll split up the team and take you back.' The old man walked into the woods and looked at my foot. The shoe was full of blood. He said, 'Put some brown sugar on it.' That stopped the blood. Later on he told me, 'When I'm an old man I must give that secret to my daughter.' But we got to living away from one another, he died at eighty-two in Newberry, and the secret was lost. He could stop toothache too. He got the secret from his mother."

Alec now was minded of another kind of healer. "August Caulier had the gift of drying up goiter," he said in his slow, sincere way. "He was a switch engineer for the Isle Royale Mining Company, and I fired for him for two years. The section foreman's daughter had a goiter hanging down to her chest. Finally he asked his permission to cure her, without carving, for no charge. The foreman laughed, but said it was all right. That evening he went to the girl's home, and every night after that, and ran his finger over the veins of the goiter. A couple of months after he started her neck was perfectly smooth."

The talk swung back to bloodstoppers, and how they acquired the gift. Mr. Belfry quoted a local bloodstopper, old George Coty, as saying that a passage in the Bible would tell one all about it — if one knew the passage. Herm Manette added, too, that babies born with veils over their faces, like tissue paper, which choked them and had to be cut off by the doctor, would receive the power when they grew to a certain age.

A group of out-of-town men working for the County Road Commission entered the room, having finished their dinner late, and joined the conversation. The most conspicuous newcomer was Reuben Rowe, a burly florid ex-undersheriff born in Calumet, whose parents had come to the Copper Country from Cornwall. Reub bellowed when he talked, and he talked a good deal, emphatically and vociferously, filling up the room with noise. On hearing the subject, he promptly declared he knew a blood charmer in his home county.

"We had an old Frenchman up north could stop blood by seeing you or by having a person tell him that somebody was bleeding to death, whereupon he would mumble a few words. Whether it was scriptural, or he had sold himself to the devil, no one knew. He was the seventh son of the seventh son. He couldn't tell anyone or he would lose the power, until he was ready to pass out of the picture. I've seen him do it, in Mohawk, for a person suffering a very bad nosebleed after a very bad fight one day."

Subsequently I received a letter from Miss Bessie Phillips, also of Cornish parentage, in Keweenaw County, describing a charmer and faith healer who seems to be the man Rowe was talking about. I quote her letter verbatim.

• There lived a man by the name of John Buddo, a Frenchman, in Mohawk, Keweenaw County, Michigan, who had the power to heal. He claimed to have been the seventh son of the seventh son and he had the power to draw the pain from his patient to his own body, and in so doing he would perspire freely, his body would be all of a quiver and articles in the room would vibrate due to his emotions.

He could stop the flow of blood, toothache, nosebleeding, or stop pain in any part of the body. It was not always necessary for him to visit the home. If a toothache, he could cure that over the telephone. Ofttimes someone would rush to his home to notify him that some member of the family had a terrific nosebleed and could not stop it. He would talk to the caller and while doing so would rub his hands over each other and in a few minutes he would say, "The bleeding has stopped," and upon their returning home found it had stopped at that same time he had said it would.

He is known to have cured such cases as Saint Vitus Dance

which doctors could not seem to do much for. The party is now well and working and I have never heard of it ever returning to her.

If he visited the patient he would just place his hand on the person while talking to him and thus seem to transfer the pain to himself. There are several people here he has cured of various aches and pains in the past.

His reward for his services was by donations. He would make a charge for his services and the medical doctors tried to have him stopped with his cures, but he carried on; and as a joke by his friends he was known as Dr. Buddo.

By just talking over the telephone or to the party who called for him, he would come under a "faith healer" evidently, but when he visited a patient, a "charmer."

Heads bent closer together in the little sitting room of the Victoria Hotel as one confidence unlocked another. The talk of bloodstopping drifted to other mysteries, to haunted mines and walking ghosts. These grown-up men, who had earlier spun grisly accounts of knife-fighting Finns and eye-gouging lumberjacks, clustered like children comparing eerie frights.

Herm Manette had seen a ghost, face to face, in Munising. "I was walking all alone in the street just when Mrs. Shilling was dying. She used to go walking down that street, before she took to bed. This night I didn't feel no air in my head at all — it was cold like. The old lady come by me, all dressed in black, although I knew she couldn't stir a leg out of bed. I said hello, she never answered. Right at the corner of West Superior, around the corner from my house; eleven-thirty at night, in the fall of the year. We were all alone on the sidewalk. It didn't take me long to make tracks for home and tell my folks. You can ask my father now. We both had the same distance to go home, but I beat her to it.

"Next day the old lady was dead."

A hush fell when Herm stopped, but Reub Rowe jumped into it, literally. Where the Canadien had spoken in low and solemn tones, the Cornishman leaped to his feet, danced his heavy girth about the floor, punctuated his speech with explosive "bloody's" and emphasized his story by slapping his hat down at his feet.

"I've been out in the bush, in cellars, everywhere where there are dead bodies, doing police work. But I can't go near a cemetery at night — I'm scared. Now figure that one out."

Reub had his reasons to be scared. "Walking home with my wife in 1918, a big gray animal appeared in front of me. I threw a rock at him — it disappeared. That night the house was tore apart — a pounding noise went through every room. When I chased it upstairs, it went downstairs; I followed it downstairs, and it was upstairs. I moved out bright and early next morning.

"Only thing we can account for it is that an old fellow was living in that house previously who caused the death of his daughter through abuse."

Eventually the yarning ended and the group broke up. I walked across the street to the Piehl Hotel with Rowe and his friend on the road crew, Jim Hodge of Negaunee. Jim had worked in the mines as a carpenter and above ground as county coroner; he was a Devonshire man, straight and spare, with aristocratic features that deceived a stranger. Jim brimmed over with Peninsula yarns, and gave me more mining lore than anyone else I met. We sat down in the narrow parlor of his hotel, and he now disclosed a bloodstopping item he had been holding back.

"I heard the miners tell of a man who stuck a pig in the throat. The pig started to bleed, then stopped. The man turned around, looked at the group, spotted a fellow who had that belief, or faith — I wouldn't call it a power — and said to him, 'Jump across that stream of water.' It was running in a ditch close by. The man jumped over, and the pig started to bleed."

An old folk idea turns up here, that crossing flowing water will break a malignant spell. A witch cannot follow the track of one who leaps across a brook.

Jim unbottled another, more personal example. "Over in Idaho young McCann fell off a horse, and started to bleed through his nose and ears. Dr. Donovan came over and plugged him up. When the pressure built up, the bleeding started again. Mrs. McCann rushed in to her neighbor, who was my mother, and told her, 'Eddie is going to bleed to death.' 'No, he is perfectly all right. Go back and see.' She went back and he was sitting up, and no blood flowing. I know that for an absolute fact," concluded Jim positively. "Dozens of times she stopped the bleeding."

A severe-looking stranger in the parlor had listened attentively to this account, without offering a comment, and I felt some uneasiness at his probable contempt for our talk. Suddenly he spoke up.

"My aunt in Appleton, Wisconsin, had that power. She was born with a veil."

Jim Hodge grew excited and confidential. "My mother could stop it just that quick," he said to the stranger, and then added dramatically, "There's one right in this house that can do it!"

Reub Rowe caught on before I did and bellowed, "You?"

"Me," said Jim. "When Duba cut his hand, in Butte, making a wedge, I folded the skin back, wrapped it in paper to keep the dirt out, and told him it wouldn't bleed. It didn't. He went to a doctor who said, 'That'll heal all right.' I've stopped my children when they had nosebleed. My mother and grandmother were the same way. It's got to go from male to female to male. It went from my grandmother to my uncle to my mother to me. There's hardly a town in the United States but somebody has the ability to know what to say or do."

Reuben exploded. "Wait a minute," he said, and voiced my thought. "How far is this thing going to go? Why didn't you stop the blood when I cut my hand this afternoon?"

Hodge made no reply, but when Rowe had gone upstairs somewhat huffily, he turned to me and explained, "It wouldn't work on that fellow because he doesn't have belief."

It struck me that Reub's skepticism proceeded more from a

little rivalry with Hodge than from actual disbelief. A man who had moved from a haunted home (and when I reached Calumet later I checked Rowe's story) should not sniff at charms. But he harbored a Cornishman's pique at his neighbor county, and had earlier confided to me that no Englishman was as dull as a Devonshireman.

Later in the evening I wandered through town, and in a saloon came again on the stranger who had said his aunt in Wisconsin could stop blood. I talked with him at the bar and he said his name was Jeff Corvette and hers was Jonas, and he began to describe some of her powers.

"She was the seventh daughter of the seventh daughter. She was born with a veil. She'd be about eighty now.

"She'd make lids jump on a cookstove just by holding her hands over it. She could make a table dance on the floor.

"A horse cut his fetlock on a barbed wire fence. Blood was running out the artery. She went in alone to the barn — no vet around for miles. When she came out the horse was fine.

"Her grandchild, nine years old, had a sty on his eye. She took her wedding ring out in the moonlight. In three days the sty was gone. She cured ringworm the same way.

"She could lift her grandson by the hair and swing him around. If you or I did it, he'd holler his head off.

"And that's no goddamn lie."

Next morning I called at a fruit and candy store in town kept by Abe Artibee, who Reub had told me knew some bloodstopping experiences. Abe was puttering out back, a tall, hawk-nosed old man with a fiery manner, none too popular in the town. Once he ran for mayor, and on election eve bragged to his wife, "Tomorrow you'll be sleeping with the mayor." She replied, "I'll be sleeping with Tom Jones then." Abe finished a bad second, but the story stops there.

Abe reacted at once to bloodstopping. "I could have learned it from Rose Sweeney fifty years ago in Cheboygan," he declared emphatically. "Her brother and sister had the same power. I was mowing hay with Frank Sweeney, when I was sixteen, and I fell into a ditch on a sidehill. So I had to untie the traces, and unhook the neck-yoke from the mare — the neck-yoke was bolted to the mowing machine pole. I unhooked the mare first, the horse wanted to follow her, she pulled up and hit me in the nose with her foreleg. Frank seen me there bleeding so much. I used to have a nosebleed all the time, was afraid even to play with the other boys. All at once the blood stopped. I never had the nosebleed since. Frank said, 'If you ever have the nosebleed again, think of me and it will stop.' It was the biggest miracle I had ever seen. Only Catholics have the power to do that. [Nevertheless the same claims were made to me by Finnish Lutherans and Cornish Methodists]. You've got to do a little penance after it too."

Speaking of miracles reminded Abe of one that had happened at Cheboygan, below the Straits, some fifty-five years before.

"Father Manion cursed away all the army worms into the Cheboygan River. The worms rained on the ground from the air, and the ground for twenty miles square was alive with worms. So the people held a mass, and Father Manion pronounced the curse, and everyone paid ten cents, except one fellow who said the priests were only quack doctors. The worms ate all his crops on the way to the river. They rolled hooplike into the river, and covered it like a velvet rug. They filled the whole twelve miles from the sorting gap to the paper mill at the foot of the rapids on Black River, and the men had to rake worms off the guards fending the logs from the sidewheels. All the worms drowned in the river."

Abe peered at me closely and said, "You can ask my sister in Cheboygan if it didn't happen just like that."

That is what I heard about bloodstopping, and other occult

matters, in the space of thirty-six hours. Throughout the rest of the trip I made a point of asking about the "power" at every opportunity, and found it widely known among all the Peninsula's ethnic groups.

A salty Canadien from Escanaba, Joe Boyer, astonished his son and daughter-in-law by revealing that he had the gift. He got it from his sister, who got it from Joe's brother-in-law out in Fall River, Massachusetts. Splitting wood one time, Joe cut the cord of his second toe ("If my foot wasn't dirty, I'd show you") and the blood poured out. Suddenly he thought of his brother-in-law Alphonse, and the bleeding stopped. Alphonse wrote him that day asking if anything had happened. Joe wouldn't tell me Alphonse's prayer, which he now possessed (he said it was about five minutes long) for fear he'd lose the power.

A French lady at Lake Linden, Madame Le Beault, confided that her aunt had stopped blood and healed burns over the telephone, to points as far as Detroit, although she worried a little that an intervening lake might break the charm. A pious Irishwoman in Crystal Falls contributed a new bloodstopping wrinkle. Mrs. T. J. Murphy said that the local charmer wrote her maiden name, her father's name, and her mother's maiden name on a piece of paper, and then placed both hands on her forehead, whereupon her nosebleed stopped. A Swede at Vulcan, named Johnson, said his father in the Old Country could stop the blood at long distance if he knew in which direction the bleeding person lay.

But it remained for a Finnish magazine editor to give me the secret charm words. Peppery little John Rantimaki, who edits the *Suometar* at Hancock, seemed too educated a person to know peasant folk beliefs, but he had learned the prayer from an old woman of Torstila in Finland, back in 1902, when he was working as a shepherd boy. One of the other boys cut himself with a knife, and Rantimaki repeated the prayer to himself — not aloud, for fear of their ridicule — and the bleeding promptly stopped. He wrote the charm in my notebook, both in Finnish and English.

"Seisota veri, *seisota veri*! Niikuin vesi Jordanissa, kun kristus kastettiin."

"Stop, blood, *stop, you blood*! As the flow of river Jordan when Christ was baptized."

Some bloodstoppers also heal burns, and once in a while a pure burn specialist turns up. My Canadien friend from L'Anse, Bert Damour, greatly respected a burnhealer his family often consulted half a century earlier in Lake Linden. This was Louie Toine, "an old common laborer, big powerful feller, who would go out in de woods in de dead of winter and chop timber. What dat old man used to do, it was a miracle. I didn't believe it till he done it to me." Bert had once been badly scalded when a bull chasing a cow in heat had scared a dog which jumped on a crossbar and upset a boiling kettle of maple-bark water. The water splashed on Bert's hand and he ran to Toine in great pain. Louie told him to sit down while he went up to his room, "to pray, or whatever he done." When Louie came back in about fifteen minutes the burn had gone. His hand hurt for a while but it no longer smarted.

Still a different type of charmer came my way one evening when I talked with a Pennsylvania German probate judge in Vulcan. For an hour we sparred conversationally, but the thickset man with the pop-eyes and unsmiling face had no tales for me. He seemed so matter of fact I mentioned bloodstoppers only as a last resort, but he came to life on that, and informed me that he had the power to charm warts. He had cured a bookkeeper in his office who had such a bad wart on his finger that he couldn't hold his pen. The little McCarthy boy, seven years old, was covered with warts; the judge took him on his lap, concentrated, and shortly after every wart had gone. "You can go right down the street and ask the family if that isn't so," added Arthur Meyers excitedly.

"Oh no," I protested. "Can you tell me though just how you make the warts go?"

"In curing warts I make my mind blank to the whole world, except that one thing. Then in a second it's done. There must be no noise or anything to attract the patient's attention. It's just the transmission of your mind to the other person, which sets those little cells laying dormant to work — that's the secret of the whole thing. People have come to me from all over, from as far as Milwaukee, and I cured them. The longest it ever took was three months. I make a reasonable charge, with a guarantee if the warts do not go away. No one ever asked for their money back."

But the most potent manifestation of power I came across went deeper than any of these charms. Sam Colasacco told me about it in a slurring Italian accent, behind the bar of his newly decorated tavern in Hurley.

"Do you know the *fattura*?" he asked me.

"No."

"You can tie up the blood of a man who marries a virgin for life. First you say the prayers from the prayer book, and then tie knots from a horse-tail's hair. That's called *fattura*. One fellow can tie you up and another what got more power can loosen you up.

"There was a man in Old Country, in Calasko, could loose those knots — John Berdino. He got married and his blood was tied up. So he had his wife pad herself out to look like she was in the family way, a little more each month.

"One day a stranger comes to him on the street and says, 'God-dam, I don't believe in that *fattura* any more.' 'Why not?' 'Well, your wife's in the family way.' And the stranger showed him the hair knots where he buried them. Berdino loosed the knots and he was a man again. So he shot the other one dead. And he never got anything for it, when the town heard how it happened.

"You can stop the *fattura* if in the church at the wedding you put some wheat or fishnet knots in your pocket."

Sam knew an Italian living in Iron Mountain who used the *fattura* on his son for a practical joke. "When this young man got married, his father tied him up. In the morning he asked his son, 'How did you make out last night?' 'I couldn't do nothing.' "

Since both charmer and victim believed the spell controlled the flow of blood on which virility depends, I submit that the *fattura* takes the prize for bloodstopping prowess.

PART III
THE NATIVE TRADITION

8

TOWNSFOLK

Few legends spawned in American history can match the story of the lynching of the McDonald boys at Menominee, Michigan, in 1881. It involves a brutal bloodletting orgy and a bizarre superstition.

In Menominee, a sawmill town on Lake Michigan's Green Bay, just above the Wisconsin line, old-timers have spun the grisly yarn of the McDonald lynching to pop-eyed youngsters for more than sixty years. Echoes of the tale float around Michigan and her neighbor states, and can be heard in saloons and boardinghouses when lumberjacks and lakesmen talk about knife-killings and witch-healings. No two granddads tell quite the same story, for this is strictly a family tradition, never frozen in print, and unceasingly distorted with the vagaries that grow from hearsay and surmise. But on one point, the very heart of the legend, all the storytellers agree: that every ringleader in the lynching died with his boots on.

The Lynching of the McDonald Boys
• On the afternoon of September 26, 1881, the two McDonald boys stabbed to death a half-breed named Billy Kittson. Billy belonged to a family that had been burned out in the disastrous Peshtigo fire of 1871, moved to infant Menominee, and seen it mushroom into a bawdy lumber town. He had an English father,

an older brother Norman who later became janitor for a church, and a husky two-hundred-pound half-brother named George, who started the McDonald-Kittson feud by arresting the McDonalds at Quinnesec while serving as a deputy sheriff.

Everyone called them the McDonalds, although they were actually cousins, and the tall slim one was named McDougall. One tradition describes them as "very fine fellows, except when they were drunk, when they were always fighting with knives." During the spring drive on the Pine River they got into trouble, and assaulted the Menominee sheriff, a man named Ruprecht who had a glass eye. Ruprecht then deputized big George Kittson to arrest the troublesome pair.

After their release from jail, the McDonalds worked two days for the Bay Shore Lumber Company, in Menominee. They then relaxed at a saloon, the Montreal House, in a section in the west end known as Frenchtown. One of the boys swore to Norm Kittson, who was tending bar, that he would "get" his brother George, and pulled out a spring jackknife significantly. Leaving the saloon, the McDonalds drifted up to the Frenchtown whorehouse. A trail ran off Bellevue Street, on which only two houses then stood, through a tangle of jack pine to the whorehouse.

Billy Kittson was in there, drinking whisky with the whores out of quart-size pop bottles. The men fell to quarreling, and Billy hit the little McDonald over the head with a bottle. Then he walked out into the street, toward the Montreal House.

Norm Kittson and three or four others were standing on the corner by the saloon. They saw the McDonalds coming behind Billy, and Norm shouted out, "Hurry up, Billy, they're after you."

"I'm not afraid of the s.o.b.'s," answered Billy.

The McDonalds closed in. "Don't do nothing, boys," pleaded Norman. Big Mac knocked Billy down on his hands and knees with a peavy club. Then he drove the blade of a six-inch dirk into his backbone.

Norman went to help Billy and little Mac stabbed him in the neck. Billy, staggering, went to help Norm in turn and got stabbed again, in the head. Norman, who had been knocked down, almost fainted, but managed to roll over and pull a .32 caliber revolver out of his pocket. He fired twice and hit little Mac in the calf of his leg.

Billy was so drunk he did not know he had been hurt. He walked a block to the Montreal House, and blithely ordered drinks for the crowd. One hanger-on, seeing that Norman was being attended to, said, "You better look after Billy first." A blanket was laid down by the stove for Billy, but he walked to the window first, suddenly shot his hands up over his head, and dropped dead.

After the stabbing the McDonalds ran back for a rig, and then drove to Dr. Phillips, in Finntown near the depot. They were caught there and put in jail.

At the Forvilly House on Ludington Street, the largest hotel in town, men gathered, drank steadily, and talked ominously all the next day. Hearings had been postponed while the prosecutor rounded up witnesses, and the lumber bosses chafed at the delay. Max Forvilly was in the group, supplying the liquor, and Bob Stephenson, superintendent of the Ludington, Wells, and Van Schaick Lumber Company; Robert Barclay, the sheriff, who ran a livery stable; Louis Portvin (usually called Porter) and Tom Parent, boom bosses; and Frank Saucier, a dray-man. Someone spoke of a lynching. These McDonalds were trouble-makers: hadn't they beat up a sheriff? — and here again two days after release from jail they had murdered a man, a son of the second oldest settler in town. How could the companies operate with confidence when such desperadoes roamed the streets? Teach them necktie justice! (The lynchers did not reason that the lumber companies had blocked all the bridges, so that escape was unlikely, and that the evidence against the McDonalds seemed irrefutable.)

Bob Stephenson said he would furnish the rope. Frank Saucier offered to supply a big square timber to force entry into the jail. In his dray cart, with which he peddled water at ten cents a

barrel, he had just hauled some timbers to a space directly behind the courthouse. Early in the evening the group of determined
men marched on the courthouse, lugging a large timber. Two
deputy sheriffs guarded the jail. One, Jack Fryer, said he would
shoot the first man who approached. But Louis Porter grabbed
the gun out of his hand and threw it on the grass, saying, "You
can't kill all of us." The gang crowded into the courthouse with
their timber. They battered down one cell door and found it
empty. They tried a second. The taller McDonald stood there.
"Boys, give me five minutes to talk," he begged.

"Dog, we wouldn't give you one minute," the answer came
back.

A rope was thrown over his head. Louis Porter walked up to
the smaller McDonald and started to put a noose around his neck
too. This McDonald had a penknife, with a blade an inch and a
half long, which one of the whores had given him. He stuck it
through Porter's hand. Porter turned to Laramie, a redheaded
Frenchman standing by, and said, "Give me that ax." He smacked
the smaller McDonald with it and killed him on the spot. The
two men were dragged out of the courthouse basement and
thrown over the iron gate. The taller McDonald's neck caught on
an iron post, and stretched a foot.

Some of the lynch party grabbed the noose ends and hauled
the pair by their necks down Main Street. The others jumped up
and down gleefully on the moving bodies, gouging out chunks
of flesh with their heavy caulked boots. They scrapped and swore
for standing room and a free ride on the McDonalds' legs,
groins, stomachs, and chests. Max Forvilly rode most comfort-
ably of all by sitting down and straddling a corpse.

A crowd speedily formed beyond the Fire Department, whoop-
ing and hollering at the fun. The streets in no time became alive
with shrieking women and drunken lumberjacks, and shrill with
the tooting of whistles and the clang of church bells. Mothers
held their babies in the air to goggle at the parade. For frontier

Menominee, this beat any camp meeting revival or fourth of July jamboree.

The lynchers stopped at a railroad crossing sign that said "Look Out for the Cars," and strung up their prey. The taller McDonald twitched as he was being raised, and a woman shouted ecstatically, "Good! You didn't struggle like that little girl!" It was believed he had raped a young virgin. The crowd threw stones and refuse and spat curses at the dangling McDonalds.

But Sam Pelthier, who kept a lumberman's home, argued with the leaders. He said the fluttering corpses would scare the horses, and the women and children, and cause accidents at the crossing. The leaders, men of business, saw the weight of the argument. Now a really ghoulish idea attracted them. They pulled down the bodies and dragged them back to the starting point of the crime, the whorehouse on Bellevue Street. They dumped the corpses on a bed and forced the girls — some twelve or fourteen of them — to lie with their earlier customers. Some say the fight had originally begun when one McDonald accused Kittson of chiseling on his girl. If so, the two-timing gal now had a chance to prove she still loved her man. Next the gang whipped the whores out of the house, and burned it. Then they strung the McDonalds to two little jack pine trees outside.

A photograph exists, that shows the McDonalds hung to the jack pines. George Premo has seen the picture. He is a tough man, but he says that the picture is more than the human stomach can stand.

No trial was ever held, no arrests were even made, of the ringleaders. But it would not be correct to say that they never received justice. Sentence had been passed even before they reached the crossing sign with the dying men. Father Menard, whose church stood only a block away from the courthouse, pleaded with the gang to desist, as they careened down Main Street. When the bloodied men laughed in his face, he denounced them with this curse: that all who rode the bodies would die with their boots on. So say the French and Irish Catholics. Men of other faiths feel that divine vengeance visited the curse on the lynchers.

In the ballad that the folk made and sang on the event, the McDonalds become wronged, misguided youths, who pay with their lives for their innocent fun, and the men who resorted to lynch law are the transgressors.

> *To make a declaration*
> *   As best we think we can,*
> *You know liquor had the best of us*
> *   As it has of many a man;*
> *And if we acted in our own defense*
> *   Let Mercy lend a hand,*
> *And if we're guilty of the crime*
> *   The law can us command.*

But the law is not permitted to take its course.

> *The jail is broke, the mob is in;*
> *   Give us one word to say,*
> *Take a message to our mothers*
> *   Who live in Canaday.*
> *It will make them broken-hearted*
> *   And cause them grief and pain*
> *To think they never more shall see*
> *   Their own dear sons again.*

In the years since the lynching, a sequel has been added, which many folks solemnly repeat. The curse has been fulfilled, and all the leaders have died strange and violent deaths.

Bob Stephenson, who furnished the rope, died first, within a year after the lynching. A fire started in his lumber yard, among piles of four foot slabs, then used to fuel the lakes boats. The space of a wagon road separated the two flaming piles, each several hundred feet long. Stephenson wanted his men to go between the piles and tip them over, to save the slabs. Neither they nor Randall, the fire chief, would enter the inferno.

"By God, haven't you got guts enough?" asked Stephenson.

He walked in between the piles with a hose. Flame swept across his face. He opened his mouth and gasped for air. Stephenson was full of whiskey. He inhaled some flame and his alcoholic breath caught fire. He ignited, like a human blow-torch. "Boys, I'm done for," he sobbed.

He lingered three days and died in slow misery. He was given a fine Masonic funeral.

Louis Porter was going out with his crew to Paint Dam in the spring, to drive logs on the river. He said, "Go on ahead, boys, I'm tired. I'll be out dere in a liddle while." The crew never bothered about him, because he had not been sick, but he did not show up all day. When the mule drivers came back that night, after unloading, the mules stopped at the hill where Porter had sat down to rest and refused to go further. The teamsters found him still sitting there, his back against a tree, his arms folded, his legs crossed around a cane, his head resting on his arms. But now he was dead. Some say a venomous water snake bit him in the foot. Porter's name is marked on that birch tree today, two and a half miles outside the wilderness village of Amasa.

Dunn was adjusting a head saw in a sawmill in Green Bay, Wisconsin. He thought the carriage was locked. Maybe the catch was not fastened, or maybe a setter touched the lever. The saw swung back and he went through it, sliced like a pickle.

Frank Saucier died on a train going from Iron River to Menominee, while on a carpenter job. He died without apparent cause.

Albert Lemieux, a timber cruiser, was playing cards in camp with Dune Cruikshank, when he suddenly got up, took a knife, and slashed his own neck.

Alfred Beach, whom they called Long Beach because he was so very tall, tipped over in a boat and drowned.

Some men boasted they would never die with their boots on.

One was George Chandler, a boomer. He was in all kinds of accidents and sicknesses, but pulled through after being in bed for about three years. His first day up he took a little walk, and just as he got back to the gate of his house, he toppled over and died.

Barclay, the ex-sheriff, was another who swore he would cheat the curse. One day he drove a team of horses in a surrey from his livery stable to a family reunion. He tied up the horses, walked to the front gate, waved cheerily to the group, and slumped down dead.

Max Forvilly, whose whiskey primed the necktie party, lost his hotel and everything he had, went crazy, and died on a little farm on Peshtigo Sugar Bush.

No other prisoner has ever occupied the cell that held the McDonalds. When the WPA rebuilt the courthouse, the bloodstains could still be seen on the wall.

How Crystal Falls Stole the Courthouse from Iron River

• The best known story in Iron County is a matter of local political strife that has many counterparts throughout the United States. The battle for the county seat — and, on a grander scale, for the state capitol — is often waged with all manner of cunning and chicanery, and leaves its wake of bitterness and rage. For the patronage of county offices may determine the life or death of a town.

Crystal Falls and Iron River are mining communities of equal size that lie at the east and west ends of their county. When Iron County was carved out of Marquette County in 1885, rivalry flamed high between the two for the coveted county seat. Just what the events were that shaped the decision, no one can say with absolute certainty. But every old-timer in Iron River reacts to the topic with a grimace and a sad shake of the head. And the veterans of Crystal Falls grin slyly and smugly, and look fondly along a Main Street that climbs from a valley up a hill at a dizzy angle, to the handsome lemon-colored building that sits smack on the top. Both sides agree that Crystal Falls "stole the courthouse."

My questions about the theft of the courthouse brought, along with the knowing smiles, many contradictory stories. I asked county officials, families of the participants, the town characters, and strangers in saloons, who had stolen what, for obviously the building itself had not been lugged the intervening fifteen miles. One native said the theft involved the blueprints for the courthouse, another the cash on deposit for its construction, a third the county papers. The accounts all have one consistency, that a theft occurred, which made possible the transferring of the temporary county seat at Iron River to the present permanent one at Crystal Falls. Further, the theft was unusually audacious and it was sanctioned by an unusually fraudulent election. No sneaking corruption here, but the bold and open lawlessness of frontier democracy.

Here is the composite tale, spliced impartially from versions from both sides of the county:

When the state legislature assigned the county courthouse temporarily to Iron River, pending a county election, certain indignant and imaginative men of Crystal Falls plotted to abduct the safe containing the records of the county treasurer and county clerk. One theory has it that the object was to steal the records in order to destroy the registration list and make possible an illegal election. These men were no ordinary riffraff, but elected agents of the people: the school supervisor, the sheriff, the county clerk and the county treasurer. At a scheduled meeting of the board of county supervisors, at Iron River of course, the Crystal Falls group jovially challenged the opposition to a poker game with manly stakes.

After the meeting, accordingly, the supervisors adjourned to the Boyington House, and were soon immersed in serious gambling and drinking. As the night wore on, and the stakes and the curses grew larger and manlier, two Crystal Falls men, Frank Scadden and Dick Hughitt, yawned obviously and headed for bed. The proprietor, Andy Boyington, a pioneer settler and Civil War veteran lacking an arm, suspected their intent and made several visits to their room, stealthily carrying a chair on which he stood to peer into the transom and listen to their feigned snores. Eventually Andy went off to bed too and the pair, hearing from the noise and laughter downstairs that most of Iron River had congregated to see the game, lowered themselves out the window to a shed below, and stole silently off in the darkness to the shack that served as courthouse. At the Boyington House the Iron River supervisors and citizens exulted, for the cards seemed to be running strongly in their favor.

Scadden and Hughitt plowed through snow up to their waists on this twelve below zero night, entered the shack, whose back door had been purposely left ajar, opened the safe and loaded the records onto a hand sled. They made for the railroad yards, where a Crystal Falls conductor helped them stow sled and records into a boxcar. Next day the county records reposed in Crystal Falls. The courthouse had been stolen.

Iron River boiled over with chagrin and rage, and talked of shooting it out. But Crystal Falls swore mightily to fight back, and formed a vigilance committee to defend the records. An Iron River sheriff named Ball boasted he would arrest the thieves on New Year's Eve; friendly parties drank with him all evening to strengthen his resolve. Then at midnight they told him his term had expired. Finally Iron River decided to settle the issue legally by winning the imminent election for the county seat, through all possible means fair and foul.

Both sides prepared thoughtfully for the 1888 election. Iron River imported five hundred lumberjacks from Gogebic County, and Crystal Falls scoured the Upper Peninsula for floaters and ringers. The dead were resurrected from the graveyards, and their names entered on the registration rolls — although it was claimed that Crystal Falls unfairly preëmpted names from the Iron River cemetery. The Australian ballot made it possible for a man to vote his honest opinion as many times as he desired, and many men did. The timekeeper of the Mastadon mine sat beside the polling booth and checked off his miners as they entered the

polling booth; if Crystal Falls won, they received a day's pay, if
Iron River, a day's docket. The Sipsons zealously got out the vote
in Iron River, for they owned property on Hammer Hill and
wanted to sell it to the county, at a reasonable price, of course, as
the permanent site for the courthouse. Never had a local election
commanded such civic enthusiasm. Three thousand odd votes
were counted for Crystal Falls, which then harbored some three
hundred all year residents. And so evenly were the sides matched
that the vote, as counted in the temporary Crystal Falls courthouse, showed Crystal Falls the victor by only five votes.

But no sooner had the long-pending question been duly and
democratically settled, when disconcerting cries of dirty work
and double dealing were heard. These concerned not the manner
of voting — after all, both sides had equal opportunity to inflate
their record — but the count of the votes that found their way
into the ballot-boxes. Rumor asserted that Iron River ballots,
whose number would have tipped the close returns, mysteriously
disappeared from the Iron River ballot-box which Bill Tully was
carrying over to the county seat; thereupon the court set aside
the tally sheet. Some say that Bill fell and broke the seal on his
way over. Of course everybody knows that Bill, a native son of
Iron River, became the first regular county sheriff after Crystal
Falls won the election.

To be fair to Bill Tully, other candidates did arise for the dishonor of deceiving the voters. One was the supervisor of Bates
township, Kleinstuper, who was supposed to have stumbled downstairs carrying a ballot box. When he arose, and reinserted the
ballots, Bates, which was solidly pro-Iron River, had experienced
a change of heart and votes. And Kleinstuper became the pump-
man of the Crystal Falls waterworks.

Or maybe the renegade was a "pettifogger lawyer," an Iron
River justice of the peace named E. P. Locke, who, when the
vote was running close, mislaid a ballot box containing an Iron
River precinct, so that the court disallowed the tally sheet which
would have given the vote to the west side of the county.

But most judgment affixes the guilt to Billy Tully. In later years Tully returned to Iron River and built himself a fine home there. One day Tully stood on the street watching road workers resurfacing the road. An old fellow, Sullivan, was raking up the coarse stones in little piles along the sides of the street, preparatory to laying down a gravel top. (Iron River had many pioneer Irish families — the Kellys, Lolleys, O'Briens, Kinneys, Tulleys.)

"When they going to remove them stones, Mr. Sullivan?" asked Tully, who was now an important man.

"When they grow big enough so we can build a courthouse, Mr. Tully," answered old Sullivan.

A teamster was seen hauling an outhouse from Crystal Falls west to Fortune Lake. "Where you going, Patty?" asked a friend.

"I'm taking the courthouse back to Iron River," said Patty. This remark especially hurt, seeing that Crystal Falls had purposefully built the finest courthouse in the Peninsula.

During the second World War, Iron River refused to take advantage of the free headquarters room for the county rationing board available to them in the hated courthouse. Because they had the population edge, Iron River was entitled to the rationing board, and by God, it would be located in Iron River, even if that meant paying forty dollars a month rent for a room. And by God, it was.

Newberry Politics

• Politics in a post-frontier town is apt to degenerate from a high standard of lawlessness to petty boss rule. Especially when the town loses its economic energies, the county and township political offices loom as the surest jobs, and attract strange candidates. Some good political stories start traveling then. I heard several in Newberry, an inland community of under three thousand persons, which once manufactured thousands of tons of pig iron annually, but now depends for survival on a lone sawmill and a State Hospital for the insane.

Newberry had an economic boss, the owner of the sawmill, who ran the town in an unofficial way but wished to legalize his power. He entered himself as a candidate for the Board of Supervisors of the (Interior) Township. There seemed no way of stopping him from taking over the local government.

Duncan Cameron appeared against him. Duncan had just been released from prison, where he had served a term after being convicted on an embezzlement charge.

In his campaign speech Duncan blasted at the economic tyranny of the sawmill owner. He ended up by saying, "You are all forced to pay a tax on his mill."

Someone in the crowd cried out, "No, no, that's not possible."

"All right," said Duncan, "look on your tax receipt. See if it doesn't say, 'One mill.'"

He was elected. Now as chairman of the Board of Supervisors he runs the town.

They claim that's an actual fact.

The Poles in Newberry held a dance around election time, and everybody got pleasantly drunk — no one more so than the County Treasurer, Jimmy Morgan. He got on a table and made a speech to his constituents.

He said, "I'm crooked, and you know I'm crooked. But so is everyone else. You might as well elect me and pay me the County Treasurer's salary, because I have nine children, and if I'm not elected you'll have to support and feed us anyway, when I go on relief.

"Besides, you might elect some crooked fellow smarter than I am."

Jimmy is still treasurer.

Prospects for reform in Newberry are not the best. The Board of Supervisors guards its prerogatives with paternal zeal. At a town meeting to present nominations, Pat Quinlan's brother, who was not on the board, moved that the existing members be retained. Pat, who was Probate Judge, moved that nominations be closed. Mr. Hendrickson set out from his home at the eight o'clock whistle to attend the meeting. When he arrived at the hall, four minutes later, the meeting was over.

The City Never Born

• Why towns get born, flourish and wither, change face, strangle rivals, or perhaps never throb into life at all, make subjects for community legends. For the rural American regards his town as a second family and its history as scarcely less personal than his own genealogy.

Bill Bryer told me one such legend when I drove out to see him in McMillan township. I say "township" advisedly, for there was no town, only two frame houses catty-corner from each other at a country crossroads, close by a small round lake. Newberry, the largest inland town in the Peninsula, is thirteen miles away, and the road between passes increasingly empty land and wild-looking scrub. The Bryers, calm, elderly folk, sat in the kitchen looking out over the cleared farm land, for it was a drizzly day, and Bill began to recall, in a matter-of-fact way, the rough pioneer experiences of his father. His wife, the first white child born in Luce County, in 1881, cheerily added details.

Robert Bryer took up the first homestead in present Luce County in 1876. He came down from Canada, where his English mother had married an Irish lumberjack, as a young man of twenty-four trying to make a stake. Homesteading in the heavily timbered wilderness, where not a single stick had been cleared, presented fantastic difficulties. Bryer had to lug in his supplies over twenty-five miles of tortuous Indian trail from Naubinway, an Indian fishing village to the south on Lake Michigan. After working all day on his farm, he walked in to Naubinway, loaded up with seventy-five or eighty pounds of flour, pork, sugar, and tea, walked back during the night with the pack on his back, and next morning pitched in again on his farm chores.

To aid him in clearing timber from his land, Bryer bought a

yoke of oxen from a lumber jobber at Naubinway. He loaded
them with provisions and set off through the woods, fording creeks
with the oxen trailing behind, driving the team right over little
trees which bent down before the yoke and sprang back again,
and chopping big ones enough to make them yield. By instinct,
for he scorned a compass, Bryer reached a spot about eight miles
east of his homestead when night fell. He turned the oxen loose
to browse on buds and branches while he lay down for a snooze.
He dozed uneasily, since it was severely cold, and so jerked up
at once when an object grazed his ear. His eighteen hundred
pound ox had planted a foot directly alongside his ear, and could
as easily have crushed his face like an egg. Bryer found himself
nearly frozen to death on awaking, and to renew his body heat
began to chop vigorously at a great hemlock on a ridge. He
chopped it half through before his blood ran warm again, and
for thirty years after, passersby marveled at the notch and little
suspected that it represented the margin of a man's life.

When dawn came, Bob Bryer led his team and wagon to his
homestead. He covered the eight miles in half a day, arriving at
noon, and set to work clearing and burning the timber, for there
was no market for hardwood then. Unaided, he built his log
cabin, chinking moss and mud between the logs, and shaving
shingles for his roof from two-foot blocks with a double-handled
drawing knife. All his furniture he made himself. When son Bill
was a boy of seven or eight, in 1874 or 1875, the family moved
from Naubinway to the homestead permanently. Winters they
never saw a soul. Bob lived till he was ninety-two, dying in 1941,
rugged and hearty to the end. As his son says, "Men were like
whalebone then. The generations are weaker and wiser now."

But Bob Bryer, the homesteader and pioneer farmer, had his
gobbet of wisdom. He did not force a passage into the woods just
to grub a farmer's living. Bob planned to pull a business coup,
and grow wealthy in a way that Henry George would have
sputtered at. He intended to buy up homesteads at the government price of a dollar and a quarter an acre, and resell them at

zooming figures. Bob would be in on the ground floor of a great land boom.

He figured this way. When he left Canada as a young man to seek a fortune on the west coast, he had stopped off at Detroit, and by chance seen a survey drawn up by the South Shore Railroad Company for a track from St. Ignace at the southeast foot of the peninsula diagonally across the timber and iron lands to Marquette on the north central edge. Bryer looked carefully at the projected route, and noticed that it touched only one lake in the entire distance across the Peninsula heartland. His imagination promptly took fire. Obviously a town would rise here, the biggest town in the Peninsula, bigger than Marquette or the Soo, an industrial and trading center. The railroad would bring iron ore to the city from the Marquette range, the dense woods would supply hardwood for charcoal, kilns and furnaces and sawmills and stores would mushroom forth. The railroad would carry out iron goods and white pine logs to St. Ignace to be shipped across the straits and downstate. As the peninsula grew, so would Round Lake City, its economic and geographical heart. And Bob Bryer, selling town lots to industrialists, would grow very rich.

So Bob bought a homestead of a hundred and sixty acres at the north end of Round Lake, and waited for the railroad. But the panic of 1873 wiped out the company, and the contractor lost his charter. Another company secured it, but meanwhile the state resurveyed a route four or five miles north. The new Duluth, South Shore, and Atlantic Railway Company then constructed a railway with the aid of state grants of sixteen sections for each mile of road completed. The company mortgaged half the land, filled with the finest white pine, to finance its construction.

Even while the railroad was being built in 1881 and 1882, Newberry began to spurt. She became the site of a camp for the railroad workers, and in time the location for sixty-four charcoal kilns, an iron-furnace that manufactured millions of tons of iron, and an active sawmill. But Bob Bryer and son Bill believed that their unborn city, abutting on Round Lake, would have grown to three or four times the size of Newberry. Newberry has faded off since the hardwood gave out and new processes were introduced to smelt the iron.

Instead of selling town lots, Bob Bryer pitched in and cleared his homestead. Son Bill bought the nearby acres, and today he and his nephew across the way are still farming the land. Round Lake City is now a dead dream, an historical might-have-been.

9

LUMBERJACKS

THE LUMBERJACK CODE

THE white pine lumberjack has grown into legend, the legend of a swashbuckling, ferocious, tenderhearted superman. "There were men in those days, by God," a pioneer mail carrier swore to me reverently; "Ain't one like 'em in the country today." "The typical lumberjack was the most independent man on earth," said Moonlight Harry Schmidt, one of the few loggers left in the Peninsula. "No law touched him, not even smallpox caught him. He didn't fear man, beast, nor devil." Then he looked around at the quiet lollers in his camp and added with scorn, "Young shoots we call second-growth jacks."

The life of the jacks followed an unwritten creed, and he who violated its articles suffered dishonor and dismissal from a proud fraternity. This creed or code resembled somewhat the cult of the medieval knight in providing standards of valor, honor, justice, and chivalry. The teamsters cherished their horses and the axemen their broadaxes as ever the armored knight his war steed and broadsword. Both the knight and the lumberjack spent a good deal of time fighting viciously for sheer fun. But unlike the noble, the jack never considered it a disgrace to work for a living.

More surely than any union contract, the lumberjack code extracted from the woodsmen unslacking, prodigious toil. "They

worked all day from the first light until deep into night; they'd
work their heart out for you," Moonlight Schmidt said. To be the
Number One jack in a camp was a coveted honor; to haul the
most board feet of logs into camp was an incentive that spurred
rival teamsters; to belong to the best camp was a proud assertion
backed up with flying fists. A true jack could jump into any woods
job: a log-cutter, felling the logs on a dime; a swamper, cutting
trails through the brush so the fallen logs could be skidded out; a
cant hook man, decking logs twenty feet high in rollways, there
to lie until the spring drive. Herb Larsen tells of the jack in Iron
County who bet he could fell, limb, cut into four-foot lengths,
split, and pile a cord of hardwood in an hour. He did it with six
minutes to spare — a job that would take a modern jack, dependent on the crosscut saw, a whole day.

Skill and superstamina being taken for granted, the code next
stressed the ability to brawl and the necessity to get insensibly
drunk. The lumberjacks have been aptly styled "whiskey-fighting
men." Every spring when camp would break, a jack must leave
the woods where he has lived in monastic seclusion for six or
seven months, hike to the nearest town, and blow his entire stake
of four or five hundred dollars on rotgut whiskey. During this
spree he visited the brothels and mauled other jacks. When he was
dead broke he made his way back to camp, to recoup his stake
by working as a river-driver (or river-hog). Many jacks never
escaped the woods because they blew every stake they made for
liquor. Nat Kavanagh spent twenty years trying to see his mother
but never got beyond St. Ignace. Just why the jack had to spend
all his earnings thus futilely none of the old woodsmen can quite
explain, all accepting the matter as fundamentalist doctrine quite
beyond inquiry.

So as a point of honor the jack must drink, and treat his fellows
to drink, while his cash lasted. Lanky Archy Garvin carefully explained some of the drinking ritual to me in the lobby of the
Richards Hotel at Menominee. A rigid custom required that the
bartender never ring up thirty cents. If he did he would be fired

and the saloon would be boycotted. Whiskey sold for ten cents a glass, three drinks for a quarter, four for forty cents, so drinks were bought in threes. A jack who bought a drink just for himself was known as a "Dick Smith," and six honest jacks would summarily toss him over the bar, whereupon he would automatically be compelled to stand treat. "Come on, boys, belly up to the bar," the well-heeled jack roared out when he entered a saloon. Barney Waters, a genial timber chopper well known in the western counties, coined his own treat cry. Waving a handful of bills as he strode up to the bar, he sang, "Balance two and how do ye do, and away goes Barney Waters. Come on, boys, and we'll snow the road. I'm foreman over all foremans. Give the boys another snort." "Snow the road for Barney Waters" became a popular bar saying around Sidnaw, Trout Creek, Bruce's Crossing, and Ewen.

Saloons often reserved special quarters, the snakeroom, for lumberjacks drunk stiff, since the law forbade throwing them outside where they might freeze. Poli Venne of Newberry, fifty years in the woods, saw them piled up in the snakeroom at Rexton, where a big camp once operated. A teamster there received eighteen hundred dollars from his folks in Germany, and blew as much as he could on a big drunk, helped along by some thieving "sharks." He was deposited in the snakeroom and lay blissfully on the bare floor with a couple of dozen other comatose axemen. But even in his stupor he intuitively clenched his roll in his right-hand pocket. The prowling sharks could figure out no way to break his grip. Finally one tickled his ear with a straw. The poor teamster put up his hand to his face, and when he returned it to his pocket, his wad was gone.

Some wild tales arose to describe the lumberjack's passion for whiskey. John Nelligan, a pioneer lumberman around Menominee, tells about the logging crew that ran short of grub in the middle of winter. They selected some of their number and entrusted them with cash to buy supplies for the balance of the winter, at the nearest town. Eventually the committee returned, and presented the starving jacks with several cases of whiskey and a couple of loaves of bread. After staring silently at this exhibit, one jack dourly remarked, "What're we gonna do with all that bread?"

Deprived of whiskey, especially during Prohibition days, the woodsmen resorted to any plausible substitute. They have been said to drink Hinkley's bone liniment, Sterno, Hoffman's drops (a cough medicine full of ether), Snellman's colic drops, varnish, and Jamaica ginger. Nelligan tells, for true, how Bob Starr and two other tie-loggers working in St. Louis County near Duluth, Minnesota, customarily drank raw alcohol for stimulus. Their last drinking occurred when they sent a message to the closest drugstore by an Indian asking for "one gallon of good alcohol." But the druggist interpreted the badly written note to read "wood alcohol." The tie-loggers were found some time later, quite dead.

An old Seney tale on the same theme relates how Paddy Joyce, a veteran jack, was pumping water vigorously from the town pump, with no results, since he had forgotten that it must be primed. At length Paddy said to the pump, "I don't blame you for not giving me any water. I only come to you when I'm broke."

The whiskey-drinking tradition continues still. While I was talking to Moonlight Schmidt at his camp outside Newberry, some jacks came in and said, "Alfred's drunk in the ditch down the road." Moonlight sighed paternally and cussed mildly, saying, "Well, I oughta let the s.o.b. lie there and rot, but that ain't human, so I guess I'll have to get him or he'll freeze to death."

Then turning to me, he added, "Two years ago that fellow worked for me at a camp near Grand Marais, and spent a hundred and fifty dollars on a drunk. Another feller said to him, 'That's too bad you spent all your money with winter coming on, you'll need some clothes.' He just said, 'That's Moonlight's worry.'"

Moonlight said this rather proudly.

A cheery jack standing by — Ike Perry, who had worked for Moonlight since he was thirteen — wisecracked, "Tie a rope around his neck and drag him in; he'd never know the difference." Then he recalled a case in evidence. "Old Joe Donor of Eckerman lay out in the ice in thirty below weather and never froze. He got drunk in the Soo and was crawling along Ashmun Street [the main street in Sault Ste. Marie] on his hands and knees, right in front of the whole town.

"A passerby said, 'Can I give you a lift? You've got more than you can carry.'

" 'By God,' said Joe, 'if I can't carry her, I can drag her.'

"He crawled back to his shack and lay outside in the snow all night. The snow melted, dripped on him from the eaves, and then froze again. When he woke in the morning, sober, he was frozen in and scared to death. He hollered like hell, and they had to chop him out of the ice."

As a lumberjack must drink, so must he fight. Whiskey was the prelude to battle, in which belligerent jacks for little reason flailed each other with bruising fists as long as a man could stand. And then the upright mauler planted his caulked boots on his prostrate opponent's face and twisted his foot, leaving his caulk marks there as permanent scars in the flesh, and giving his victim a smallpox look. Above all, the lumberjack tradition required toughness, and a jack proved he was tough primarily by savage and brutal brawling. But the tradition also insisted that he harbor no grudge against his foe. The fight was not so much a personal matter as a test of valor.

The woods storytellers describe fight after bloody fight. Eighty-four-year-old Albert Neilsen, who looks like a shaggy Santa Claus, lived through the heyday of such flaming lumber towns as Seney and Grand Marais, and prizes this ringside memory.

Albert Neilsen speaks

• De toughest, bloodiest fight ever seen was between Black Tom McCann and Pikey Johnson, in Grand Marais in 1894. I just come in Marcotte and Wan Kip's saloon, and I got up in de corner so I wouldn't get a punch in de nose — I remember dat.

Pikey only weighed 130, and Black Tom was 190, but de liddle feller had de staying power and wouldn't quit — you had to kill him. He was like a wildcat. Pikey had no clothes — dey was all tore off — but he didn't care if he was naked; he'd fight at de drop of a hat. He was a nice fellow when he was sober, but quarrelsome when he was drinking. He knew Tom was a good man, and he started it cause he was drunk. In fact he was so drunk when dey started dat he could hardly stand up, but he kept getting soberer and soberer.

Dey fought and fought and fought, until dey fell in a clinch on de floor in deir own blood. Tom said, "Let's quit." But Pikey said, "I'll never quit, goddamn you." And he didn't, until dey was parted.

Dat Pikey was de goodest liddle fellow you ever met.

Biting and gouging played a regular part in the unrestricted mayhem of the lumberjack fight. Gabby Aaron Kinney of Iron River tells of a confirmed biter who finally met his match.

Aaron Kinney speaks

• Billy Winter, who had a farm one-half mile up the road from the lake here, had a skull half an inch thick. You could pound it and he wouldn't feel it — he didn't have much feeling anywhere. In a fight he would chew the other fellow's ears and fingers and thumbs until he cried. You'd see jacks around town with their ears half chewed off and their thumbs all bitten up.

But one time he got stopped. He came into the Boyington barn when Al Hunter from New Brunswick was there. Al could lick anything that walked. Billy went up to Al, grabbed his hand and stuck his thumb in his mouth. "Let go or I'll gouge your eye out," said Al. But Billy wouldn't let go and kept chewing the thumb. Al stuck his other thumb in Billy's eye and laid it out on his cheek. Billy still didn't let go and Al popped out the other eye. "Let go or I'll tear 'em off and throw 'em away," he told Billy. Finally he had to choke Billy to make him let go.

Doctor Bond (Carrie Jacob Bond's husband) and I were just across the street. The fight was over by the time we got there. Doc put the eyes back in while I held Billy's head. His left eye was always a little crooked after that. Billy just grinned a little bit when Doc put his eyes back. He just didn't have any feeling.

In the fight tale of "Bruce's Challenge," a miner successfully tangled with a braggart lumberjack.

Jim Hodge speak

• One time John Sullivan's boy cleaned out six or eight men in a saloon. He came back with a little cut on his cheek and a black eye, and his dad bawled him out. "Whin I was yourrr age, me bye, there wasn't a man could put a hand on me," John told him. And he told the truth.

As a young fellow John worked as a blacksmith at the old Jackson iron mine in Negaunee, where iron ore had first been discovered. Word reached him that a lumberjack named Bruce had made the brag in Marquette that he could lick any man in the county. So he got up Sunday morning at three o'clock, and walked twelve miles into Marquette.

Mrs. Sullivan asked him, "Be ye going to mass this early, John?"

"I have a spot of business to attend to afore," he said.

When he got into Marquette he asked a policeman, "Mr. Officer, could you tell me where there's a man by the name of Bruce around here?"

And the policeman, who was another Irishman, named Dingy Hogan, said, "That's him standing over there."

Sullivan walked over to him and said, "Mr. Bruce, I understand you said you could lick any man in Marquette County. Now that covers a lot of territory, and I'm only one man, but I'm ready to try ye."

The fight took place at the corner of Front Street and Baraga Avenue. Dingy Hogan said it was the cleanest fight he ever saw. Before it started he went up to Bruce and said, "Now you're a lumberjack, and there'll be no kicking or stepping on a man when he's down. It'll be a fair fight."

Sullivan licked Bruce to a fare-thee-well. Then he walked the twelve miles back to Negaunee.

Jim Hodge told me that story as a fact, in a boardinghouse in Munising. Yet it closely resembles the long-standing tale of the saloon bully who boasts he can lick any man in town. When he hears no takers, he increases his boast to include the county, and finally the state. Thereupon a bystander slaps him down. "That time I covered too much territory," the fallen hero admits. And there are accounts of determined men who walk great distances for the privilege of fighting. John Single, never licked in a rough and tumble, is said to have walked over fifty miles from Big Bull Falls to lick Jack Cudahy at Grand Rapids (now Wisconsin Rapids), for beating up his brother. He left after supper and arrived before breakfast. After mashing up Cudahy he walked back home. Tradition says "he was a highly respected citizen and peaceably inclined."

T. C. Cunnion, as tough a jack as ever lived, was known as the man-eater from Peterborough. "I knew him very well," Archie Garvin told me in a hotel lobby in Menominee. "He had double teeth all around, a smashed nose, and was cross-eyed — the fiercest looking brute you ever saw. When he gritted his teeth you could hear him all over; his teeth were all wore down from gritting. In Saginaw one time he picked up a baby, and told its mother, 'I'm T. C. Cunnion, the man-eater from Peterborough. I haven't eaten a man in quite a while, guess I'll have a lunch.' He opend his mouth to bite the baby and the woman fainted."

In its most extreme form the tradition of toughness ran into degeneracy, and the most degenerate lumberjack who ever walked the northwoods was P. K. Small. He must have gotten around some, for I spoke with old jacks in Newberry, Seney, Grand Marais, Manistique, and Munising who knew him personally, and tell disgusting tales about him. His name arouses much more talk than Paul Bunyan.

P. K. Small had no taste. "I seen P. K. Small eat a live snake from the tail up for a drink of whiskey," said John I. Bellaire. "He'd eat horse manure for a drink of whiskey. He'd drink sow beer till he was insensible. One time I found him in the street with vomit all over him and hogs rooting at him. He bit the head off a boy's pet crow once and handed him back the body with blood spurting all over him. In the American House here [in Manistique] Mrs. Miller gave him a ham sandwich. He handed a piece to a dog. The dog slobbered it out on the floor. He cuffed the dog, picked up the ham, and put it back into his mouth. Miller threw him out of the hotel."

"He had a stomach made of steel," said Alec Belfry in Munising. "He'd go down the street and pick up a big dried-up slab of manure and eat it, for a drink. He'd pick stuff out of the spittoon in his hands and eat it. I saw him with a live mouse in his mouth, the head at one side and the tail at the other and blood running down his cheeks. He had everybody vomiting. Once he held up the train from Shingleton to Seney with an old rusty pistol with no silver in it, for a drink. I took him to the St. Mary's hospital at Marquette after. Next morning I saw him in a saloon with the bandages all ripped off — he had a broken collar bone. 'I wouldn't stay in that goddamn place,' he said, 'it's too dry for me.'

"You could smell him half a mile. He was the toughest beast that ever lived."

"I shacked with P. K. Small all one summer in 1894," Charlie Goodman told me at Grand Marais. "He'd froze his left foot one time and lost all his toes when he lay down drunk in the snow to sleep. He wore a number eight shoe, so that about two inches of his shoe stuck out in front. Whenever the boys caught him drunk they used to nail his shoe to the floor and make him perform before they'd let him loose."

In a fight with Small his opponent clinched with him, bit the end of his nose, which had been once broken, completely off, and spit it out on the barroom floor. Dr. Scott replaced the dismembered nose with such good effect that some time later, when he was arraigned in court before Judge Steere at the Soo, the judge, who saw him frequently in court, remarked, "This mishap has made a better-looking man of you."

Even children knew of P. K. Small as a noisome ogre. He was

said to have snatched a goose from a little girl in the Soo and bit its neck off. Thereafter children chanted, "P. K. Small eats them, feathers, guts, and all." (Girls substituted "skins" for "guts.")

The case of P. K. Small quite oversteps the boundaries of the lumberjack code, for although he was tough, he was also despicable. A self-respecting jack had ideals and integrity. For instance, for all their fighting in the towns, the axemen never scuffled in camp. When the fight could not be avoided, the combatants immediately departed from camp. At Fiborn Quarry, north of Rexton, a sawyer and a little toploader quarreled over a girl. They had it out in a quarry two and a half miles from the camp, stripped to the waist, pummeling each other with bare fists in a circle in the snow about thirty feet in diameter, ringed by silent jacks. Each knocked the other down more than once, but the fight continued until one could rise no more. As the Irish boss put it, "They fit and fit and fit until one was licked." Then each clothed himself and they marched off in opposite directions, never to return to camp.

Toward women the woodsmen behaved with a scrupulous decorum. This attitude seems odd in view of the widely celebrated whoring activities of the jacks, for whose benefit, says a tenacious legend, a stockade with girlies penned inside and guardian wolves yowling at the gate adorned Seney, Marinette, Hurley and other tough lumber towns. (Ed Grondin, who ran a hotel in Seney in its palmy days, told me that the stockade story was a complete fabrication, devised to appall a temperance woman from Detroit lecturing in Seney to a respectful and thoroughly unrepentant audience.) But the jack never trafficked with nor molested women outside the profession. A school teacher at Rockland remembers that drunken lumberjacks would sweep off their caps when she passed them on the street, so strenuously that they frequently fell flat on their faces. And Arthur Quirt tells how three Sisters of Charity once called with impunity on riverhogs driving the Brule River, to solicit donations for an orphan home. All profanity ceased, each man glared for the sign of any suggestive look (two of the Sisters were young and attractive), and everyone promptly pledged a dollar from his pay.

Proud in his honor and ability, the old-time jack could suffer no keener disgrace than being fired, and believed the stigma would follow him to hell. Other jacks remembered the man who had once been fired, talked about him slurringly, and avoided his company. If a weakling came in early on a rainy day the foreman said never a word until the following morning, when he handed the man his check in front of the crew — the crowning shame. Even sickness lowered a man's stature. The lumberjack gloried in his superman role, as an old story illustrates. A family from lower Michigan stopped off at a tavern, and the father told his little girl that lumberjacks were sitting in the next booth. She peeped around and said, "Aw pa, them ain't lumberjacks, them is men." One woodsman overheard her and answered, "Oh, girlie, you're wrong, we're lumberjacks. Just pour some whiskey on a bale of hay and see if we don't eat her."

CAMP BOSSES

Cycles of lumberjack tales cluster chiefly around the local camp boss — not around Paul Bunyan. The merciless and the wily boss become traditions, and identical anecdotes get attached to different salty figures in northwoods lumber history. No doubt because they prided themselves on being tough, the jacks took equal pride in the toughness of their boss — much as sailors cussed at and secretly admired the captain who reigned over them for many monastic months each voyage.

Legends about hard treatment of the jacks are rooted in facts. One retired lumberjack gives this thumbnail sketch of his woods life.

• I worked in the woods from daylight till dark, seven days a week. The only time I saw the camp in daylight was on Sunday. All the time they fed you on red horse and sow belly and baked beans. You had to work six months or longer or you didn't get any pay. In the spring they paid you off with a 'white horse' slip. Then you had to walk thirty miles to cash it, at the company office. Then the company would deduct ten per cent for cashing it, and tell you to vote the Republican ticket.

The saying went that a lumberjack's life was worth no more than a chipmunk's. One tough boss from Newberry, Norwegian Jack, when told that a jack had been killed that day by a falling tree, is supposed to have said, "Isn't it lucky it wasn't a horse? The hauling is just getting fine."

CON KULHANE

In the Deer Park to Emerson area on the south shore of Lake Superior, which from 1890 to 1904 bristled with lumber jobbers, legends cling to Con Kulhane, the wild Irishman. Con started as a horse logger, hauling logs on sleighs to Lake Superior, or to rivers down which they could be driven to the Lake in the spring, and then rafted to Muskegon and Saginaw. About 1893 his wife, Betsy, who was nearly as well known as he, bought a locomotive which the lumberjacks promptly named "Ma's Machine," and Con then hauled by rail. This locomotive ran over and killed him in 1904. Many landmarks are named after Kulhane in Lake Superior State Forest: a lake, a dam, a trestle, a grades, while Betsy is memorialized by a river in Chippewa County and the largest lake in Luce County.

A typical old-time lumberman, Con displayed a big heart and a heavy hand. He drove his men hard, and got the timber out in millions of board feet each year. While he swore and fumed at his jacks, Betsy nursed them when they ailed, and sewed up their axe wounds, often putting in as many as ten stitches. When Con went on a rampage and fired the whole crew, she promptly hired them back. (Con thought so much of Betsy that when she came back to camp after spending some months on their farm in Canada, he shaved and changed his shirt.) Half of the babies in Finland are named for Con. The Finnish families knew him well because he went over so often to get men for his camps.

Con was husky and powerful; men claim they saw him lift a four-hundred-pound barrel of salt pork into the back of a wagon. His byword (during the Cleveland panic, when labor was plentiful) to greet any man who came to camp looking for a job, was "Me bye, can you fight?" And if the applicant put up a good scrap Con gave him a job. Once a solid young jack licked Con; he got Con's head between his legs and tore off the seat of his breeches. Con was so pleased he made him straw boss.

Con liked spine in his men. He tells on himself the story of the tote teamster for whom he wrote instructions, to deliver supplies to four of Con's camps. But the teamster could not read, and he botched up all his deliveries. Con lit on him like an angry god on a sinner, cussing him up and down. But he stopped when the man replied with spirit, "By damn, what do you think, has a man got to have a college education to drive this damn tote team?"

In the early lumbering days, the teamsters and loaders who were obliged to haul by sleigh worked a long day, often fourteen to sixteen hours. Con worked his teamsters just a little bit longer. A young farm boy newly hired to do camp chores went in to Con's office one evening and asked, "Mr. Kulhane, what time shall I wake the teamsters tomorrow morning?"

"Any damn time you catch them asleep from now on," Con told the boy.

Con never bothered with elaborate bookkeeping, even when his operations greatly increased. One time he had a large contract for taking out logs for a Muskegon company, and as was customary, had received a substantial advance. Along about midwinter one of the company executives thought it would be a good idea for a representative to call on Con. The young man on arriving at the camp asked to see the books. Con reached in his hip pocket and pulled out a memorandum book, in which he kept track of the board feet he got out each day. "There she is, me bye," he said genially.

"That isn't all the books you have, Mr. Kulhane!" the lad asked aghast.

"She is all there, me bye, except a few things I have written on the door of the blacksmith shop and on the barn."

In spite of his success, Con never put on airs, and when he went to Muskegon and Saginaw to order thousands of dollars worth of supplies for his camp, he dressed even worse than his lumberjacks. Once he was arrested as a vag and tossed into jail. Next morning in police court he was ordered to furnish a fifty dollar bond for release. Con told the police sergeant to call up the First National Bank and ask them to go his bond. After some argument the sergeant, thinking he was drunk or crazy, did so. He asked the cashier, "Do you know a man named Con Kulhane?"

"Yes."

"Will you go his bond?"

"Yes."

"For how much?"

"For one hundred thousand dollars."

Con was released.

Accounts of Con's death from his logging engine vary. Some say Ma's Machine backed up when he wasn't looking. Others say he fell on to the track while wrestling with his brakeman, and a car cut his legs off. And still others think he took a notion to run along the empty rustle cars up to the locomotive, a daredevil feat since the cars had only cross beams to run on. He fell between the cars and six or seven rolled over him. At any rate he died thumbing his nose at death, like a real lumberjack.

JOE LEMAY

Around Escanaba many jocular stories are heaped on Joe Le-May, a crafty French-Canadian lumber jobber who cheated his men and his competitors impartially. "He was a big burly fellow, uncouth, uneducated, who couldn't read or write but was quick at figures." Today LeMay is the best remembered pioneer in Delta County.

On Joe's broad shoulders gets hung, inevitably, the omnicurrent legend about the Canadian jack lost in the woods who hears an owl hoot, "W-h-o-o, w-h-o-o" and answers, "I'm Joe LeMay, de big lumberman from Lake Brulay." Or maybe it was "I'm Joe LeMay, de big cedar jobba from Escanaba, lost in de woods." The owl-answerer in Kenton hollers, "I'm Joe Mouffreau, lost in de wood. Give anybody two dollar and a half cash money in deir pocket to come find me out. Hoo-hoo." In Newberry a lost Irishman carrying the lunch on the river drive cries, "I'm Mickey Hayes wid de lunch, you son-of-a-whore." Or a cabinetmaker for the Newberry undertaker replies, "You don't know Bill Obey — make de cedaire for Underwood?"

Joe had various tricks for doing his men out of their wages. A Canada boy who had worked all winter for Joe was anxious to get his money and go back to spend it, but was bashful about asking Joe for his pay. Finally he told Joe that he wanted to go home and see his mother, as he hadn't seen her in a long time.

"Well, dat's fine boy, want to see his mothaire."

The boy timidly mentioned his pay; he needed it to get back.

"Pay? Don't worry 'bout dat — you strong boy, got good clothes, well fed — how'd you get over here?"

The boy said he had worked his way over on a boat.

"Well, Joe get you job on boat going back."

Joe was a jobber as well as a logger, and bought lots from piece-makers. He was to pay the piecemakers' wives while their husbands were off in the woods, so they could buy groceries. But he didn't explain what the money was for when he paid the women — and they understood it was for something else. When their husbands came home and told them about the contract, they couldn't very well complain about Joe.

Joe trespassed on land belonging to the powerful I. Stephenson Company, "cutting over the line" as it was called. The superintendent warned him and threatened to sue if he cut over the line again. Next year Joe found a little swale so that he didn't have to cut a road in, and he gutted the company forty from the inside. A cruiser going across country spotted the cutting and told the superintendent, who reminded Joe of his warning.

Joe protested, "I no cut over de line, I cut in de centaire now."

Joseph Mallman remembers that one time LeMay had the nerve to ask him to pay for trespassing on his land, as he was going to sell out. Mallman said, "Joe, after all the trespassing you've done in your days, why should you try to collect from anybody else now?"

"Dem days is gone forever," said Joe.

BIG ERIC ERICSON

In L'Anse I sat around in the Liberty boardinghouse after supper with a group of Ford timber cruisers, roomers, and local boys, and listened to a storyfest that lasted till midnight. At one point, among the tall tales and dialect yarns, someone mentioned the name of Big Eric Ericson, who ran a lumber camp at Skanee. The group exploded with laughter, and instantly the room filled with queer whines and sobbing noises. One after another told a Big Eric story, in a tearful, high-pitched accent that all had down pat. The star performer was Norm Thompson, gangly, sandy-haired, long-faced, and a fountain of jokes; he told three to the group's one, hours on end, spilling them out with a drawl, a sigh or a snap; when he did a Big Eric his voice quavered up to falsetto and his cheeks hollowed out with grief, convulsing his audience. This imitation of Big Eric's own Swedish singsong has become a standard second voice around L'Anse for describing the eccentric acts and sayings of the celebrated boss.

Norm Thompson speaks
• Big Eric is six foot three or four, all humped over. He is the biggest contractor with Ford around here. (Ford owns the saw-mill in L'Anse.) He's happy when losing money and grumbling when making it. If you meet him in the woods where he's boss he's dressed up in oxfords, dress pants and a silk shirt. In town

he dresses like a lumberjack, very ragged. He cut off the pants legs of a new eighty dollar suit in a saloon, to show he was one of the boys. "Sesus Rist, none of my friends know me," he said.

Eric was checking over the cook's list. He came to loganberries. "Logging berries — dat's fine — order a carload of dem." Then he saw New England ham and crossed it out. "Isn't American ham good enough for dese damn lumberjacks?"

Big Eric signed up with Ford along with four other operators, including Sirard, a man who kept race horses. When Eric was making out his income tax he was asked what his resources were. "I ain't got any rees-horses," he cried, "but Sirard has. But I got eight damn good teams."

The gasoline companies deliver gas to the lumber camps, for use in tractors and other equipment. A representative from one company visited Eric to try to get the concession for his camp. Eric asked him what kind of gas he sold.

"City Service."

"Citee Service — what good will Citee Service do me out in de woods?"

When he made his money he bought a home in Houghton on the main residential street, where professors and business men live, and filled it with overstuffed furniture. "Sesus Rist, dey tink I'm a big shot now — I live on College Avenoo," singsang Eric. When his pals visited him, they saw him sitting in a big living room spitting in an old tomato can. If the can were not around, he lifted up the rug and spat under that.

"MOONLIGHT" HARRY SCHMIDT

It was my good luck to see, in real life and in action, a colorful north-woods boss, "Moonlight" Harry Schmidt. His name Moonlight does not come from logging off other people's woods by moonlight, he claims, but because he woke his men up so early in the morning. Moonlight has logged in Chippewa, Mackinac,

Luce, and Schoolcraft counties, and even in Canada. He now
bosses a camp eighteen miles out of Newberry on the Deer Park
road, and I drove out to see him there.

Moonlight deserves his Rembrandt. I saw a lean, hawk-faced,
white-haired man, with a swaggering, pigeon-toed walk and a
crinkly smile that broke through his tough crust whenever he
made some telling witticism. He cussed furiously at all times in a
husky voice, spat constantly, and handled his men with a gruff
paternalism; they all called him Harry. He was the living incarna-
tion of the traditional lumberman, a store of woods tradition himself, and a practicing exponent of the old woods ways. I had
supper at the camp in the complete silence that was a standing
rule for meal time in the first camps.

In the course of his talking — and he talked freely and vividly
— Moonlight told some anecdotes on himself, including ones I
had heard about earlier bosses like Con Kulhane.

• A blankety-blank lumberjack said to me once, "I want to take
Saturday afternoon off."

I asked him, "Why, are you going to town?"

"No, I want to see what this place looks like by daylight."

A fellow came up hunting last fall and told me, "I worked for
you thirty-five years ago. You bawled me out one time for over-
sleeping, when it was four o'clock in the morning, and you'd gone
seven miles from headquarters to my cabin to catch me."

Had a feller once who I sent down to get supplies at the siding.
I didn't know he couldn't read or write. He went down to the
siding, where the railroad crew had unloaded supplies for several
companies, and he came back the eight miles with another company's supplies. So I bawled him out. "Goddamn it, couldn't you
read the label?"

So he said, "Goddamn it, does a man have to be educated to
drive this goddamn tote team?"

I bawled out a young fellow once, in the time of the first war, and warned him he'd be overseas soon. "I'll be right at home," he said. "They drive you there till you fall, and you drive me here till I fall."

What do I want a big house for, Moonlight asks rhetorically. Hell, all I want is a packsack and a frying pan. I can't afford to live in the city. Yeah, it's expensive, but it ain't that — I went home one evening and found thirteen roomers and twenty-four star boarders.

WOODS TALES

Yarns in the woods grow fierce and tall, like the giant pines. Men who cut, haul, search for, sell, and buy timber hear and tell many extravagant tales, for there is much esprit de corps and a great fondness for the prize marvel among these gentry. The witty raconteur is worth his weight in radio tubes and movie celluloid.

Around Newberry, still an important logging center in the Upper Peninsula, I speedily met some straight-faced old-timers with crooked tongues. They gather in Surrell's garage and auto-parts store, sitting in four green leather aluminum chairs that face the window in a semicircle, high-lighted by a spittoon in the center, while a green and yellow parrot squawks in a cage alongside. As soon as I located this hangout I edged into the group every time I saw them in action. Eighty-five-year-old Matt Surrell, the pioneer mail carrier and livery stable operator, frequently dropped in to his son's place — he was a striking old man, tall and stoop-shouldered, deep-eyed, halting in his speech, and troubled by a painful cough. His special pal, Joe Nantell, a French-Canadian camp cook, talked and spat companionably with him; Joe had the thick set of a wrestler. Bill Perry, an insurance man somewhat younger than they, but still white-haired, with a deep, slow-breaking laugh, attended the sessions pretty regularly. Various others dropped in at different times; Bernard McTiver, a ruddy State Ranger from Deer Park, who talked loudly and confidently, and spat particularly well because his front teeth were missing, came in once while I was there and easily topped all the stories told that day.

Bernard McTiver speaks

• My dad could tell some pretty good yarns. He lumbered from Alpena to Cheboygan in the Lower Peninsula, came up here in 1911, and then went west to cruise for Weyerhauser in Minnesota, and he picked up all kinds of stories. His best one — I knew it was a damn lie but I couldn't help believe it — was about the time he was cruising timber in Minnesota. He drew lots with his partner to see who would go back for supplies, and he lost. He knew where Weyerhauser had a little camp a quarter of a mile from a lake, with a man and a wife as caretakers all year round, so he headed for that in his canoe. (There are so many lakes in Minnesota that the cruisers worked inland from the nearest lake.)

As he beached the boat, he heard a woman hollering and screaming, and he ran up to the camp as fast as he could. There was a man inside astraddle a woman, holding her hair and pounding her head down on the floor. Dad pulled the fellow off, and they started to fight. The man was pretty husky, and they were having an even match of it — hard to tell who was getting the better — when the woman went over to the sideboard, picked up an iron skillet, and hit Dad over the head with it. The bottom fell out, leaving the rim around his neck, and he had to walk twenty-six miles through the woods, lay his head on the anvil, and have it knocked off with a cold chisel.

That's the last time he ever interfered between a man and his wife.

The group laughed and spat appreciatively, and the ranger told another.

• I was raised with my uncle on a little farm near Sudbury. He grew mostly peas, which he soaked in a barrel and fermented for his hog. He always put an old washtub over the top so the bull wouldn't get in. But one time he forgot and the bull got in and ate up the whole barrel of soaked peas, and was all blown up. It was expensive to go for the vet to get the bull's wind up, because the vet lived thirty miles away. So uncle stuck a horn up the bull's rear, and the wind started to come out. It blew the horn and frightened the bull so that he ran off and jumped into the pond. The water ran into the horn and drowned the bull.

"That sounds like one of White Pine Tom's stories," said mild Bill Perry.

• Tom was a great axeman, when he worked, and a great joker. One time he was shacking on the Sucker River, and catching fish to sell to the cook at the camp. The cook found there was about two pounds of sand in each pike to make them weigh more. Tom would pour sand down their mouths before selling them. The cook asked him about that sand. Well, Tom said, the lake is so deep they had to take in ballast in order to get to the bottom.

The borderline between reality and romance is often hard to draw in the north woods. In the lobby of the Falls Hotel in Newberry I sat in on a different group, lumber jobbers and landlookers in a gabfest, nodding wisely at each other's odd experience and adding a still more remarkable example, for as a matter of honor none must acknowledge ignorance or surprise on any branch of woods lore.

Pete Dumours did lift some eyebrows when he began recounting his wilder experiences as a timber cruiser. At seventy-five the incredible Pete, a spry, effervescent, lightly built Frenchman, still walked the woods with the best of the younger cruisers. Pete told how he had stayed with a fellow-cruiser, John Hick, in a tumbledown shack near East Lake, outside Mackinac City, under primitive conditions. "All we had was a little board with some straw to sleep on. John was bigger than I and had to sleep edgeways on it. Old man Jersey, the cook, used to tell us to turn the plates over so the mice wouldn't get in them [a storm of laughs]. That's right, no josh, he didn't wash the plates for a week."

To silence the skeptics Pete then told about Jay Gould who homesteaded back of Rapid River and never came out for seventeen years. He had twenty-five dogs and cats, and made his wife's dresses himself; he made them all so tight her back-side showed through. When they moved to Gladstone, after their long isolation, Mrs. Gould complained of not feeling well. A neighbor woman gave her a bath — her first in seventeen years — and killed her. [Removing her crust exposed her to germs, I suppose.]

But the evening's honors went not to Pete but to a deliberate-speaking wood buyer named Dave Howard, who ground every word out with a solemn fury.

"The fish in the little ponds in Spanish and Mass," said Dave, when the talk swung around to fishing, "up in Canada, a hundred and twenty-six miles east of the Soo, have big heads. There are so many fish in a lake that only their heads grow. You can see fish piled right up on top of each other like this [and he spread the fingers of one hand vertically to indicate the successive layers]. Fact, although you won't believe it unless you see it. I heard a fellow tell for a fact, that up at Spanish fish would eat berries that hung on bushes over the water. I couldn't question it. Well, I've reeled up plugs and had pike jump out of the water at them."

And Howard glared around at his awe-struck audience so belligerently that not one twitched a face muscle.

"I'm so poor I can't buy a rassling jacket for a louse," said knotty Jack Pohlman, who lives in the woods beyond Gwinn five miles from a house or a paved road. His lumberjack idiom pays tribute to an important woods personality, for the louse makes himself felt in the winter camp and on the spring drive.

"On the river drive," Jack recalls, "I got so tired washing our clothes to get the lice out I just lay down, told my partner I'd get an hour's sleep anyway, and slept until they woke me. Then I shook my shirt out and went to sleep for another hour."

Joe Boyer of Escanaba found a way to lick the lice, though.

"Working on the drive and sleeping outdoors, my clothes'd get full of lice. I'd pick lice off on my suspenders. I used to wear heavy woolen underwear, all homemade, thick as leather, so I turned it inside out and it'd take them two days to walk through."

The lice did serve one useful purpose, from a barber's point of view. In the spring when the hirsute jacks came into town for their annual haircut, the barbers never had to worry about carting off the great masses of hair and whiskers they sheared — the lice walked away with the cuttings.

The Finnish humorist of Palmer, Herman Maki, who got his start in America in the lumber woods, recollects an epic experience with lumber camp lice.

Herman Maki speaks

• This happened in the year 1903; I had just come from Finland and was told I could get a job in a lumber camp at Big Bay. When I got there, whom should I see, to my great surprise, but a man I had last seen in Finland, and whom I believed to have died long ago. As soon as he saw me he yelled, "Halloo, podner."

Larry told me there was one bad thing about the lumber camps in America, and I soon found out what it was. There were many lice in the camp. The straw in the bunks rose and fell as the lice wrestled within them.

I tried to do things as the others did, but although I saw all the older lumberjacks take off all their clothes to go to bed, I, being a tender young man, wore my underwear. I was unable to go to sleep; the lice were so old they were toothless, and I spent the night scratching them up a little meat for their supper.

Larry soon saw how his "podner" was faring, so on Saturday night he came in with a large ten pound bag of salt. He told me to take off my underwear, which I did, and put the ten pounds of salt as a layer between the underwear and my skin. I did not understand this, but I had been well trained in the Old Country, having been fed snowballs by winter and rain water by summer, and I knew he was trying to help me.

The next morning I awoke to find some of the salt still in the bunk, the rest clinging to my skin. At last when our Sunday dinner was eaten, Larry took me with him to the other side of Independence Lake. I was a little afraid of him, and even the weather seemed gloomy — it was a cold gray day in November. He led me to a steep path where a big beaver slide ran into the lake, and here he began to peel off my clothes. At last the salty underwear, the last piece of clothing, lay on top of the beaver slide. A windfall tree lay near, and we sat behind this to watch what happened.

As soon as we were out of their sight the procession began. The lice started to travel in a great horde toward the lake, and at last only one straggler remained limping along slowly behind the others.

The old man, Larry, sighed with relief. "That's the last one," he said. "You can put your clothes back on you again. We'd better hurry back to camp before they finish drinking water. I knew they'd get thirsty if we'd feed them enough salty meat!"

In his summer cabin outside Escanaba old Joe Boyer, a hale, confident Canadien with rugged good looks, described to me a number of cures he had learned in his half century of woods life.

Joe Boyer speaks

• For kidney trouble cut up the dried kidney of a beaver and drink it in a pint of white whiskey. I did it once and my back never bothered me since. It tasted like poison.

Dried beet leaves draw the poison out of a nail-cut. When I stepped on a big iron square-nail in the garden, my mother pulled it out and put the leaves on the cut, and it never gave me any trouble.

Press your axe on the blisters on balsam trees. A little pitch comes out on the blade, and I lick it to clean my blood. But it's hard on the kidneys.

Use hemlock bark juice for harness blisters on a horse.

In May, boil hemlock, tamarack and mountain ash bark and drink the juice to purify the blood. Mother always gave it to us in Canada.

A poultice of pine pitch is good for a sore back. Just place it low down on your spine, and it will crawl up your back to where the pain is. You can put the poultice above the ache too, but then you'd say it slid down. Pine pitch is good to caulk canoes also.

I cured myself of piles when I was driving on the river. The blood was running down my legs, so I put a cheesecloth in a gallon of turpentine and shoved it up my rear as far as I could. In about half an hour it started to needle, and I pulled it out. I've never been bothered with piles since.

Joe Shuster gave me a recipe for dog-skin disease. It had creosote, kerosene, and a lot of other things in it. One time I had the itch and I said, By gosh if it works on a dog it can work on me. I went to the bathroom, stripped, and put that stuff on. Oh God, did it burn for an hour! But it fixed me up.

10

MINERS

MINING TALK

ABOUT one-third of the way across the Peninsula, swinging west, mining talk begins. Until one reaches the great ranges in the western counties, conversation turns chiefly on the lumber woods, the farm land, and the Lakes. It was in Munising, on the edge of the iron belt, that I first heard underground tales.

In a boardinghouse parlor Jim Hodge reeled off a string of mining superstitions to a companion, which I copied surreptitiously in my notebook. Later I learned he came from Negaunee, in the heart of the Marquette range, had been born in Devonshire, and was now working on the county road commission. Tall, high-colored, trim, clean-featured, Jim looked out of place in the north woods, but he spoke with the dead seriousness and nonstop fluency of typical Peninsula tale tellers.

Jim Hodge speaks

• I walked in the Negaunee mine once a-whistling. The miners told my father they'd tell the mining captain if I did it again.

There is a reason for these things. They allowed women down in the Negaunee mine once, wives and sisters of the company officials. Down in the mine women's voices sound altogether different, shrill, and high-pitched. A miner got scared and walked right down into the cross-cut and fell into the raise. Bill was going out to investigate the noise, and figured he was walking into the drift. Just something out of the ordinary threw him off.

To kill a rat in the mine is worse than murder. Rats know ahead when ground is breaking; they can hear it. Tommy Waters got fired in Negaunee for killing a rat, forty-six years ago. We used to eat at a cross-cut connecting the main drift with the raise, and this big Frenchman, Pedro, raised this rat, used to feed him, called him "Peter, Peter," and the rat would come running. The rats kept everything cleaned up around the mine, you know. Tommy Waters was a mule skinner who ate before the miners, and he was scared to death of rats. He picked up a piece of lagging and killed Peter. That Frenchman went crazy and would have killed Tommy if he had caught him. He chased him right clean out into the shaft. The mining captain sent Tommy home, and he was laid off for ten days, and when he came back he wasn't on our shift.

Miners never worked on the 24th of June, which is Whitmonday or Midsummer Day. In 1896 they were asked to work half a day on Midsummer Day. At eleven o'clock that morning Johnny Gribble and his boy were working together, when there was a fall of ground, and Johnny Gribble was killed. They've never worked on that day since, until the present war. On the 26th of December, Boxer Day, miners won't work. We had orders to work once that day. I told the boss, "No." Christmas was on a Monday, and father said, "Remember, you don't go to back to work till Wednesday. You won't work on Boxer Day." But miners will work on New Year's Day; they figure they'll work the whole year then.

Later when I made Jim Hodge's acquaintance he added mules to the list of mine traditions. "Things happen in a mine that you can't believe," he said. "Now take mules. Mules worked the same shifts as the drivers. When I worked as a mule driver, before I graduated to a regular miner, I had a pet mule named Maud. Nobody could ever haul as much ore with that mule as I could. She'd foller me all over. If I asked a miner for a chew of Peerless and he wouldn't give it to me, I'd say, 'Go get him, Maud,' and he'd open his mouth and start after the man with the Peerless; he'd back him against the wall until he gave up the cud. We had all the mules trained to eat Peerless."

Ghostlore abounds in the mines, where death lurks in the stopes and timbered drifts, and noises and shadows fill the deep tunnels. Jim, who had absorbed every kind of mining yarn like a sponge, had a ghost story too.

• The Negaunee mine was a funny one to work in — damp and cold, and the posts would get all covered with white fungus. Back in 1899 this Joe Cornish, one of the timber trammers, was sent to get some timber, and he was running along the drift when he saw a ghost. Joe ran back, and he was so scared he couldn't talk. The assistant mining captain asked him what the matter was, but he couldn't say a word, and he just wouldn't go back. Later the shift boss told us someone had painted a face on a white post, and the minute Joe turned the corner in the drift he ran smack into the face. Tricks like that were easy to pull then, you see, because so many of the miners believed in ghosts.

Behind these underground traditions which men like Jim Hodge had breathed in from childhood lies a vivid mining history. In 1840, physician Douglass Houghton reported finding copper ore in the Keweenaw Peninsula to the Michigan state legislature. In 1844, surveyor William Burt announced the discovery of iron ore in Marquette County to the United States Government. Their discoveries precipitated an overland and overwater rush to the western half of the Peninsula that strewed the north Michigan wilderness with mining locations and charmed forth the long tentacles of Boston bankers. The Keweenaw finger poking into Lake Superior became alive with copper-mad prospectors, and the great Calumet and Hecla mine started its downward climb, bringing the world's purest conglomerate copper up from what was to be the world's deepest copper shaft out of one of the most profit-able mines in any ore. A triangle of iron centers developed with the opening of the Marquette, Gogebic, and Menominee ranges, and for proud years Michigan led the nation in iron ore produc-tion, and dreamed of great furnaces and mills. Today copper is dead and iron is languishing, but their glory lingers in the towns they bore: Copper Harbor, Iron River, Ironwood, Iron Mountain.

The mining booms generated a rich human history and lore. The doom of disasters and cave-ins, the bitterness of racial feuds and labor strikes, the delirium of lucky finds and the heartbreak of tragic misses are still live talk in the Peninsula, for few old-timers in the western counties lack mining experience. All Europe poured into the mines; first the Cousin Jacks, skilled in the tin mines of Cornwall, later the cheaper muscle of Finlanders, Swedes, I-talians, Bohunks, Poles, Irish, mutually hostile and sus-picious, penned within their own tongues — a situation not dis-pleasing to the mine owners.

But a common craft formed a common tradition, and the veteran miner talking of underground death speaks a group lore of drill and pick, drift and stope, pump and stull, be he Scandinavian or Slav or Englishman. He learned group words too.

"Kaikki menne mita tulle eika pusaken," became a general say-ing among miners who knew no other Finnish, and a ready answer to the greeting, How are things going? The thought penetrated all languages: Everything goes that comes, and it isn't enough. Swedes and Finns understood what an I-talian meant when he stuck his forefinger and little finger in their faces and swore "Dio Christo"; he was mad, mad enough to put the evil eye on them. (I-talians got so mad when a tram car left the rails they would bite the cars.) Lush curses floated through the shafts in half a dozen tongues. When electricity was first introduced into the Sun-day Lake mine at Wakefield, a practical joker hooked up the electric wires to the miners' lunch pails. When they reached for their pails the Finns yelled "Satana Parakela," the I-talians "Sacramento Cristo," the Swedes "Diavelin Verbunda," the Poles "Shockraff," and the Cousin Jacks, "Damn the bloody buggers."

Whatever their nationalities, Copper County old-timers talk about the great strike of 1913 from a common American experience. The tensions between strikers and soldiers and scabs and company officials tore towns and neighbors apart, and stirred up stories that are now half legend. In the saloons, lodges, and other hangouts, men from the mining locations talk grimly yet about that mortal strike.

• I saw the fight between Big Annie and Big Kate, an Austrian and a Finn woman, when they rolled down in a sewer ditch. One was union, the other anti-union. They were both two hundred pounds — either one of them could have licked Joe Louis. They pulled out chunks of hair, scratched each other till the blood ran, fought like dirty, filthy animals. And they had damn little clothes on when they hit the ditch. Big Annie smeared General May, commander-in-chief of the National Guard, with pails of human s - - - when he rode past on his white horse.

• Big Annie was a great big derelict of a woman. Every morning there'd be a union parade and she'd walk in front slapping her rear and saying, "This the one-man machine." The Company had been taking off one of the two men that handled the drilling machine for the dynamiting.

• Big Annie was some great big old Austrian. There's no man used language like she did — you couldn't print the things about her. She led a parade of bulbish women like herself, and stopped men from going to work. They'd parade down Waterworks Street, and women would turn the water engine on her to get her back where she belonged.

• My dad was a scab all through the strike. He never believed in unions or strikes. He had six kids. This Finn woman who had been his friend for forty years yelled " 'Cabby, 'Cabby," at him every morning when the cavalry escorted him to the mine.

• During the strike the union gave a Christmas party for the men who had been out of work since August, in the Italian Hall in Red Jacket. All the children were to get a little bag of candy. Someone yelled "Fire." The union said it was a company man, but the townspeople always said it was a union man. The union wanted to get sympathy, and funds. The crowd rushed downstairs, but the door opened inwards and they all piled up at the foot of the stairs. Eighty-four children died. There was no fire.

• My father was going to Italian Hall with his two children. He got as far as the bridge and turned back to get something. When he got home the teakettle was singing. He said, "Something terrible is going to happen; we will stay home." Finns always believed that the kettle whistled in a funny way when a man was going to die in the mines.

LOST LODES AND LUCKY STRIKES

Much mining talk deals with fabulous fortunes lost and found in the ore beds. In the early land-grabbing days of the boom, before the shafts were sunk and the business of mining had swung into grim routine, every shoestring prospector dreamed of stumbling on the mother lode. The legends of sudden riches are double-grained; one cycle deals with the near-misses, the golden chances that slipped away; the other with the crazy successes, the overnight millionaires who found a fortune they never sought.

Strangely, the frustrated ore hunts often concern silver and gold. Jim Hodge told me of a mislaid gold mine in one of our first bull sessions.

Jim Hodge speaks

• A fellow named Larsen was traveling north of Teal Lake, Negaunee, picking berries — lots of berries on the hills. He picked up a piece of quartz, attracted by the specks in it. If he'd been a mining man, he would have known there was gold in it. He put it in his pocket, and cut across the hills back to town, to his brother's saloon. There was a mining man present; he said, "Show it to me." After he looked at it he said, "I'd like to show that to a friend of mine." He sent the piece to an assayer at Houghton, and it was assayed at two hundred dollars a ton in gold.

But when Larsen went back to look for the quartz he couldn't find the spot, or even the hill.

Geologists have been intensively surveying the country all around, and they admit there is gold. Some day they will probably find Larsen's vein.

Later I heard many such stories. That of Peter Paul's gold mine which I heard from Aaron Kinney, the bard of Iron River, typifies the general run.

Aaron Kinney speaks

• Peter Paul's Gold Mine is on the south branch of the Paint, right below Uno dam. Peter Paul came from Canada where they had gold, and here he found a piece of quartz that looked like gold. He was telling my father he'd strike the gold in a few strokes. He blast-drilled, sunk a shaft, single-jacking, twisting the drill himself. When he came down to water he had to quit, because he had only a hand pump.

He was going to sell blueberries on the land around there to make a stake to develop his gold mine. People could pay him so much a quart to pick themselves. There were blueberries a solid mile up the river, you see. The dream of the gold mine never left him, but he never got a stake. He dug till he was too old to dig, and died without making a fortune. His place is still called Peter Paul's Gold Mine.

These gold veins may be fables, but banker's gold lay in the iron drifts, and they too inspire tragic legends. The one that old-timer Arthur Quirt (who set down his memories of pioneer days in the Peninsula in a rare little booklet, *Tales of the Woods and Mines*) recalls about an Irish stumblebum tops all the rest.

Arthur Quirt writes

• I see by the *Iron River Reporter* that the mining company is sinking a shaft on what is known as the Sherwood property. There's a story connected with that property that very few now living remember.

An old Irishman named Mike Ryan homesteaded the land in 1882. Mike went to Iron River in the fall of 1880 when the nearest point on a railroad was Florence, Wisconsin. From there to what is now Iron River was a thirty-two mile hike through the woods. I'd been there a few months before he came. I judge he was about forty-five or fifty years old while I was a little past twenty.

The town was laid out and building started in the spring of 1882. The railroad reached there in the fall of that year. There was a homestead craze started that fall and everyone was filing on a homestead. Mike filed on four forties in Section 23, Town 43, Range 35. Had he been able to see through the hundred feet of surface he couldn't have followed the iron formation any better. There was an iron mine on every forty.

Mike had his periods of drinking and his periods of sobriety. In his sober spells he'd raise a garden, keep some chickens, and by doing odd jobs eke out an existence. When he had his drinking spells he'd go down to the hotel kept by Old Kate, who was never known to turn anyone away that was broke. Sometimes she'd get paid, but often it would be a dead loss. Mike, I know, lived there off and on for years and in order to square accounts deeded to Kate two forties which are now known as the Sherwood.

Kate sold the two forties to Sherwood and others. What she got for them I don't know; probably not more than what Mike's bill came to. Up to that time no one dreamed that ore existed north of Iron River, as the overburden was well over a hundred feet deep and there was no sign of ore on the surface. It was different to the south in Spring Valley, where ore cropped out in several places. All exploratory work was carried on in that vicinity. Some local fellows formed a pool and took an option on Old Man James' forty, which joined the Sherwood forties on the north. They put down a test pit and struck the ore formation, but their money played out and they had to quit.

Old Man James tried to get a company interested in the property. The company sent an expert to examine that part of the country and he reported iron ore couldn't exist north of Iron River. Today there are ten or twelve of the biggest mines in Iron County operating there. So much for the opinion of experts. By giving a mining company an interest in the fee, Old Man James got them to do some drilling, and ore was discovered. Soon all the properties around were under option and diamond drills were running everywhere.

Mike, after selling two forties to old Kate, deeded the other two forties to his son-in-law, with the right to occupy the place during his lifetime. His son-in-law sold twenty acres to a grocer for a couple hundred dollars; the other sixty acres he traded for a small house worth about three hundred dollars.

To give you some idea of the value of the Sherwood forties, where they are now sinking a shaft: the mining company spent fifty thousand dollars drilling in 1910 and 1911. In 1912 they took a lease on the property for fifty years, paying two thousand dollars a year minimum royalty on each forty. The two forties were assessed at $1,200,000, making their taxes fifty thousand dollars a year.

Mike Ryan was found dead in his shack in the summer of 1889. I had worked with him in 1880, digging test pits along the side of Stambaugh hill, where the Riverton mine was opened up and the first iron ore was shipped in the fall of 1882. I didn't like to see Old Mike, as we called him, carted away to his grave in a lumber wagon, so I hired Boyington's hearse to convey him to his last resting place. All who had been lucky enough to acquire an interest in Mike's homestead are living in ease and luxury, either in California or Florida, while old Mike sleeps peacefully in an unmarked grave covered only with grass and weeds.

On the reverse of the shield, fate deals her favors with equal irony and paradox. The unsuspecting turn up ore when it is least on their minds; the ignorant become overnight millionaires through the mining stocks that cost experts their shirts.

Folks say that Daddy Fisher — Hiram Damon Fisher — found the Fisher mine when he threw his pick on the side of a hill and picked it up streaked with red, from hematite. In Norway the deed to a worthless mine was given to a minister instead of two dollars, for performing a marriage ceremony. It turned out to be the wealthy Chapin mine. An unemployed miner named Moore, thrown out of work by the panic of 1873, was looking for pine land in the Gogebic country. There wasn't any. He sat down on a hill to rest and curse his luck, and saw beneath the roots of a giant tree felled by a storm a smooth surface of black rock. Moore had found the Gogebic iron range, which has produced eighty million tons of bessemer ore, and he himself bought the successful Colby mine. In the Copper Country they still tell how a bush farmer spotted the rich conglomerate ore of the famous Calumet and Hecla mine, when his sow showed up with her snout all bloody. He followed its trail and came onto outcroppings of the copper where the pigs had been rooting. Some say that the sow littered in a hole left by the tornout roots of a pine tree blown down by the wind. When the owner descended into the hole to catch the piglets, he stumbled on chunks of copper lying under the leaves and rubbish.

So the stories go, building into romance. For a classic example of the lucky strike legend, consider the discovery of the Wakefield mine by a "Bohunk" named John Honusek. By chance I met a former neighbor of Honusek, Arthur M. Gilbert, now a state welfare commissioner, who remembers the affair clearly, if ruefully.

Arthur Gilbert speaks

• John Honusek wanted to sell me two cutover forties in Wakefield for a hundred and fifty dollars. I said, "What'll I do with it?" He said, "Raise cattle on it." But I wouldn't buy. He couldn't sell it in 1910, and he was tired of paying taxes on it, so he fenced it off and raised scrub steers. Then in 1912, ore was found on the south side of town, one hundred and fifty feet from the surface. They scooped the overburden out and open-pit mined it. Honusek sold his land for half a million dollars plus twenty-five cents on every ton taken out.

The iron ore of the Gogebic range had been lost at Ramsay; there was a four-mile fault there. Some upheaval had turned the vein over. The Mikado Mine was digging under its pit, and couldn't understand where the ore was. Selden Rose of Marquette, a geologist, knew the ore lay south, running from Hurley to Watersmeet. By studying the surface outcroppings he became convinced that the ore, at a sixty degree angle, had turned over and lay flat on its back. That's how he picked up the fault between Ramsay and Wakefield.

Honusek was a big, rawboned three-hundred-pound man, who made a living as a small timber jobber. A Bohemian. He'd been a miner and saloonkeeper in Ramsay, which only had half a dozen houses then. He bought eighty acres to supply wood to the Mikado Mine; paid three hundred and fifty dollars for them. Then when he'd cut the timber he tried to sell the land. I remember when he came running into the mine office at Ramsay and said, "Jesus Christ, Jesus Christ, they struck whores on my land," in his thick guttural accent.

They say that in spite of his wealth he still lived in his old log cabin on his forty, with a bucket of beer in front of him. His daughter had modern ideas, drove around in a Cadillac, and had the lawyer get a beautiful house in Ironwood for John. The lawyer showed him all through it, the sun porch, lovely tapestries, and so on, and then asked him, "What do you think of it?" "Not so much," said John, "not a goddamn spittoon in the place."

DEATH IN THE MINES

To the men drilling and hauling out ore a thousand feet under the earth's surface, the fear of premature burial always hovered in the air. Sudden death could come in many ways, through fall of rock or timbers, from gas, fire, flood, or other accident. Mining stories from the early flush times are strewn with narrow escapes and ironic tragedies, and embittered by company callousness. When the tensions became unbearable, the miners found relief in laughing grimly at corpses.

As in the lumber woods labor counted for less than horses and peavies, so in the mines a man mattered less than a drill or a mule. "We used to have two, three, four men killed a day in the copper mines," said Reuben Rowe. "The boss would say, 'Go on, get back to work, it's only a man. Men is cheaper than timber.'"

Jim Hodge tells a series of somber death tales from his youth in the iron mines of the Marquette range.

Jim Hodge speaks

• Dad told me how the first man was killed in the Negaunee mine, in 1888. He and a partner were working two hammers on a drill, while George was twisting the drill. Father heard something fall, although the stope had been trimmed of loose rock. He went one way and his partner went another to see what it was; George said, "I'll sit down here and wait for you." A rock came down and killed George right where he was sitting.

Up to 1902 only nine men were killed. But when the water rose up to the main level I quit and went to Butte. That was in June. Next January 7 I picked up the paper in Butte and read, "13 Men Entombed in Negaunee Mine." They were all my old gang — Sullivan, Johnny Pierce, Billy Williams. I told Sullivan before I left, "You'd better get out of this mine. It's going to cave in." They all died. One of them was only a foot from the main drift when the sand and water came in — it was a cave-in from the surface. If he'd kept his mind he could have shoveled through the ore with his carbide candlestick. But he lost his head, went crazy — was completely naked when they found him. They didn't find him for five months, although they looked all over. Then a car passed along and loosened or jarred the sand so that he just fell out into the drift.

In the Queen group of mines they averaged one death a day. I remember one fellow they fetched up and sent to the dry man (who took care of the changing house, and would prepare the bodies for burial). After he finished with the body the dry man said, "That fellow's never been so clean since the day he was born. After I washed him an hour I came to a second pair of socks."

Tommy Davie was always groaning, from habit. He was working in a four-man crew on a timbered stope on the seventh floor, fifty-six to sixty feet high. But that day I figgered it wasn't his voice. I climbed up the stope and found Matt Eskola with his scalp hanging down over his face. A chunk of iron ore had come down on his head and knocked his scalp right off. The other three men had gone off after timber. I got him down and the shift boss had us take him to the dry and send for the doctor. After a while the doctor comes out and Mort Conway says to him, "Is there any hope, doc?" "Oh, that fellow isn't hurt so bad," he answered. "No," says Mort, "I meant, is there any hope of him dying." The tension had lifted by then, you see.

In 1895 Captain Dick Edwards sealed a burning mine, when the men were within seeing distance. He saved the mine, but didn't figure about the men.

There was a similar disaster at the Hartford mine in May, 1911. The Captain ordered the water turned down the shaft, and the fumes and smoke suffocated the men. One miner on the surface offered to break the connection to the timber shaft so that the trapped men wouldn't be choked by the fumes when the firemen turned the hose down the main shaft. They wouldn't let him, although he knocked down the mine captain and the company clerk. Eleven men were lost. Sam Steinaway carried his son on his back half a mile, and saved him, but gave his own life. (Young boys went down to the mines then; I went down when I was only thirteen. Now you have to be twenty-one.)

The Captains wanted to save the mines, you see, and weren't

responsible for the men. If there had been compensation they wouldn't have done that. Next year compensation came in.

Each man who worked underground in the early days carries with him such a private stock of death and accident tales. On a broader scale, the mass disasters burn brightly in the folk memory of entire communities, whose families still share the sense of a common tragedy. Around the cave-in of the Mansfield Mine, for example, has crusted a grim body of legend.

In Crystal Falls, a tilted town carved out of iron, angry, eerie talk buzzes yet about the twenty-seven drownings of September 23, 1893, when the Michigamme River poured into the Mansfield shaft. There are people in the town today whose husbands and fathers lie buried in the drifts, and I met one veteran miner who worked the early shift on that fatal day.

Mrs. Lydia Pearce, a dried-up, childish old lady, relives the tragic day with single-minded clarity, for her husband substituted for another man on the cave-in shift. She recites her story in shrill and rhythmic tones, as if it were a dirge.

Lydia Pearce speaks

• My husband and I came from Penzance Lelant, near St. Ives, in 1887. William Henry Pearce was his name. He was a time-keeper at the Croton Dam in New York for three years. Then he came up here to see his brother Tom. All the mines were closed down except the Mansfield. I told him, "Pearce, I don't like you to go there, it's too far away." He said, "I'll come home every Sunday, and when I'm on night shift I'll stay home Monday too."

That week he stayed home twice to haul in the potatoes. But on Thursday he went. His partner Buzzo wanted him to change shifts with him because he had a headache. Pearce prayed twice that night, Buzzo said; usually he prayed only once, before he left the rooming 'ouse. Walking back to Crystal Falls, Buzzo felt some great force whiz past him, and he was terribly scared. After he thought it was a sign that Pearce passed out.

At seven o'clock in the morning I was lying down in bed beside Flora. I got up as usual to light the fire, cook the breakfast, and send the children to school. A man who had lived downstairs, Patek, a lawyer, came around. I said, "What brings you round this morning?" He said, "What would you think of a woman who came over from Germany yesterday and found out the next day her husband had been drowned in the mine?" "In what mine?" "In the Mansfield." "Where is Pearce, my husband?" I said. "He's gone too, Mrs. Pearce," he said. "Mr. Patek, what did you tell me that for?" I said to him. My little boy, just seven, was listening at the top of the stairs, and he fainted, tumbled head over heels down the stairs. "Now you've killed my boy," I said. He turned and ran out. Then he sent his wife up.

Flora the daughter, stout and queerly streaked across the face, perked up when her mother mentioned her name, and now interrupted. "I felt hands go over my face six or seven times that night. I was two years and seven months then. They stroked my face all the way down. They must have been my father's; he always liked to fondle me. I think it was mental telepathy; when you're dying you think of someone you like."

With surprising vigor the aged mother declared this was nonsense. Flora kept repeating her conviction that she had felt her father's caressing hands. I watched in bafflement at the skepticism of age and superstition of youth.

Mrs. Pearce finished the sad, simple history.

• Four years later Lew Henry saw some of the bodies when they turned the river from its course. He thought he saw Pearce. I asked him why he didn't take me to see him. He said, "You wouldn't want to see him, Mrs. Pearce. His flesh pinched like putty. Besides, I can't say for sure it was he." I said I would recognize him by a red chest protector I knitted for him; he was delicate in the chest. But he wouldn't take me.

I was left with three children to bring up. The company never gave us anything, although they were thought to be at fault. C. T. Roberts was inspector of the mine, but he hadn't inspected it for several weeks.

Two Swedish sisters still resident in Crystal Falls lost their father in the Mansfield. Jean Carlson and Regina Raben, although smiling, plump housewives, nurse bitter grievances about the blow.

Regina Raben speaks

• The miners could hear the water rumbling while they worked. When it started coming in they raced for the ladder, and a few climbed up and lit brooms as torches for those below. Mother said when the river went in they could hear the rumbling at Crystal Falls, miles away, and the dishes rattled.

The mining officials declared bankruptcy, and the families never got the miners' back pay and overtime. The men had three months pay coming, but the widows never got anything. My mother had to raise five children — the fifth child was born in the April following. She had to sell milk, rake hay for her cows, wash clothes. She would walk to Balsam ten miles to cut hay, and walk back again next day to spread it. She got five dollars for a mid-wife-scrubbing-housecleaning job.

You can imagine it was pretty tough coming up against that water. There were three miners left in the sixth level who never made it. Four years later, when they reopened the mine after shifting the river, I said to Henry Anderson, "I'm going to look for those men." I found a rubber boot with nothing in it but clean bones. The three skeletons were found later. The men must have been hit by dirt, and couldn't make it to the ladder. It was said bones were found mixed with the ore and dirt when they started mining again.

But the mining captain and the superintendent always had money. Lustfield, the mining captain, started a dry goods store. John Erickson, the superintendent, became superintendent of the

Dunn mine. It was always suspected they took the miners' wages. Lustfield died of cancer of the stomach, screaming night and day in the hospital — my sister worked there. Erickson died of softening of the brain. Mother always said, "They're suffering for their wrongs."

Shades of the McDonald Boys! But this family tradition of retributive death collapsed in half an hour. Mrs. Raben excitedly took me over to the house of Matt Johnson, a fellow-Swede who had actually worked in the Mansfield mine at the time of the flood, and who promptly scotched her story. No one had ever solicited from the seventy-year old miner his unique information on the disaster. Yet bean-pole Matt spoke easily and drily. The immigrant Swede boy who risked his life underground had grown into a seasoned old-timer, wise to America.

Everyone knew the danger of mining so close to the river, Matt said. But it was 1893, the depression year, and the new Oliver Mining Company alone had a mine in operation. The captain, Louie Ashelman (not the cancerous Lustfield), must have foreseen the catastrophe. Matt went on to tell his story.

Matt Johnson speaks

• I started in the mines when I was seventeen, when I come to this country. My sister and brother-in-law were in Crystal Falls, so I came here and worked in the mines. I was on the day-shift at the Mansfield mine when it flooded. I came off at five-thirty, the flood started at nine. My partner and I worked on the fourth level, in the east end of the mine, where your father [this to Regina Raben] and Olie Carlson were caught.

At nine we heard the whistle blowing, and knew something was wrong. We ran over to the shaft. There was just a little hole, about seventy-five feet, when the river started coming in, but in fifteen or twenty minutes the center of the mine caved down. It took about sixty minutes for the mine to fill up. There were forty men on the shift, and thirteen came up to surface. The sixth level, the bottom, didn't cave in, and the only men who were saved were trammers on the sixth level. They were tramming dirt from the chute, and climbed up the ladder. Their clothes were torn off, their hats off, their lamps out, but they made it — all husky young Swede-Finns.

Matt turned from narrative to analysis.

The pressure in the levels was so much that the studdings, or sprags, made of spruce or tamarack, that held the ground up until the timbers were put in, broke off like matches when hit with an axe. The whole thing was settling down. You could plainly see on the fourth level that it was going to go. The way I figured it, the fourth and fifth levels caved in first. There was nothing but timber for about three hundred feet; the ore had all been taken out down to the fourth level. On the sixth level the chutes were about ten feet apart — the miners would dump ore down the chutes for the trammers — and the level was solider.

"We never knew there was a mining inspector," Matt said, when I asked him why no questions were raised. "The miners hardly spoke a word of English, they were mostly I-talian, Finn, Swede. So the men couldn't talk much."

This was the human report of the tragedy. What did the documents say about the matter of culpability, either of the Oliver Mining Company officials or of the Mining Inspector for Iron County? Strangely, the 1893 bound volume of the "Diamond Drill," the Crystal Falls weekly paper, was missing from the files in the newspaper office. But in a family scrapbook I came across the key clipping, containing the report of Inspector C. T. Roberts on the Mansfield cave, as submitted to the Board of Supervisors of Iron County. It is a masterpiece of wriggle.

The report begins with a statement of the "terrible catastrophe," followed by a list of the twenty-seven workmen who perished:

the customary Upper Peninsula blend of Cornish, Swedish, and Italian surnames. There follows the hypothesis as to the cause of their deaths. The evidence of the survivors is conflicting, for "No two have the same story to tell." That many of the men spoke little or no English, that they were of course panic-stricken at the time of the cave, and that they might have agreed very equably on the long-range causes, Mr. Roberts does not suggest. He proceeds to develop a theory of his own.

"The break occurred at what is known as the timber shaft. This shaft is located within twenty feet of the river's edge and extends down through all the workings of the mine. This shaft was used for the admission of heavy timbers into the mine, and equipped for an exit for the miners in case of accident in the main shaft.

"The shaft was in constant use for sending down timber and I am of the opinion that certain of the timbers of the shaft were dislocated in the progress of the work, unbeknown to the management, which is within the range of possibility. The timbers thus removed would form a breach in the support of the shaft, allowing it to cave. The river then rushing down the shaft carried everything before its great pressure."

So management is absolved. Mr. Roberts had examined the shaft regularly three times a month, and "heard no complaints from any of the men working there." This is probably true. Matt Johnson never knew there was a mining inspector, and Roberts truly never heard him complain. Furthermore, Roberts' deputy, Captain James Rowe, was in the mine three hours before the caving, and "saw no disturbance of an extraordinary nature or nothing indicative of imminent danger." Captain Rowe might very profitably have talked with Matt Johnson. The report arrives at this sensational conclusion.

"I am of the opinion that no loss of life would have occurred and the damage would have been small, if the water from the river had not rushed into the mine when the cave occurred."

That is, no one would have drowned if there had been no flood! But Roberts has already stated that the timber shaft lay twenty feet from the river's bank, so that any cave, even if it proceeded from an independent cause, would surely invite the river's entry.

All the traditions of the early mining disaster are present in the story of the Mansfield cave: signs and jinxes, criminal negligence and folk justice, the fraud of owners and travail of widows.

11

LAKESMEN

THREE Great Lakes wash the Peninsula's shores, and their stretching waters are never far out of sight or out of mind of her folk. Almost every town of size curves around a bay, a harbor, a channel: the Soo, Grand Marais, Munising, L'Anse, Marquette, Ontonagon, face Superior; Manistique, Escanaba, Menominee, front Michigan; while St. Ignace commands the Straits of Mackinac joining Michigan to Huron.

Especially does Superior, the Great Cold Lake, with her savage icy storms, her clutching depths and her immense expanse, grip the imaginations of men. Superior is a prized friend and a relentless foe. Through the Soo locks, accommodating traffic between Superior and the lower Lakes, annually passes more tonnage than the Panama and the Suez can jointly boast — and Superior freezes over five months of the year. During the second World War the Army guarded the St. Mary's locks with fantastic precautions — not so fantastic, for one well-placed bomb could have crippled American steel production, fed by the iron ore shipped from the head of the Lakes down to Ohio and New York ports and thence by rail to the great foundries at Pittsburgh, Youngstown, Cleveland. But Superior, an unparalleled highway for commerce, is also a graveyard of twisted ships and swollen corpses, for as the legend says, the Great Cold Lake never yields up its dead.

Old lakesmen can yet remember the last days of sail before the coming of steel freighters as an heroic era filled with fresh-water epics. They may be retired captains and crewmen of Lakes ships; commercial fishermen who still drag the Lake beds for whitefish, trout, herring, pike, muskellunge; Coast Guardsmen and lighthouse keepers and locks workers living along the shores. The Lakes exert a strange compulsion on these men, and their memories are crammed with marine legends and sailing sagas. Some become devoted fans of the Inland Seas, collecting and treasuring their traditions, amassing logs, photographs and clippings about favorite vessels.

The foremost devotee of Lakes' lore I met was Edwin T. Brown of the Soo. Although never a sailor himself, because of frail health, Mr. Brown — who bears a striking resemblance to roly-poly Charles Winninger of "Showboat" fame — has lived in closest intimacy with Superior and her ships. His father sailed the Lakes in the heyday of the sailing schooners, and boated his family from Bay City in lower Michigan up to the Soo in 1887, where they lived on shipboard until he could build a house. Three of the sons became Lakes captains, a fourth was a steward, while Edwin worked at the St. Mary's locks, eventually becoming chief clerk and statistician. In that key listening-post he met every captain who sailed the upper Lakes, chatted with them for hours while their ships were waiting to be locked through, and took occasional cruises as their guest. To him they revealed sacred confidences, for the captains were sensitive to the point of superstition in talking about the experiences of their ships. Each trip had its quota of danger, in the old days, and each safe delivery its memory of strain and doubt.

"In a storm you can see the ship weave, writhe, and twist like a thing alive — the steel ripples like water," Mr. Brown said matter-of-factly, explaining the tensions of the voyage. "Sometimes a ship shed fifty thousand rivets, and came in practically ready to fall apart.

"The captains wouldn't talk about things like that. Not one

ever told me about waterspouts on the Lakes. None ever spoke about the land birds which boarded westbound ships about fifteen miles out of the Soo, stayed on board until they reached Duluth, and then flew south down the Mississippi, every spring. If a ship went north to Fort Williams, in Canada, the birds would know and always desert."

Retired now, Mr. Brown spends much time adding to his excellent collection of wreck photographs and arranging them in his albums. He can pause at any picture and give you the biography of the ship up till the day of its doom. Every ship has its story, he says, and he files away their careers in his mind as carefully as he pastes their prints in his scrapbooks. Frequently schools and lodges and socials call on Mr. Brown for a cycle of Lakes legends, and he willingly obliges. But he will just as willingly share his marine lore with you in his own parlor, fondling through his albums, and soberly detailing their stories.

SAVED BY A BATHTUB

Edwin T. Brown speaks

• Captain John Duddleson of the "L. C. Waldo" told me this. He was out on Superior during the great storm of November 9 to 12, 1913, when twelve or fourteen big ships were lost, on every one of the Lakes.

In attempting to seek shelter in the lee of Keweenaw Point, he ran on the Presque Isle rocks. It was too stormy for the coast guard to get to them. The bow was high on the rocks, the aft was awash, the fires had all gone out. It was freezing temperature. The men had to seek shelter in a chain locker — thirty all huddled down there. They knew they would freeze to death if they could not get a fire going. They took the captain's bathtub, turned it upside down, and let it rest on some bricks, to give a draught. They chopped up the captain's cabin — the ship was of steel but the cabins were of wood — with their emergency axes, and carried the wood down. They pushed the wood underneath, chopped holes in their emergency fire pails, cut a hole in the bottom of the tub, and placed their pails over it, one on top of the other, to make a smokepipe. They curved the pails so that the end of the pipe went out through a deadlight.

Then they were able to build a fire. When the storm subsided, the Coast Guard came out for them. Their lives were saved by a bathtub.

THE SAGA OF THE *BAUTZEN*

Few ship biographies can match the uneasy and ironic career of the "Bautzen." She was built in the first World War when the French government ordered three ships from the Fort William shipyards on the Canadian shore of Lake Superior. Sailing to the Soo, across the Lakes and out to the Atlantic, her two sister ships, the "Cerisolles" and the "Inkerman," foundered on the unknown reef that had wrecked the "Bannockburn" in 1902 and given rise to a Flying Dutchman legend on the Lakes.*

The French government suspected chicanery and sent over a commission to investigate in the fall of 1917. The commission arrived at the Soo just as the big Lakes steamers coated with ice were coming in on their last trip of the year. "I was in the group with the Locks superintendent that received them," Edwin T. Brown recalled. "We asked them if they wanted to take passage to see for themselves what a fall voyage on the Lakes was like. They took a look at the incoming ships and said they didn't think they wanted to go. They went back to France and gave an unsatisfactory explanation. The French government didn't know what a Great Lake was like. They couldn't understand a ship being lost on inland water. No trace was ever found of their two ships, not even a stick of wood."

As for the "Bautzen," she continued on her indestructible way. After serving for the French as a transport ship during the war,

* "Nothing was ever found of the "Bannockburn" except an oar," John Keast told me in Marquette. "The newspapers carried tales of seeing her again, and captains reported sighting her on moonlight nights, bound for Duluth."

she was sold to fishermen on St. Pierre and Miquelon Islands, the vestigial remnants of the French empire in the New World. Mac-Millan, the Arctic explorer, next purchased her, rebaptized her the "Peary," and sailed off to the North Pole to continue the explorations begun by her namesake. After this expedition, a Cleveland millionaire dreaming of a sequestered isle in the South Seas bought the "Peary" to search for his Shangri-La. He never found it. The ubiquitous vessel next serviced rum-runners operating from the West Indies during Prohibition times. Captured by the Coast Guard, she was sold to the United States Lake Survey, and brought back to the Lakes where she had been spawned. Ironically, she participated in the survey that located the offshore pinnacle of rock, Superior Shoal, that had killed her newborn sister ships. Today she still pursues survey work, in tame old age serenely contemplating her lurid past.

THE BULL AT THE SOO

Among Superior's legends one singular happening at the Soo locks commands an unrivaled celebrity. This is a story of a ship that ran amok, bankrupted her company, caused the smash-up of a sister vessel, and wrecked a lock. I heard it from burly Howard Crooks, a retired lakes captain living in Menominee, and the encyclopedic Edwin Brown in Sault Ste. Marie.

• In 1909 the freighter "Perry G. Walker" of the Gilchrist line approached the Canadian lock at the Soo from the St. Mary's River, bound up to Lake Superior with a load of coal. The upper gates were open and a big passenger ship, the "Assiniboia," was entering the locks from above, followed by the "Crescent City," a Steel Corporation vessel. Accordingly, the lower gates were closed, and the "Perry G. Walker" was supposed to tie up some distance below and wait her turn for locking. Through some mistake in the signals between her pilot house and engine room, the engineer misunderstood his orders and went full speed ahead instead of backing. His ship rammed the lower gates and smashed the hinges. Lake Superior, with a twenty-foot head of water above Lake Huron, rushed through the locks. A torrent of water hurled the "Perry G. Walker" backwards, and carried the "Assiniboia" and the "Crescent City" downstream in a mad rush.

Behind these two a third ship had tied up above the locks, awaiting her turn, the "Manitoba," a passenger vessel belonging to the Canadian Pacific Railroad. The force of the current snapped her mooring lines and swept her through the locks in spite of herself. She passed through safely, not drawing enough water to hit the sill. Her captain rang up "Full Speed" and maintained steerage way right down the river.

The "Crescent City" was not so fortunate. Heavily laden with ore, she struck the lower lock-gate sill, unduly exposed by the decrease of water, with such force that her bottom was flattened from one end to the other. She careened on down river, struck a protruding rock, and sank.

The Gilchrist Company, being held for heavy damages, went bankrupt. The Interlake Steamship Company bought a number of her ships and renamed the "Perry G. Walker," in memory of her exploit, "Taurus," the Bull. She sailed the Lakes until 1945, when she was scrapped at Hamilton, Ontario.

Aboard the "Assiniboia" the passengers, not knowing what was about, thoroughly enjoyed the excitement, believing that they were witnessing regular locking procedure. Said an Englishman aboard, "My goodness, but they do things demned fast in America."

LAKE SUPERIOR NEVER GIVES UP ITS DEAD

Every lakesman and those landsmen living close to Superior know that a drowning in the Great Cold Lake means an irrevocably lost body. Never has a body been recovered from the frigid depths of the Lake, they say, and many offer evidence.

Edwin T. Brown speaks

• Lake Superior never gives up its dead. The temperature is uniform at forty degrees, winter or summer; bodies don't decay, and are probably eaten by fishes.

The "Henry B. Smith" went down in November, 1913, in one of the greatest storms in the history of the Lakes, and about thirty-five bodies aboard were never recovered. The chief engineer was later found buried on the north shore; he had a life preserver on, and floated. She left Marquette against the advice of the dock men, and when she was just out of sight her volume of smoke suddenly disappeared. She sank right down in the ordinary lanes of traffic, and no floating bodies were ever seen.

The "Superior City" was lost three or four miles within shore, with the Coast Guard station at Whitefish Point in sight. It was a bright sunny day, and she collided with another ship, the "Willis L. King," through mere negligence; the ships should have been half a mile apart. Both pilots lost their papers. The Coast Guard boats put out right away, but no body was ever found; twenty-eight men were lost. Their relatives employed boats for weeks, thinking the bodies would float, without any result. Two men were picked up alive by the other ship, blown a hundred and fifty feet by the explosion. (Some claim there never is an explosion.) One had all his clothing blown off. The other was Captain Storey; he was just eating supper, and came on deck from the galley on hearing the jar and was carried away by the explosion.

The St. Mary's River connecting Superior with Huron will yield its dead, and Mr. Brown while talking at the Carbide Dock about a recently drowned man saw his body come up through the locks. Bodies float up in the other Lakes too. The spell applies only to Superior, and it applies most rigidly — even to parts of bodies. A cable snapped in a ship at Duluth, in '41 or '42, and took off a sailor's head. The head was never found.

An old lakesman, now a commercial fisherman, barrel-built,

Ora Endress at Grand Marais, later spoke somberly of the tradition.

• Lake Superior never gives up her dead, in deep water. I've known well over a thousand men that's been lost in the Lake, in over forty years I've been on it. More bodies have been lost from Keweenaw Point to Whitefish Point than in all the rest of the Lakes put together; it's known as the Graveyard of the Lakes. That's caused by deep water and different levels of currents. The deepwater fish there have two or three inches of fat to protect them.

And Captain Endress handed me a list of wrecks he had compiled that had occurred in the Graveyard, and from which no body had ever been recovered. "That list covers a radius only of twenty-five miles north and perhaps a hundred miles east and west," he noted.

• Two men drowned at the end of the pier last summer was the only ones I know of that ever came ashore — very unusual. It was a fishing boat; the men were McDonald and Tornibish. I told the captain at the coast guard station it was useless to look for them. Since then I say the Lake doesn't give up her dead in *deep* water.

I heard that as young as I could remember. All the sailors believe it. If the Lake did give them up, where did they go? Maybe it's an old tradition, but it's been proved. Most of the bodies has been found on Lake Huron, now.

NINE MONTHS TO THE DAY

"Most everybody that's drowned around here, in nine months they find their bodies. Everybody around here thinks that the body will come ashore in nine months."

This was Charlie Goodman talking at Grand Marais, a lonely bay town on Lake Superior. Before 1908 Grand Marais hummed with lumbering activity, and her harbor bustled with steamers and barges. But the town died when the white pine went and the railroad pulled out, and today a coast guard station and a few hundred souls maintain a community.

The waters about Grand Marais have seen disastrous wrecks and valiant rescues, and the uncanny memory of Charlie Goodman records them with a scholar's precision and a pulp writer's verve. So he relates a coastal saga whose echoes are frequently heard from Grand Marais to Newberry, the storm-driven voyage of a barge named "Smith."

Charlie Goodman speaks

• Dan McLeod had a lumber camp at the mouth of the Sucker River, with twenty-three miles of railroad running into the woods. One tug and two scows had come up from the Soo and were un-loading flat cars, steel, hay, oats, provisions, and supplies for the lumber camp. After they'd been unloading two days, the lake got rough, and they had to pull out for shelter. McLeod just had a little dock along shore; the railroad ran right out onto the dock and connected with the rails on the scow. The scow was cabled onto a maple and a beech tree on both sides of her, a couple of hundred feet away, to hold her steady. Another cable connected the barge to the scow.

When the big northwestern wind came up — it was late in the fall, in November, 1901 — the Captain of the barge blowed a whistle that he was going to pull out and head for Grand Marais, eighteen miles away. But the men on the scow didn't know what he meant. When the "Smith" pulled out, she pulled the scow along with her, and the scow pulled up both the trees. She still had two of the five flat cars on board, loaded with railroad steel.

The scow was loaded heavier in front than behind, so she started shipping water. The men thought if they pushed the cars overboard that would bring the bow up, but in their excitement they forgot to unhook the cars. So one hung over, and one stayed on, and the bow settled still deeper, and the scow shipped more water. If they'd only pulled the draw pin, one would have gone

over clear, and raised the bow several feet. The rails fell off the
car hanging overboard — they're in the lake yet.

It was after dark, and the scow was shaking back and forth
with that rough wind. The waves washed seven of the men overboard. Five of 'em got through hanging on to whatever they
could find. Roaring Jimmy Gleason (who talked as if he could lick
the world, though he got licked every time), put his arms around
the towpost and froze right to it. The waves would wash over
him, but in between he'd get his breath back.

The Coast Guard got them about a mile from the harbor at
Grand Marais. They'd been on the scow about two and a half
hours bucking the wind, and they were so froze it was hard getting
them off. Only Jimmy Gleason and the foreman lived through it.
Gleason always made a big thing of it, and what a miracle it was
he got through. He didn't go back to work for McLeod no more —
he didn't want no more of Lake Superior.

The bodies of the seven men were found all the same day on
the beach, nine months to the day after. I found one of them on
the beach down by the mouth of the Two-heart — fellow name of
Johnnie Cascaddin. I called up the Coast Guard Station and notified them of the body, and a Coast Guard man and I carried
him up the bank and buried him. The other bodies were found in
different places, but all same day, mostly by the Coast Guard.
That was in 1902.

"Does every single drowned person turn up nine months after?"
I asked Charlie.

Sometimes they don't ever get the bodies, but most always
they come ashore in nine months.

In 1894 two men drownded here — a couple of town fishermen, John Brenith and Jake Sodestrand. I sold them the boat that
they drownded in, a forty-foot sailboat. There was no lighthouse
here then, but a fellow would hang a lantern on the pier at night.
It was so rough, with a northwest blizzard blowing, that he
couldn't hang the light out that day. So, when they were coming

in, their boat struck the east pier and split in two lengthways. One half floated in the bay, the other half floated sixteen miles down the beach. The sail and one spar were found the next day at the mouth of the Sucker River.

The bodies were found nine months to the day after. They showed up at the east end of the bay, at the same place where the sail had been found the fall before.

Baldheaded Charlie, the only fellow to try to walk to Grand Marais from the wreck of the "Curtis," was found nine months to the day after, on the pier in the bay. He died right on the stones, in November, and two town kids, Palmer Masse and Archie Larou, found him the next summer, nine months later.

CAPTAIN TRUEDELL'S DREAM

For over half a century the tale of a young lifesaver's eerie premonition has stirred the folk in the Soo country. Its chief actor still lives, and I drove to his woods home two miles east of Grand Marais, and another mile into the forest from the gravel road. Taking the wrong turn, an easy thing to do since any opening in the trees might pass for a road, I followed a wilderness path that after a while petered out completely, and sat bleakly in my Ford convertible looking up at the towering hardwood giants, listening for bears, and wondering what would happen if I got a flat. But the car pulled through, and I fled back to town, to meet Captain Benjamin Truedell next day in a store, and follow him cautiously back to his retreat.

Captain Truedell was a stubby, gray-haired man with a preacher's gravity. In the excitement of talk his pale blue eyes lit up with a mystic glow. He had commanded the Life Saving Station at Grand Marais for twenty years, but was retired now, had time to burn, and appeared most anxious to tell me his story.

"If there ever is any event of importance happening, I dream about it in advance — I always have," he began, once we reached his new frame house, ringed about by great pines and hemlocks. "My mother was the same way. She told me I would be gifted with unusual things. Anything important in my work, in my business, I dream of, and when it happens the next morning, I remember it. It's not exactly the same, you know, but the conditions are similar."

Captain Truedell speaks

• During my second year in the Life Saving Service, in 1892, I was stationed at Deer Park [a ghost town east of Grand Marais, but once a busy lumbering area]. I was called to go on watch at twelve o'clock midnight, so I went to bed and slept from eight till twelve, and the dream happened at the very time a sinking was going on.

I dreamed I met a man on the beach, coming towards me. He appeared to be an acquaintance, yet I was doubtful as he got nearer. He was very nicely, finely dressed. As I approached him, he held out his hand to shake hands, but his hand was cold and clammy and I couldn't hold the grasp. Then he turned and walked towards the water and dissolved in the surf.

I was awakened standing in the middle of the dormitory, wet with perspiration. The relief watch was holding a lighted lantern up to my face, asking, "What is the matter?"

That morning at the breakfast table, seven of us were messing together, and I recited the dream to them. They laughed at me, but I said, "Watch out." As the day wore on and nothing happened, they all began to make fun of me, even the captain.

It was blowing a three-day gale, with high seas from the northwest. About two o'clock that afternoon a man stumbled into the station, stating he had been on a wreck and had been washed ashore, the only survivor. Not knowing the direction of any town he followed along the beach until he arrived at Deer Park Life Saving Station (the Coast Guard did not begin till 1913). I was called to take the beach patrol west, and I was the first one ashore. There was the body of a man lying on his face, stretched out. He was finely dressed, and appeared to be an aristocrat. As we rolled him over, his hand flipped over and struck mine. And I saw he was the man of my dream. The resemblance was very noticeable. He had a mustache, but no chin whiskers. His clothes were not wet in the dream, though.

He was Peter G. Minch, millionaire owner of the "Western Reserve," the first steel ship to go down in the Lakes.

The "Western Reserve" was the flagship of the Minch fleet of fourteen cargo vessels, a record-breaking three-hundred footer. On this trip Peter Minch was taking his family pleasure sailing from the Soo to Two Harbors, Minnesota, there to load up with ore. Proud in the strength of his ship, he sailed beyond Whitefish Point and Point Iroquois into the storm, against the advice of Captain Albert Myers. The decks buckled before the gale, and about nine o'clock, the evening of April 30, the steel freighter split in two. Passengers and crew scrambled into a metallic lifeboat and a yawl, and when the lifeboat capsized, all clambered into the yawl. A steamer passed to the west and the huddled group tried to burn a shawl as a signal, without success. The yawl coasted from this point, about twenty-five miles north of Grand Marais, until seven-twenty the following morning, when it overturned in the surf, some fifteen miles west of Deer Park and the Life Saving Station. All the occupants were drowned except the wheelman, Harry Stewart, who snatched a life preserver and made shore at Lonesome Point. It was Stewart (a cousin of Truedell) who lurched into the Station bringing news of the wreck, and verifying Benjamin Truedell's dream of disaster.

SAILOR SUPERSTITIONS

"My dad was a fisherman at Whitefish Point and Copper Harbor" (two of the loneliest outposts on Lake Superior), Ora Endress told me in Grand Marais. "So I got my training from an old sea dog. I been here a little over twenty years, and I was on the Lake twenty years before that. I was born and raised in Sault Ste. Marie. During the depression I took a job on a passenger boat from the Soo to Grand Marais — that's how I came here. Been in commercial fishing, on harbor tugs, passenger barges, ore barges, any kind of a thing that floats — I've got an unlimited master's license. During the war I handled all the priorities for the commercial fishermen on the Great Lakes." He did not tell me, but Ora had won a Congressional Medal of Honor for heroic rescue work on the "Reynolds" in 1919, making four trips through crashing breakers to take off the helpless crew.

Endress looked like a small barge himself, heavy, solid, dark, Teutonic. His white porticoed frame house stood not far from Charlie Goodman's bleak shack, but across the gravel road on the bay side; the lonely waters of Superior rolled past his windows, while the forest lay at Charlie's door. One man's life lay in the water and the other's in the woods, and each was a master of his element. Ora had compiled a logbook of wrecks; Charlie treasured torn lumber camp account books. But where Charlie unloosed his experiences in a ceaseless gush, Ora could only marvel helplessly at his own life history, not knowing where to begin. I would ask a question, and he would answer, and that would be all.

Ora did have a sheaf of sailor superstitions on the surface of his mind.

Ora Endress speaks

• The most superstitious people is the sailors. They'll never take a boat out on a Friday, on her maiden voyage. As a matter of fact we never take any boat out on a Friday. We have a chief engineer won't even leave Grand Marais on Friday. And Friday the thirteenth is Black Friday. That covers both ends of the boat.

The 1913 blow, one of the fiercest blows ever on the Great Lakes, some twenty-odd boats lost — was on a Friday. I was on a freight boat then, drove down from Caribou Island to the Soo in a blinding snow; two foot of snow on the lock wall in November.

A sailor will not go to work on a boat that is considered a hoodoo — commonly called a Black Cat. Some ships always have full crews, while others were always hiring men. You'd hear a man say, "I only stayed two weeks on that Black Cat."

A rat won't stay where there is water, if the ship leaks. I've seen sailors throw potatoes or carrots at rats to drive 'em back into the boat. It may be that a rat has knowledge that a human being doesn't.

In foggy weather you see little men jumping on the bow of the boat and dancing on the upper deck. They call that the loup-garou. I've heard that so many times — don't know how to spell it or what it means. It's caused by currents of air or a change in the atmosphere that makes cold and warm spots in the air. Easterly weather, with the reflection of the sun on the water, causes a lot of things to be seen that really isn't there.

You generally see that at night with the lights of the boat shining. I heard some sailors say it's a warning; when you see that, something's going to happen. A man'll be at the wheel or at the pilot house and he'll say, "Lots of loup-garous tonight — there'll be trouble." The wheelman is in the right position to see it, where a man at the bow wouldn't see it. Everything that happens at the forward end is blamed on them. For instance, if the boat runs aground they'll say, "That's that damn loup-garou last night."

On the score of deserting rats, an actual case is supplied by Dr. J. F. Deadman of the Soo.

• I remember when twenty-seven rats ran off the breast line of the old steamer "Sault Ste. Marie." Captain Mondor was in charge and Henry Doench was cabin boy. The boat was loading up when the rats left, one after another, running out on the line. Half the crew deserted at once. The boat was on her way up the lake with winter supplies. A great storm came up in the night and the next morning she was on a sand reef outside of Grand Marais. But by lightening her cargo she made port safely.

LAKE SERPENTS

About half a mile north of Munising we stopped the car, got out, and walked toward the photogenic bay that curved in a semicircle around Grand Island. From the road nothing seemed to be between us and the water, but as we descended the little hill, a tiny colony of shacks suddenly came into view. The nearest was a lopsided crazy structure of boards and sheeting with a stovepipe chimney, obviously patched together from the city dump. Down a ways we came across a husky young fellow splitting wood, and my newspaper friend asked him if Bill Powell was at home.

"Well I cain't say as to whether he is or not," he said very gravely. Lew thanked him and we walked fifty feet further and found Bill in the next house all right. Since this was Powell's Point, and no one but Powells, a New England bred clan of commercial fishermen, lived there, the young fellow certainly knew that Bill was in. "He wouldn't tell you because he didn't know whether you mightn't be the law," Lew explained.

Bill Powell was sleeping in a living room waist high in debris. His house was solid and roomy, but it apparently had no housekeeper. Bill jumped up at once, apologizing for the litter, very friendly and pleasant-looking, a short sturdy man, tanned, healthy, quick-eyed, open-faced, well-spoken. Lew said that he had told me Bill Powell was cram full of all kinds of fishing superstitions and stories.

Bill looked interested, and agreed that he ought to know a good many, seeing that he had spent his life fishing in Superior, and tried to think of some, and couldn't. He rubbed his head, and thought, and glanced at Lew in some embarrassment, and gave up. We all three felt disappointed, and small-talked for a few minutes to cover it up. Lew and I were saying goodbye when Bill remembered an unusual experience he had often heard from a fellow fisherman.

Bill Powell speaks

• Angus Steinhoff and Van Dein were lifting gill nets on the west side of Trout Bay from near Black Point along the Grand Island shore. Angus was a young fellow then working for Van Dein, the owner of the boat, a man about sixty. They were coming toward Munising, and sighted a creature swimming fast. They took after it in their boat, the "Viva," a gas boat; it made eight and a half to nine miles an hour. The creature zigzagged back and forth. A good part of it was out of the water; it had an angled head, looked like a big snake or serpent, made quite a wake. It was broad daylight so they could see it clearly. Nothing in the lake could go that fast. Van Dein said something similar in the Old Country, Sweden, took after him once when he got too close. So they turned the boat across the bay and went by the Thumb home.

Van Dein said he always hated to tell anyone about it because they wouldn't believe it. I heard Angus tell it two or three times though.

That Bill Powell did not regard the story skeptically became at once apparent, for he knew two similar mysteries.

At Au Train Lake, better than seventy years ago, my dad was jacklighting deer in a canoe with his brother. (You use a pitch pine knot that burns like a torch; there is a blind behind the light so that the deer, when he is drawn by the light, can't see your motions.) This creature, like nothing they had ever seen, circled the boat two or three times; he was about a couple of feet out of the water; they could hear his teeth chatter. It couldn't be a turtle because it buzzed so fast. They hit it with a hardwood paddle, sounded like hitting a rock. It went down to the bottom. There must have been lots of it in the water, since it kicked up quite a little wake.

I saw a peculiar spouting in Basswood Lake, in northern Minnesota, once. It repeated three or four times. No beaver would make that unless it were twenty-five feet long.

And Bill Powell, who had lived his life on the lakes, could offer no explanation for these matters.

We next hunted up Angus Steinhoff, the creature's eye-witness, and eventually met him coming out of a grocery store. He stood in the entrance, a ragged, angular Swede grinning vacantly, and told a story somewhat at variance with Bill Powell's.

Angus Steinhoff speaks

• It was some kind of a fish or something that made a wave like an airplane or motor boat. It went faster'n we could travel. We couldn't get close enough to see what it was; we got within three hundred feet. There weren't any outboard motors on Lake Superior then. It resembled a goose or a loon, but bigger; traveled to beat hell, spray shooting out on both sides.

We were going out to set nets about nine-thirty, in June, about twenty years ago. When we seen it, we tried to catch up with it; it'd wait for a little while, we'd gain, then it would go like hell. It follered the shore line all the way, eventually disappeared; we lost it at the east point of Trout Bay, by the north light of Grand Island.

We talked it over many times. Van Dein had fished all his life; he said he'd seen a reptile in Sweden that made a similar wake, from wigwagging.

Angus half grinned uneasily, and left us to consider the obvious hypothesis.

12

SAGAMEN

S OMETIMES a fluent storyteller launches into a stream of highly colored personal experiences that enthrall his audience as much or more than any folk tale. In his autobiographical sagas he plays an heroic role, overmastering the hazards and outwitting the dangers presented by vicious men, ferocious beasts, and implacable nature. These narratives rest on explicit factual detail, and yet they are strongly flavored with romance.

In the Peninsula I met such sagamen from time to time, old woodsmen, homesteaders, prospectors, gifted with talk beyond their fellows and, from their own statements, kin to the pagan heroes who battled armies, monsters, and demons. The chronicles of Swan Olson will serve my point.

Swan in 1946 was a seventy-three year old mason, plasterer, bricklayer, and carpenter, but he had worked in the fields and forests and mines in the heroic age of the north woods. I met Swan in a barber shop in Negaunee, an Upper Peninsula town astraddle the Marquette iron ore range. Waiting my turn, and listening to the casual conversation about me, for any wind in the Peninsula is apt to bear a folk tale, I heard the man in the chair say " fly pie." He was relating the following story as a personal experience of his youth.

SWAN OLSON

• Down below Lake Linden, I was traveling on the road, forty-eight years ago. A farmer's wife asked me to come in and have some coffee. There was only one room in the house. It had a table made out of planks, and planks for seats all around the table. After she poured the coffee she came over with a pie plate. I thought it was huckleberry pie, because it was in the fall. When she came close, I looked at it and saw heads, wings, and feet sticking all over. If there had been any frosting on it, I might have taken a bite.

I asked her what it was. She told me it was fly pie. I told her I thought it was huckleberry pie. Then she told me, "Oh, that pie is good! We got a hired man working for us, and I have to make him one every day."

She had six fly traps in the room, made out of a bowl with a funnel. The open mouth narrowed into a small hole, like a bee-hive, and the flies flew into the funnel and through the hole, and then flew around inside without being able to get out. She had the windows and doors of the house wide open to let the flies in, and they were singing and flying around to beat the band. She took the flies out, killed them, dumped them out of the back door, fumigated them, and made pie out of them.

I said, "Well, I think I don't try the fly pie, and I don't think I try the coffee either."

When Swan finished his haircut, I went up to him and inquired into the story. He affirmed its truth most solemnly,* and even added a little sequel.

"Another time I passed that woman who made the fly pie, and she was standing in the door, with dough dripping from her hand, holding it over her head to look down the road. I was going to a sawmill four miles below. I asked her for a drink of water. She recognized me, and said, 'There's a lake behind the house. Go down and help yourself.'"

* Grasshopper pie, I am told, is sometimes eaten in the plains states.

Swan was now cautious, and the lady sensitive.

I made a date with Swan to meet him that evening, when he would tell me some more of his experiences. And he did, talking to me in a booth in a beer tavern steadily from nine till two a.m., a gentle old man, whose head swung sideways in the slow rhythm that sometimes visits elderly people, and who walked tentatively, like a child. Swan looked like a monk, with his long, ascetic face and benevolent eyes, while he talked of desperate deeds. He spoke with the clumsy tongue of the immigrant, and the singsong cadence of the Swede, but his words pictured high drama and derring-do. In his sagas of the past he lived and acted like a giant, and then at the end of our evening he declared with glee that he had finally satisfied his wish to stay up until the saloon closed.

Without preamble Swan began a narrative dealing with his first adventures in the United States.

• I came from Stockholm, Sweden, when I was just confirmed, about 1890. I was seventeen. I landed at Quebec and went to Litchfield, Minnesota. I came there in harvest time, and worked for a farmer, Eric Ericson. He drank clear alcohol with a dipper. No one would work for him more than two or three days; he would go crazy and threaten to murder them, and his wife, and me.

We took some big barrels of eggs thirteen miles into town to sell for three cents a dozen. The storekeeper sold them for five cents, but Ericson could only get two cents. Well, he went into a saloon and told me to get three cents for the eggs or take them back and bury them in a hole in the manure pile. I couldn't sell them, so I went back to the saloon, and he was dead drunk — couldn't walk.

So I had a couple of fellows help me lift him up into the wagon, alongside me, and let the curved iron side hold him in place, slumped against it. So we started back, and I let the horses go as fast as they wanted to. It was a spring wagon, with springs under the seat, which fitted over the sideboards. The wagon hit a deep rut, and gave a big bump from the spring, and he went from the bloody wagon clear up in the air, and landed plunk in the bloody sluice alongside the clay road.

It took me a while to slow up and go back, and I couldn't figure out how to get him up — he was like a dishrag. So finally I unhooked one of the lines from the horse's bit and tied it under his arms, and then I went up in the wagon and began pulling him up. I got hold of him by the neck and the collar and pulled him the rest of the way. Then I put him under the bloody seat and left him there the rest of the trip.

So we got back to the farm and drove up to the front door. Then I went into his room, looked under his pillow and pulled out his gun, emptied all the cartridges and put them in my pocket. Then I went out and unhitched the team and put them in the barn. I had one harness off, and was just hanging the other up on the peg when he came in the barn holding the gun.

He said, "You son of a bitch!" and pointed the gun right in my face, and clicked the hammer — click, click, click.

Then he said, "Don't you drop? You son of a bitch."

I said, "Not for your gun or you either." Then I dropped the harness, grabbed his gun and hit him right in the mouth, and the blood squirted all over him and right in my face. I knocked out one of his teeth. He fell backwards over the doorway, and I thought I killed the bugger. I listened to his heart, heard it beat. So I got a pail of cold water from the galvanized trough and poured it over him, and he began to hiccup. Then I helped the bugger up to the house and seen him get undressed and get to bed.

Then I went back to the barn, after wiping off and feeding the horses. I couldn't sleep up in the attic of the log house — only two rooms in the whole place — so I slept in the barn in the hay. I slept with two blankets and a pillow, and in the morning I was covered with snakes, ice-cold snakes. They wanted my heat, so they curled up all around me, up to my neck and my face. When

I'd wake up I'd take one of the bloody buggers by the tail, when his head was under my neck, and break his neck. They were slippery and cold, but not poisonous. (One time when I was pitching hay, I pulled on one's head, and he just squeezed tighter round my neck, and I had to grab his tail with my other hand.)

About three o'clock in the morning I heard a holler of "Murder" from the house. So I threw off the snakes and put some overalls on and ran up to the house. Eric was standing over his woman (his second wife — his kids ran away 'cause he said he'd kill them) with a stove handle in his hand, ready to kill her. She was lying down on the floor stretched out. He had hit her once, was going to finish her up. I grabbed the stove pipe from behind him and hit him over the head, right on the coconut, so he dropped down on the floor. Then I picked him up and put him over an Old Country chest he had in the corner (I got two of them at home — they're rounded at the top) and laid him across it on his stomach, and pushed the trunk against the wall with all my strength, so his head was caught between the trunk and the wall. Then I took the iron rod from an old muzzle-loader he had, about four feet long, and pulled it out over the barrel, and beat him with it on the hind end and the legs and all over.

The woman said, "Just keep it up."

When I was finished, I was all perspired. He fell over the side of the trunk on the floor, and I picked him up and put him back in the bed.

That was Saturday night. I got up early in the morning, milked the cows, fed the horses. Then at breakfast the woman said he wanted to see me. So I went up into the bedroom, and he showed me all his bruises; he was black and blue and green.

So I said, "Well, that's what you get when you go to town. They was going to beat you up in the saloon, and I saved your life."

Then he asked me to hand him his pants. They were on the chair right alongside the bed, but he couldn't reach them, he was so weak. (He stayed in bed for a week.) And he took a silver dollar out of his pocket — they had no paper dollars then — and gave it to me for saving his life.

That was the only time he paid me all the time I was there.

Observe that story: its combination of economy and detail; its series of climaxes — the fall from the wagon, the knockout in the barn, the trunk whipping; its minor sensations — the alcohol drinking, the cheapness of eggs, the snake-bed; and its marvelously ironic O. Henry ending. To my mind it is a classic in its genre.

Swan in his time had handled other unruly customers, and thus describes the jeopardy into which he fell when his lumberjack partner ran amok.

• Down in Wisconsin fifty years ago, at a lumber camp way out in the woods, this French fellow and I was making a logging road. He was driving the team and I was swamping. We was filling up the big tank by first filling the barrels and then emptying them into the tank. We had to saw a square hole in the ice.

While I was filling the barrel he came around the tank and unhitched the neck yoke of the horse on the sleigh and went after me, with foam coming out of his mouth.

"I'm going to kill you," he said.

He chased me all around the tank and the horse and the hole till I was nearly played out. I was going round there like a bloody merry-go-round, till I nearly lost my breath. I made a short cut by jumping over the corner of the hole, and he tried to do the same thing and fell in, with the bloody neck yoke in his hand. All I seed was the cap floating on the water. The first thing to come up was the neck yoke — he couldn't let go if he wanted to. So I decided to give him a good ducking so he don't get after me till I come to the camp. So I took him by the hair — all lumberjacks had long hair — and pumped him up and down in the water. Then finally I pulled him up on the ice. He was pretty well tame. His clothes froze stiff as bark — they were rattling. I hoisted him up into the sprinkler, inside the tank, I pulled the plugs out, and let out the three barrels of water. (If I'd put him on top the tank he'd a fallen off, or frozen to death.) I put him into a barrel, and had the horse hoist him up the slide and dump him into the tank. I put the slide on the hooks and drove like a son of a gun to the camp, about a mile and a half.

They took him into town and he never come back no more.

This unpremeditated attack reminded Swan of two deliberate assaults on his person, which he countered with his usual ingenuity and daring.

• I was held up twice. When I was working for the Minneapolis Brewery Company, about 1893 (I was twenty-one or twenty-two years old), I was taking private delivery out of town. On the way back I was sound asleep, when the horses stopped. I looked up and saw a fellow standing on the ladder, and two other fellows was holding the horses. He ordered me to give him my watch and my money. They were just tramps — would have killed me just as well as a jack rabbit.

I didn't know just what to do. I had nothing except a black-snake I was sitting on (it had a short handle loaded with lead and covered with leather). I said, "My money's in my hip pocket; wait till I get it up."

So I started to feel behind the seat, by my right hand. The horses were excited, because they weren't used to anything like that, and he looked at them. Then I hit him right across the face with the blacksnake, and I didn't put any fingers in between either. I don't know whether I knocked out all his teeth or not — the blood squirted right out, and he fell flat on his back, down on the road. Maybe I killed him — I don't know.

Then I gave a lash in the air with the blacksnake, like a pistol shot. And the horses raised right straight up in the air [gesture], and the fellows lost their hold, and I rode right over the lot of them. It was on a hill, a long sloopy hill, and I rode right up to the top and tied the horses. Then I walked back and looked at the fellows and seed them lying still. When I saw they didn't move, then I was satisfied, and went back up the hill. I don't know to this day whether they were dead or alive.

They were dirty, raggy tramps. It's not on my conscience 'cause I didn't mean to kill them.

At Litchfield, at one o'clock in the morning, Swan was standing in a depot waiting for a train, when he overheard two tramps planning to hold him up, tie him to the rails, and let the train run over him. Swan, who this time had a gun, immediately pointed it at them and ordered "Hands up." The tramps raised their hands, but when one started to lower his Swan shot him through the groin, and fired four bullets in the air at the other. He set the wounded tramp against the side of the depot, until a policeman came along. Upon hearing Swan's story, the officer told him he could shoot the tramp dead, promising there would not even be a hearing, and offered his own gun. Swan refused, and insisted on taking the tramp to a hospital.

The tramp said, "Please don't kill me."

Swan told him, "I ain't a-going to do that; somebody else will have to."

"Those tramps would make the farmers' wives patch their clothes while the farmer was out in the field," Swan told me. "They'd take their pants right off in front of them. Then they'd steal turkeys.

"They'd get killed sleeping on the rods — I'd pull their boots off."

After leaving Minnesota and coming to Ishpeming and Negaunee, where the balance of his life had been spent, Swan found work at once in the mines. As a matter of course, for him, he had witnessed grim sights and experienced hairbreadth escapes during his career as iron miner.

• I seen Frenchmen, lumberjacks, take up handfuls of big black ants they found in the sawed-off stumps of hollow logs. They'd nest there in the winter and get all frozen up. But when they hold them in the hand they start crawling with life. And they pick them up and stuff them in their mouth — it made a crackling between their teeth like sand. They said it tasted like vinegar. It made me shiver to hear it.

Some Austrians were working in the stockpile at Winthrop, above Ishpeming — little black fellows. They came in cattle cars, from Chicago and the outskirts, standing on the horse manure about a foot and a half high on the bottom. I seen them kill rats with chunks of ore, then pull the skin off and eat them raw, like a cat, without even taking out the guts — the guts'd be hanging down their cheeks. I lost my bloody lunch the first time I saw that.

There was a cave-in at the Nelson mine between Ishpeming and Negaunee, when I was tending to the chute for the trammers. The boards across the chute broke off, and the mud poured out, tons and tons. I was buried under three to four feet of mud. They dug me out with their hands — a pickaxe or a shovel would have cracked my skull. They found a hair first, then my mouth. I was all covered with iron ore — looked like a bloody turtle.

In the number seven mine, between Winthrop and Ishpeming — hard ore, not hematite — I was drilling on a stope. I was sitting on the machine, which was on a tripod on three planks, on the ladders. Every time the drill struck the ore, my head bumped against the ceiling. The machine weighed five hundred pounds. A big chunk of ore, big as a boxcar, fell down from the ceiling and smashed the drill machine and broke all the ladders like toothpicks. I fell fifty feet down to the bottom of the stope. My partner was out getting water for the drilling. When he came the place was all dark; my candle had gone out. I was crawling on my knees and hands looking for my head. I asked him to help me look for my legs. He said I still had them. The circulation had stopped, I guess. If the ore had hit me, they wouldn't have found a piece of meat of me. A piece just as big as my thumb would have killed me, gone right through my head.

AARON KINNEY

Aaron Kinney is the bard of Iron River. He recites an earthy epic of the pioneer days in Iron County, filled with eye-gouging brawls, political melees, homesteading feuds, and graphic character sketches. His reputation for talk is countywide, and properly deserved. In his general store by Ice Lake (ice is one of his main sales items), he finds time a-plenty to steal into a corner and draw upon his limitless store of personal adventures and memories, given one attentive listener.

Aaron's father was an Irish Protestant from north Ireland; his mother's line is French Protestant. At seventy-odd Aaron is healthy, solid, and bouncy, with the outdoor hue of so many Peninsula men. His store teeth are his only concession to age. He looks like Boston's perennial mayor, James Michael Curley, in his prime: big-faced, always near-smiling, with a confident chirp, and a strut in his manner. Once in a while Aaron gets up during his story to imitate some dandy or cock-of-the-walk, with expert mimicry.

Frequently his narratives redound to his own advantage. Aaron has been an actor in many of the dramas he describes, and his own actions are no less remarkable than those of other giants from the past. He comes by his prowess honestly.

"My great-grandfather was a Huguenot." says Aaron. "He was put on board a French ship bound for America, and he and a fellow-prisoner were going to be hung within sight of the coast. The crew of twenty-seven got drunk on cognac, so my great-grandfather and the other man battened down the hatches, waited for them with marlin-spikes, and killed them one by one with the spikes as they came up. Then they made shore in a dinghy. Great-grandfather never got over it; he was a religious man, but he had to kill to save his life."

In the tough days of Iron River, this heritage of reluctant valor came in handy.

• A new fellow, Joe Shero, a Greek, came to town. He weighed two hundred pounds; I weighed a hundred and fifty-six — I didn't need any more.

He was peddling fine jewelry and spending money free. One night he picked up a girl at Iron River, and took her to Stambaugh to a dance. She walked off with someone. He went as far as Gaastra looking for her, and then when he came back to the dance, he had lost his horse too.

I had taken it to drive some girls home. I couldn't see his in the dark, but I knew every rig and everybody in town, so I borrowed one. When I came back he called me all kinds of names. I said, "It's too bad, mister, but I didn't mean any harm by it." He was upset though; he had had a bad evening. He called me an s.o.b., and took a wild swing at me. I wasn't there. He missed me the second time too. The third time his thumb caught me just under the eye; it closed up later.

I wasn't going to take that, so when he came again I gave it to him. I ketched him right on the breastbone, just below the neck. He went eight feet — eight feet. He landed on his back, on his neck and shoulders. He caved around, tried to catch his breath, tried to get on his hands and knees, but he couldn't make it. (He was lame for a week after.) So he asked his partner to go after me, but his partner knew me. So I tipped my hat and went off.

The redoubtable Aaron had once laid a ghost in a mine that had been terrifying the miners.

• This is a true ghost story that happened to me.

I was working in the mines, not on contract, about forty-four years ago. I heard there was a ghost up in the Riverton mine (named after John Todd Riverton of Cleveland) at Stambaugh. A man had been killed going up in the skip. Somebody crowded him, the first timber bumped him when he dropped down, the next timber cut his head right off.

This trouble happened between the first and second levels. The boys would tell how the ghost would get on the skip between levels and talk with Captain Harry Duff. He belonged on the second level; the third was the bottom. This here ghost went in on the second level, where the pumps were. The story goes that he kicked Joe White the pump man in the seat of the pants, took his dinner pail away from him, and ate it.

I said I didn't believe it. They said, "Work here and you'll see it." So I went to get a job there. I made friends with the shift boss so I could look around.

I had been working there a couple of weeks, looked at the pumps, at the place where the man had been killed, etcetera, etcetera. One hot summer night I lay down in the hot stinking dry house. It was a miserable place, the clothes all hanging on the steam pipes, steaming. I was on the night shift, and it was too hot to sleep during the day. Suddenly the cry came that the ghost was loose.

I took down a sharp pick from my locker, throwed it down into the skip, and jumped down. I went to the second level; the ghost belonged there. I was going down in the hole, when the fellows crowded back. A Cousin Jack said, "Don't go in there, the damme bloody ghoust is in there." I pushed them back, vaulted right out, grabbed the pick in one hand and a candle in the other (the candlestick was like a sword; the blacksmith made fancy ones, with nice tapered points to stick into the timber). As I walked down the drift they kept calling, "Don't go up, stay back here, we're going up."

A cling, c-l-i-n-g, was heard down the tunnel, as of a pick on a sharp rock; you could almost see the sparks. "The ghost must have hit rock," they were saying. To tell the truth I was at a tension, for I figured someone was in there. I threw my pick away on the dirt pile where I was working, and held the candle so they could see me throw it away. They yelled, "Don't throw it away, it's your only defense." But I had that candle stripped, and I meant business.

When I got to the last drift the sound changed. I held the light up, looked in and saw water dripping onto a big tin pan.

"You come on up, I've got him," I called. I held the can back in the drift, so they couldn't see what I was holding. My face was just as long as a fiddle. They heard the picking stop so they came up, scared stiff, sweating, pale as ghosts.

The crew on the second level was going to quit the mine. But after that the ghost was never seen again. When I finished out the month I went and got my time.

Aaron relates this as sober truth. In another story, however, he candidly states how he built up a too pallid hunting experience by enlarging it with a folk tale.

● Some cousins of mine in Maine had me go on a moose hunt, when I was up in New Brunswick. I bought an old felt hat, a sweater, and moccasin shoepacks, went off in the woods, picked up the trail of a moose, and snuck after him. I never made a sound, but my cousins came along and hollered out, "Here's a moose and a man after him." I was so sore I started to sweat, and it was the middle of winter.

I went off into the brush to get him on the way back. I kept so still I might have froze, but I didn't care; my legs were froze up to the knees anyway. I was afraid to move them because they would rattle. Finally I seen the moose's ear come out behind a leaf and I shot him.

Now that didn't make much of a story, so when they asked me how I got him I said: "I was waiting behind a tree when a cow moose came along and I shot it. Then I saw a blind bull right behind on her tail. But I had no bullets left — been shooting squirrels and partridges. So I cut the tail off the cow, and led the bull right back into town, tied it to the hitching post, went into the store and got some cartridges, came out and shot him.

CHARLIE GOODMAN

Grand Marais is the only harbor along a wild and lonely stretch of Lake Superior's southern shore for a hundred miles or so west of the Soo. At the turn of the century it bustled with lumberjacks and sailing ships; with the end of the white pine, and the withdrawal of the railroad, the town decayed, although it still boasts two beer gardens and six hundred hardy souls. Of these, none knows the intimate history of Grand Marais with the uncanny erudition of Charlie Goodman. For one reason, he is the second longest resident in Grand Marais, where he has lived since 1888. For another, he has a mnemonic genius and a flow of speech that men of books, dependent on others' words, can never possess.

Although eighty-three, Charlie is still athletic and springy in his walk and alert of mind. The good looks of his youth — and a photograph of Charlie at seventeen does much to substantiate his stories of triumphant romances — defy even the corrosions of age; his regular features and lean, economical frame mark him as a physical aristocrat, the pioneer hero in the flesh. He "baches" in a dingy, malodorous tarpaper shack on the edge of town, with a couple of dogs for company. Charlie knows to the last detail every event that has occurred in his north woods, from marine tragedies to lumbering operations; not a personality you can name but he has known him intimately; not a vocation of the outdoors but he has mastered it. In his sweeping, circumstantial narratives, Charlie himself assumes epic stature; for love of him, women have deserted homes and husbands; for fear of him, rowdies and law officers have cringed and fled; as a marksman, a hunter, a fighter, a lover, Charlie by his own testimony ranks with any champions of the heroic ages.

He was born in Erie, Pennsylvania, February 7, 1863, of a Dutch-Irish mother and an Irish father. His schooling was slight ("How long did you go to school, Charlie?" "Oh, I went once pretty near all week"), but his activities and jobs have been myriad. They run, in rough chronology, as follows: peeling tan bark; rafting logs down the Allegheny; traveling over the country demonstrating .22 and .44 caliber rifles for the Winchester Rifle manufacturers (he was on the American rifle team at the Chicago World's Fair in 1893); trapping beaver, otter, mink, fox, weasels, and wolves; hunting deer for the lumber camps; fishing commercially for whitefish and lake trout; picking and boating stone for bridge piers; straw push or boss over twenty-five to thirty men making log roads for wagons and sleighs; auto- and marine-engine mechanic and used-auto dealer. At one time he held seven town offices: deputy sheriff, constable, fire warden for the state, and fire chief for the town, lake captain, inspector of buildings and theaters, and town engineer.

Here is a handful of yarns in which Charlie portrays himself not unfavorably.

• I come here in the fall of '88. John Masse is the only fellow who was here then — he was three years old. His father, Old John, was the strongest man in Grand Marais. Old John would hitch up a dog and a pig to his sleigh and take his family to town. He could put a barrel of flour on his back and carry it home from downtown. Young John sold me a seven-hundred-pound single-cylinder marine engine — a Trusket — and we had to carry it from his farm out to the road to load on the wagon, about five hundred feet. We put it on a pole about ten foot long, four inches in diameter, and each took one end. About every ten feet he'd say, "Let's give her a rest, Charlie."

That was young John, and his father was stronger'n him.

That's how strong old John Masse was. Charlie modestly keeps himself in the background.

Game wardens were special anathema to Charlie, who made his living from the woods. After the wardens came around, about 1890, the lumber camps which Charlie supplied with venison put him on the books as a lumberjack and credited him with so many days' pay. He made sixty-nine and a half days for eight days' hunting, in January, 1898. A crafty warden once got the goods on Charlie. Sent up from Lansing to make a special investigation for the Department of Conservation, he represented himself as a Chicago newspaperman, asked for fresh meat for his sick wife, and took pictures of violators with deer and partridge. Brought into court Charlie pleaded, "I'm guilty and I can prove it." The city justice said, "I'll accept that plea." Charlie paid fifty dollars and costs, but no game warden ever got within talking distance of him again, for very long, as the following tale indicates. (Incidentally the above anecdote was given me not by Charlie but by the prosecuting attorney of Alger County, Ed O'Brien of Munising, who knows Charlie's reputation as the "best shot in the Upper Peninsula.")

• One thing I wouldn't be is a game warden. Every one of them is a violator; they get rich trapping beaver. I ran once from one and camped in the woods, but after that I let them do the running. Once three wardens followed me on snowshoes; I told them I'd shoot the goddamn snowshoes right out from under them.

In the winter of '95 a warden went after me. I was hunting for the Manistique and North Shore companies then. Bylo and I were living together, fifteen miles from town. We were off hunting — in February, out of season — when he came. Mrs. Bylo warned him not to follow such dangerous outlaws; she said we had killed hundreds of men. But he followed our tracks and met us coming back. I was dragging one deer, the dog another, Bylo another. He was wearing a dark blue uniform.

He stopped me and said, "I'm a deputy game warden."

I said, "You're a dead s.o.b."

I unstrapped my gun — a forty-five ninety Winchester — and the muzzle accidentally knocked all his front teeth out and knocked him down. His black mustache was all covered with blood. He hollered, "Don't shoot, I'm down."

The minute he spoke I see I had the advantage of him. His gun was strapped over his shoulder, I had mine on my shoulder, with my finger on the breech. He turned the lapel of his coat back to show the badge, when I knocked him over backwards. He had a hell of a time getting up — wasn't very good on snowshoes anyway.

He went back to Bylo's. Mrs. Bylo asked him, "Did you find him?" He said, "Yes." She said, "You look it." From there he walked six miles to Beaver, took the train to Seney, and had a doctor fix his mouth up. In the Harcourts' saloon he was telling them about it. [These were the famous Harcourts whose feud with the Dunns highlighted the blood and thunder days of Seney.] They said, "You're a lucky s.o.b. — you're the first warden ever went up after that fellow who got out alive."

I didn't mean to hit him, but he was so close to me. I never heard his name, or anything further about it.

Charlie had seen flaming Seney in all its infamy, and taken her worst in casual stride. He proved his mettle and joined the inner fraternity of Seney man-killers his very first night in town.

• In the fall of '88, the last of September, I came from the Soo to Grand Marais on a small barge bringing lumber to Burt and Gamble. I had three thousand dollars in my money belt, after staking two other fellows who were looking for a job. We walked from eight in the morning till eight or nine in the evening, and five miles barefooted in the sand. When we got to Seney I took a room in the hotel, felt pretty tired. I noticed there was no lock on the door, but the proprietor assured me no one would disturb me.

As I was laying down someone said, "Get out of bed, you s.o.b., or I'll pull you out." He'd been in the habit of coming in after everybody was in bed. I was all tangled up in the bed-clothes, but I got up and give him a wallop and knocked him end over end down the stairs. Then I went down and found the proprietor throwing him out. So I went and had a drink at the bar with Jack Liston, the proprietor — we afterwards became good friends — and then took a walk around town; I was all wide awake then. I heard a big commotion in one saloon and went in. There was the fellow I had knocked downstairs, telling the Harcourts what had happened. His name was Mike O'Donnell — I later found out he was a tough nut.* He pointed at me and said,

* 'Stub Foot' O'Donnell was a notorious Seney tough. See e.g., *Michigan: A Guide to the Wolverine State* (New York, 1946), p. 560.

"That's the feller, the youngest of the three that walked from Grand Marais. Better watch out when you're in front of him."

I bought drinks all around — whiskey was only ten cents a glass then. (If you was a good fellow in Seney you was well liked, but if you was a tightwad they'd stand you on your head and spend your money for you.) Then I wandered into the back where there was a poker game going on, and took a fellow's hand. We played till three a.m. and then all went over to the sporting house. I won a hundred and twenty dollars. That was my first night in Seney.

I've stayed up two or three weeks on end. Now the more I sleep the more I need. I sleep five or six hours now — only used to sleep three.

Charlie's amatory exploits transcend fable. He ravished women's hearts like a Greek god — but his conquests lacked the true celestial note.

• I got a dose traveling somewhere hunting up in the Adirondacks, and went to Dr. Colwell in Ridgway. While talking with him I see the best-looking woman I ever see come down a winding stair. I kind of waved and she waved back. That was Thursday. I thought about her a couple of days. Sunday I took a walk past the church; there were farmers' horses and sulkies outside. This woman, his wife, come along and says, "Charlie, will you do me a favor? I'll go to hell with you if you want me to. Dr. Colwell is in the third pew there in the rear. Will you tap him on the shoulder and tell him he's wanted at John Polley's?" I told him, and he beat me out the church. She took me by the arm and we went back to the house, and we got acquainted damn quick.

I hung to her for fifteen months. She had three hundred and fifty thousand dollars in the bank, and an income of a thousand dollars a month. That was the only time I was a gentleman. She bought me nine suits of clothes, at sixty dollars a suit. We traveled everywhere there was a summer resort. I was eighteen then, she was twenty and a half.

One time the Colwell widow and I was going to Ogdensburg, and we got snowbound ten days in Herkimer, New York. We had to stay on the train, and this Mary helped cook for us. She was a hell of a sweet looker; her father owned most of the town. She said, "I'll go any place you want to go, in the United States or Canada or Mexico." I said I couldn't very well handle two women. So she said, "Wherever you go, if you want me, send for me." Later I wrote her from Seney, and went and brought her back to the whorehouse. We got off the train together, and all the jacks followed her. She made forty dollars her first night in Seney. The first few weeks she got all the business. (The girls got half the money you know. Then they had one night of their own — they could have a lover that night if they wanted to.)

It didn't do me any good, but I had a goddamn good-looking woman whenever I wanted her. She worked there two years steady, and then got stuck on some guy and went away with him.

I never got married, but I bought a couple of women. Once I bought a boy twelve years old, and the father threw his mother in. A fellow named Theodore run away with a Belgian woman from Gladstone. She came into my place one day saying, "My husband's come up and he's going to kill me." Then her husband came in with a knife. He told me he didn't want her any more because she'd run off with Theodore, but he needed money to get back to Gladstone, and if I'd buy the boy I could have the woman. So I drew up a little contract, that he wouldn't molest her any more. The woman and the boy stayed with me that winter. Then she went off to Belgium in the spring; said she was coming back, but the war broke out then. Theodore was off in the woods; I never saw him again. The husband came back a second time and hung himself.

When she had her hair done up — it took her an hour — it looked as if she had a hat on. [And Charlie showed me a photograph of an attractive woman with a turban of her own hair.]

There was a family in town that had been hoodwinked out of their money, and I helped them along. The wife was a good looker; I gave her twenty dollars. One Sunday morning their boy comes over and tells me, "Unc', she wants to see you." I asked him, "Where are you going?" He said, "Down the road to look for huckleberries." I went over and she says, "Before my husband left this morning he said to me, 'Anything that Charlie wants you give to him. He's been too good to us.'" "Well, what have you got?" "Just what God gave me." "Well, let's see it." So that's how we became acquainted.

Fittingly enough, Charlie lived on ground hallowed by his heroic romancing. Where now stood his sullen shack, once rose an animated whorehouse. Thereby hangs another tale, which Charlie pleases to call

Seven Dining Room Girls and No Boarders

• Dave Tie and I were coming back from Sucker Lake with our furs in December, fifty-seven years ago. We got to the edge of Grand Marais, and stopped at the first house we came to. The landlady said, "Come in." We stayed there three days.

She asked us if we had had supper. I said, "No," so she had her seven dining room girls give us some. Then I said, "Dave, it would be nice if we had some whiskey." One of the girls said, "My husband always makes me bring home a bottle of whiskey. He's off in a lumber camp out of town now." Then another said the same thing. (They didn't any of them have any men — they just said that for an excuse.) We had three bottles of whiskey — it only cost a dollar a quart then. Next day it was snowing, so we stayed over, drinking whiskey, and all the loving we wanted.

Furs were the same as cash then, so we paid part of the bill in fur. The landlady wanted four beaver hides. (A weasel was fifteen cents, muskrat twenty-five cents, mink two dollars, beaver four dollars, cow two dollars, horse two dollars.) You could make change up to ten or fifteen cents. I spent about fifty dollars in the three days, and my partner spent more. When we were going, the landlady said, "Part of your change is in the woodshed." There were two cowhides there, frozen to the floor. I cut them away

with an axe. But they were too heavy to carry, so we went in to
town and I met Tom Ricopell driving a small wood sleigh. I asked
him what he'd take for the use of it, for an hour or so, as I had
some change down at the sporting house I wanted to take to
market. He said he wouldn't take anything for it. We pried the
cowhides loose, loaded up the furs, and pulled the sled back to
town.

A photographer from the Detroit *News* met us — the first one
ever up here — and asked us who we were and what we were doing. Then he took a picture of us with his tripod, and printed it
later in the paper, as "Charlie Goodman and Dave Tie on their
way to market with a load of furs."

Then he asked for a hotel. We told him of the boarding-house
we had stopped at where there were seven dining room girls and
no boarders. He went back with us that night.

The house broke up when one of the girls, Maggie Burns, shot
the landlord, Mahoney. She was tried at Au Train, and cleared,
pleaded self-defense.

My shack is on the same spot. The toilet out back is on one
corner of the old foundation.

JOHN HALLEN

The raconteur of personal history need not be a swashbuckler
to perform prodigies. He may possess superior psychical as well
as physical endowments.

When I asked for a room at an unpretentious hotel in Manistique, John Hallen, the owner and clerk, looked at me intently,
and I returned his gaze in kind. John was a nervous, bald-headed
Swede on the heavy side; his wide blue eyes, mystic's eyes, and
permanent dimples gave him an uncommon look. Later that day
he revealed to me esoteric facts about his history because, he
said, on meeting me he had immediately felt the vibrations.

John had left Warberg, Sweden, in 1906 at the age of twenty-
six and lived in New York and Pennsylvania. He has various tal-
ents; in one corner of the lobby stood an intricate ship model,

designed by his own hand, a model of the last convict ship to sail the seas, which he had once had dreams of resailing; he sang Swedish folk songs in a high, gentle voice, impromptu in the midst of his Old Country reminiscences. But his chief gift was a sense for the vibrations, which had affected the course of his life.

• I believe in vibrations. How else can you reach God, millions of miles up? We used to have seventy-nine men rooming in the hotel and I could tell about a man by his step. There was one for instance who would just go tip-tip-tip. Sometimes I can tell by a man's hand on a doorknob.

It was the vibrations that brought me here. I was in Erie, Pennsylvania, running a small contracting business, and I had hay fever awfully bad, in my nose, my ears, my throat. It was hell — I feel sorry for all hay fever sufferers. I even went to Buffalo to try to get a cure. Finally an Irish woman told me to see a German doctor there, over eighty, and he told me to get out of that climate. "Get out or you'll die." I could feel the vibrations very strong then.

Then downtown I saw a railroad car in the siding where a gypsy [Hallen pronounced the "g" hard] woman was telling fortunes. She was a high-class gypsy, about fifty, diamonds all over her neck, with beautiful features, clear, carved. I could feel the vibrations when I went in. Her body sweated, she tried so hard; she went into a — what you call it — with her eyes closed. She said, "You suffer very bad, very bad, right now." (It was in August, when the hay fever was worst.) "But you are going away, and you will work in a place where millions of dollars of business was translated [sic]." She kept saying, "Going — going — where are you going? Your sickness will get better there."

I took my wife and two children and got in the car and drove. I didn't know where I was going. One day in the barber's chair in Petoskey (Michigan) I heard someone say he had shot a lot of deer. I asked where. He said, "The Upper Peninsula." I'd never heard of it. So we drove up and my hay fever was getting better. When we got to Manistique there was no place to live, but I stopped outside a place with a painted-flower vase (all Swedes have that), and I said to my wife, "I feel in the vibrations that a Scandinavian lives here." And it was Larson — I've bought meat from him for twenty-five years. And they helped us out, found us a place at Indian Lake.

I was going down the street, and I asked a little man where I could buy a spool of twine. He pointed out the store to me, and we walked down to it, and I told him my story. And he pointed across the way to a building. "That's mine and I'm going to sell it to you," he said. His name was Leo Harman, and that was the center of all the lumbering business. He had ten clerks working for him. He sold it to me for sixty-three hundred dollars, one dollar down payment. He put a mortgage on it and sold it to the bank, and I paid the bank. That was the Chicago Lumber Company, and it has been my hotel ever since. That was in 1917.

Hallen then went on to explain that his instinct for the vibrations, rather than the gypsy's gift of prophecy, had enabled him to foresee the happy turn of events. He gave further instances of his power, and of that of his mother. But his father never possessed the true instinct, and in following a deluded vision ruined his fortune.

• I don't believe in fortune-telling, except when there are vibrations. Down at Escanaba at the Salvation Army I told a girl, "You're going to get a job offer right away." And in two minutes the telephone rang.

You had an offer — one offer — to change your business, very recently. Haven't you? [And Hallen bored his face into mine severely, and a little eagerly. The fact was I had received an offer from another university just a couple of weeks before.]

I believe in phrenology too. Jack Dempsey looks like a tiger. I saw him dancing around as a referee. He rips up and down with his gloves. Wilson looks like a mule — look how stubborn he was at Paris. Taft looks like an elephant.

[To show where he drew the line between sound and unsound instinct Hallen pointed the moral of his father's tragedy.]

My father had a very good business, quarrying; he employed one hundred men. But he had a dream about a perpetual motion machine, and he let his business go, to work on it. He had a stone at the top, and it went down back and forth on springs, and when it got to the bottom it shot up to the top again. He had it going for six months once. The owner of the "Tageblatt" financed him. The English government was going to buy it. But he lost everything he had, and we had to put him in a poorhouse, and he died there.

In Sweden on Christmas the poor people always have to eat — svagdricka (home brew), lutfisk (dried fish), rice pudding, bruga beer. We were sitting down in our room in the poorhouse, and my mother said, "Everyone is here but Karl." Just then there was a knock on the door and Karl came in from the ship, with a big turkey on his back full of presents. He was blond and tall, like you. Oh, we had a good time.

He stayed there in Warberg for a couple of months, didn't get a job. So he mustered out again. My mother threw her arms around him and said, "I'll never see you again." (The vibrations.) And weeks, months, years went by, we never saw him again. We wrote to the captain and the company, but never heard anything.

What about these stories, how do they fit into the patterns of folklore? They are not folk tales in any accepted sense, although it may be noted that all the storytellers did know some traveled tales. Neither again are they chronicles for the conventional historian, who would reject their extravagant touches in favor of the sober, deadly accounts of pioneer home-building. These are, I would say, folk narratives, folk documents of a sort, filled with the raw stuff of life and filtered through imaginative minds. All these narrators were intensely sincere; all were mentally keen; they are folk historians on the highest level, precise in fact, but seeing experience in heroic and fantastic outlines.

APPENDIX

NOTES ON THE TALES

While there have been no previous folklore studies of the Upper Peninsula, a number of books dealing with the area inescapably include references to its brawling legends and salty characters. The most skillful literary use of local lore, chiefly from Marquette County where their author served as prosecuting attorney, comes in two volumes of stories by Robert Traver, *Troubleshooter* (Viking Press, New York, 1944) and *Danny and the Boys* (World Publishing Company, Cleveland and New York, 1951), books which belong on the same shelf with George W. Harris, Rowland Robinson, Mark Twain, and such writers who drew upon the folkways and folk types of their regions. John Bartlow Martin's *Call It North Country* (Alfred A. Knopf, New York, 1945) is a reportorial job that conveys some sense of local history and flavor. *This Ontonagon Country* by James K. Jamison (The Ontonagon Herald, Ontonagon, Michigan), concentrates on one county. Biographies, autobiographies, and reminiscences often contain traditional material, and in this category can be listed Ralph D. Williams, *The Honorable Peter White* (Penton Publishing Company, Cleveland, c. 1905), an older account of a well known Peninsula personality around whom legends have gathered; and Chase S. Osborn, *The Iron Hunter* (The Macmillan Co. New York, 1919), a personal history by another Peninsula figure of heroic stature. Stewart Holbrook's human histories of lumbering and iron mining, *Holy Old Mackinaw* (The Macmillan Company, New York, 1938), and *Iron Brew* (The Macmillan Company, New York, 1939), have sections on the Upper Peninsula. For the lore and life of the copper miners in the Keweenaw Peninsula, Angus Murdoch's *Boom Copper* (The Macmillan Company, New York, 1943) deserves praise.

THE BACKGROUND OF THIS BOOK

Spike Horn's tale (p. 3), combines both a tall tale and a superstition. The elastic properties of buckskin breeches form the basis of the frontier story, "Where Joe Meriweather Went To," *Polly Peablos-*

som's Wedding, ed. T. A. Burke (Phila., c. 1851), pp. 114–118, where Joe's drying breeches gradually elevate him toward the sunset. The belief that things grow in the light of the moon and die in the dark of the moon is old in folklore; see e.g. Timothy Harley, *Moon Lore* (London, 1885), pp. 177ff.

PART I: THE INDIAN TRADITION

CHAPTER 1: INDIANS STUFFED AND LIVE

A large literature surrounds the Ojibwa Indian nation, who have benefited from descriptions by the Jesuit Fathers in the seventeenth century, and in the nineteenth by Henry Rowe Schoolcraft and his friend, the poet Longfellow. The scientific recording of Indian — and in fact of nonliterate — tales began with Schoolcraft, the first Agent of Indian Affairs for the federal government, whose meatiest collection, *The Myth of Hiawatha* (Philadelphia, 1856) deserves a high place in American literature, for Schoolcraft wrote down Ojibwa narratives with sympathy and art. A useful collative and bibliographic aid is A. Irving Hallowell's "Concordance of Ojibwa Narratives in the Published Works of Henry R. Schoolcraft", *Journal of American Folklore*, LIX (1946), 136–153. The vexed question of Longfellow's debts to Schoolcraft and the *Kalevala* produced a bulky volume by Chase and Stellanova Osborn, *Schoolcraft-Longfellow-Hiawatha* (Lancaster, Pa., 1942), that brings together the pertinent materials, and contains the authentic flavor of the Peninsula. In "The Indian Legend of Hiawatha," *Publications of the Modern Language Association*, XXXVII (1922), 128–140, Stith Thompson points out Longfellow's addition of New York Iroquois elements and his prettifying of the raw Ojibwa plots. This should be supplemented with Waino Nyland, "*Kalevala* as a Reputed Source of Longfellow's *Song of Hiawatha*," *American Literature*, XXII (1950), 1–20, which demonstrates that the metrical form of Hiawatha does not imitate the *Kalevala*.

A number of ethnographic collections of Ojibwa tales are available. A superior work is *Ojibwa Texts*, collected by William Jones, edited by Truman Michelson (Publications of the American Ethnological Society, vols. VII and VIII, Part I, Leyden, 1917; Part II, New York, 1919) which sets the Indian and English texts side by side. Of their style Jones writes:

The language of most of the material is conversational; the periods are short; sentences colloquial, seldom sustained, and often loose and incoherent. Vagueness of reference is common. The unconscious assumption on the part of the narrator that one is familiar with the background of a narrative, is one cause why so many of the statements, when taken as they stand, are unintelligible. This vagueness of effect is helped along by the tendency to abbreviate expression, — such as the frequent occurrence of a quotation without mention of the speaker, and the presence of subjects and objects without verbs, — thus rendering sentences often extremely elliptical. (I, xi–xii).

This was not my experience. Jones is commenting on transliterated English texts, while I heard the tales rendered in facile English by the best of possible translators — the bilingual Indians themselves. On one occasion, when George Cadotte was interpreting the stories of John Pete, I beheld the subtle operation at work before me, and no listener could complain about unintelligibility or disjointedness. Admittedly some knowledge of the Indian mind is necessary to make plausible such narrative elements as the power of the Thunders or the human affinity with animals, in the same way that one must understand American business methods to appreciate jokes about the traveling salesman. Only when the ex-baseball player, Archie Megenuph, obviously an unpracticed raconteur, tried to tell me stories, did they appear pointless and confused.

Comprehensive lists of Ojibwa tale collections can be found in Charles Haywood, *A Bibliography of North American Folklore and Folksong* (New York, c. 1951), pp. 834–841, and in the reference note by Stith Thompson in *PMLA*, XXXVII (1922), 12–13. The best general discussion of Indian storytelling is in Thompson's *The Folktale* (New York, 1946), part III, "The Folktale in a Primitive Culture: North American Indian." Personal narratives and histories written by educated Indians complement anthropological reports; three useful writings of this sort are Andrew J. Blackbird, *History of the Ottawa and Chippewa Indians of Michigan* (Ypsilanti, Michigan, 1887); Peter Jones, *History of the Ojebway Indians* (London, 1861); and William W. Warren, *History of the Ojibways* (Collections of the Minnesota Historical Society, V, St. Paul, 1885). The early descriptions of white travelers frequently contain informative insights into Ojibwa life and traditions; of these the most valuable is J. G. Kohl, *Kitchi-Gami; Wanderings Round Lake Superior*, translated by Lascelles Wraxall (London, 1860).

Turning to the specific themes of my material, certain references should be noted. The romantic or tourist type of Indian legend, such as the "Big Spring," although a bastard kind of folklore, deserves some study in its own right. A number of examples are given in my *Jona-*

than Draws the Long Bow (Harvard University Press, Cambridge, 1946), pp. 138–156. Another interaction between Indian and white storymaking occurs in humorous tales, both jests and tall tales. For jests see my "Comic Indian Anecdotes," *Southern Folklore Quarterly*, X (1946), 113–128. No one has looked into tall tales, although the exaggerations of Iagoo that Schoolcraft reports (*Algic Researches*, first series, New York, 1839, vol. II, 229–232; *The Myth of Hiawatha, op. cit.*, pp. 85–87) certainly show the red man's talent in this direction. The similar ways in which Winabijou and Paul Bunyan design the American landscape might well be analyzed. For this general topic see W. J. Harsha, "The Sense of Humor among Indians," *Southern Workman*, XXXIX (1910, Hampton, Virginia), 504–505; Horace P. Beck, "Indian Humor," *Pennsylvania Archaeologist*, XIX (1949), 54–60.

The reservations at Lac Vieux Desert and Hannahville have been described by anthropologists. W. Vernon Kinietz (whose *The Indians of the Western Great Lakes, 1615–1760*, Ann Arbor, 1940, is a useful handbook for the whole area) portrays the former in close detail in *Chippewa Village* (Bloomfield Hills, Michigan, c. 1947), and mentions my friends, the patriarch John Pete and George Cadotte. Even in the relatively few years since his field study, the forest community has shrunk away, and gradually shifted its base to Watersmeet. Kenneth E. Tiedke has recently written *A Study of the Hannahville Indian Community (Menominee County, Michigan)*, Michigan State College Agricultural Experiment Station (Special Bulletin 369, April 1951), in terms of its social and economic status. These studies paint in the backgrounds of such storytellers as John Pete and Alec Philemon, although their narrative genius has gone unnoticed.

CHAPTER 2: BEARWALKERS

The bearwalk tradition suggests, of course, the *loup-garou* belief of the French or the witch transformations of the English, and testifies to the universal identity of certain folklore ideas. Andrew Lang would have appreciated this evidence, and actually in his columns in Longman's Magazine, "At the Sign of the Ship" (1885–1905), he frequently referred to the world-wide notion of "the fire that heralds death," into which the flame-breathing bearwalker neatly fits. The bearwalker differs from other Ojibwa sorcerers in possessing bad power, or rather in using his power in antisocial ways, in contrast with the socially respected power-wielders belonging to the select Midéwiwin Lodge. (See Walter J. Hoffman, *The Midéwiwin or "Grand Medicine Society" of the Ojibwa*, Seventh Annual Report of the

Bureau of Ethnology, Washington, 1891, pp. 143–300). Dreaming and its rôle in Chippewa life are described by Frances Densmore in her *Chippewa Customs* (Bureau of American Ethnology, Bulletin 86, Washington, 1929), pp. 78–86; and Schoolcraft devoted a long note to Ojibwa fasting and dreaming (*Myth of Hiawatha, op. cit.*, pp. 25–26).

Preparations and potions for inducing love are common in the folklore of many peoples. The *Handwörterbuch des Deutschen Aberglaubens* has a general article on love magic (V, 1279–1297, "Liebeszauber"), and Jacob Grimm treats the theme in his *Teutonic Mythology* (translated from the 4th ed. by James S. Stallybrass, London, 1883), III, 1101–1102. Frances Densmore encountered love powders and love amulets in her field work with the Ojibwa (*Chippewa Customs*, p. 108).

CHAPTER 3: TRICKSTERS AND THUNDERS

The tales of Winabijou and Iktomi belong to the trickster culture-hero cycle which spreads among all the Indian nations of the New World. An early recognition of this dual role, marred by his solar mythology, is D. G. Brinton's "The Hero-God of the Algonkins as a Cheat and a Liar," in *Essays of an Americanist* (Phila., 1890), pp. 130–134. Different versions of the Deluge story are compared by Alexander F. Chamberlain, "Nanibozhu amongst the Otchipwe, Mississagas, and other Algonkian Tribes," *Journal of American Folklore*, IV (1891), 193–213. J. Owen Dorsey discusses the affinity between Winabijou and Iktomi in "Nanibozhu in Siouan Mythology," *idem*, V (1892), 293–304, and Martha W. Beckwith enlarges his data about Iktomi and his cognates in her "Mythology of the Oglala Dakota," *idem*, XLIII (1930), 339–442. She remarks, "The lying tales I gathered to be the Iktomi stories. They ordinarily open with the words 'Iktomi was traveling' . . . Most Iktomi stories current among the men are of such a character that my informants refused to repeat them to me . . . ." (p. 340) A good deal of the humor in the trickster stories does strike the same chords as our own smoking-car variety, but the Indian narratives are much more skillfully contrived; the well-known tale of "Iktomi and the Fruits," which apparently was not told to Miss Beckwith, grows naturally out of the forest scene, and no doubt taught Indian youths useful lessons about overeating on strange berries. Another widely spread tale, of which I collected an Ojibwa version, has Winabijou attempting the seduction of his own daughter, with laughable complications and discomfitures in robust Chaucerian vein. (See the detailed comparative study of Henrietta Shoemaker, "Trickster Marries His Daughter," in the *Journal of American Folklore*, XLIV, 1931, 196–207.)

For variant texts and comparative references to the culture-hero trickster tales given here see Stith Thompson, *Tales of the North American Indians* (Harvard University Press, Cambridge, 1928), as follows:

"The Wolf is Killed"; cf. Manabozho's Wolf Brother, pp. 10–11, and note 23 pp. 277–278, *Hero drowned by water-spirits.*

"Winabijou looks for the Wolf"; cf. Manabozho plays Lacrosse, pp. 11–14, note 26, p. 278, *Transformation to kill enemies* (D651), note 57, pp. 286–287, *Deluge* (A1010), and note 30, p. 279, *Earth Diver* (A81Z).

"The Duck Dinner"; cf. Manabozho's Adventures, C and D, pp. 54–56, and note 82, pp. 295–296, *Hoodwinked dancers* (K826), note 83, p. 296, *Buttocks watcher* (D999,D1317.3), and note 84, pp. 296–297, *Sleeping trickster's feast stolen* (J2194).

"Winabijou Goes West"; cf. Glooscap, pp. 5–8, note 17, p. 276, *Deity grants requests to visitors* (A575), and note 18, p. 276, *Immoderate request punished* (Q339) and 18a, *Modest choice rewarded* (L200).

"Iktomi and the Fruits"; see note 109h, p. 303, *Trickster eats medicines that physic him* (J2153), and note 109k, p. 304, *Trickster eats scratchberries* (J2154).

Episode A in Manabozho's Adventures (pp. 53–54), in which he dives under the flock of geese, ties their feet with basswood bark, and then is borne aloft when they fly away, was told by Alec Philemon as a variant ending to the Duck Dinner; his daughter commented, "I've heard you tell that another way." (See Type 1881 and Motif X916, The Man Carried Through the Air by Geese. William Gilmore Simms uses this motif in his literary tall tale, "How Sharp Snaffles Got his Capital, his Gun and his Wife.") Chief Welsh gave me the Teton Dakota variant of the Duck Dinner in its regular form. Alec Philemon chanted Winabijou's song to the ducks, "Quay, quake shimoke, quay, quake shimoke," according to my ear; Frances Densmore gives words and music in her *Chippewa Music* (Bureau of American Ethnology, Bulletin 45, Washington 1910), p. 206.

One theme I found prevalent among the Peninsula traditions, although only one example is here printed, concerns the monsters, serpents, or lions known to the Ojibwa as the Mizhi-bizi and the Windigoes, who terrorize the land, but are in turn defeated by the Thunderbirds on high. A local legend of a mysterious underwater creature who abducts a baby from a cradle-board, and is later ferreted out of his lair with his dam by the tribe's wizards, still thrives in the Lake

Superior areas. I heard variants from Mike Sogwin, Mrs. Feathers, Alec Philemon, John Pete — in fact practically all my major storytellers — and Jake Duggan the Sioux told me of a monster at the bottom of Stillwater Lake in Minnesota. Sogwin said the serpent's tail had been broken off by a paddler in a canoe it attacked, and that pieces of the tail circulated among his friends at a premium, because of their amuletic quality. (See William Jones, "Ojibwa Tales from the North Shore of Lake Superior," *Journal of American Folklore*, XXIX 1916, 387, "The Women and the Great Lynx.") This *Sage* particularly arouses interest from its similarity with the Bearson tale, in its Beowulf and other forms. The most dramatic Thunders tale I heard, from the lips of Alec Philemon, dealt with a band of redheaded Indians who journeyed to the very home of the Thunders, on a distant mountain, where, after various trials, they discovered a nest of the little Thunderbirds. A. F. Chamberlain refers to this story in "The Thunder-bird Amongst the Algonkins," *American Anthropologist*, o.s. III (1890), 51–54, where he concludes that the Algonkin and Siouan beliefs about the serpents and thunders run closely parallel, and deserve study, a conclusion that my own experience supports.

Scholarly recognition that Old World *Märchen* had penetrated Indian repertoires dates from Stith Thompson's "European Tales among the North American Indians," *Colorado College Publication*, Language Series, vol. II, no. 34 (Colorado Springs, 1919), 319–471, which maps a score of such invasions. Chief Welsh's "Toad-Story" belongs in this category, being a version of Type 425, The Search for the Lost Husband, combined with the Cinderella motif of the slippers test for the prince, and the whole completely Indianized, even to the faithful description of Teton Dakota burial customs. Thompson reports this tale as hitherto collected only from the New Mexico Zuni among nonliterate peoples (*The Folktale*, p. 99).

Alec Philemon told me two further *Märchen* (not included here) with interesting variations. His example of Type 708, "The Wonder-Child," has the princess drink a teacup of cat's urine and give birth to a cat, who then rescues her from the mausoleum in which the king has immured her, gets a job on a ship, compels the captain to promise to marry his mother, and finally is whipped out of his cat skin by the king and turns into a handsome young man. Thompson comments on the limited distribution of this story — Scandinavia, Hungary, and Brittany — and its nonappearance in literary form (*The Folktale*, pp. 124–125). Philemon also related in detail Type 506A, The Rescued Princess (*The Folktale*, pp. 50–51, and A. Irving Hallowell, "Some

European Folktales of the Berens River Saulteaux," *Journal of American Folklore*, LII, 1939, 167–170). Alec recognised the provenience of this tale by saying with a chuckle, "That's a white man's story," but the obvious affinities between the magic of the *Märchen* and the "power" of the Indian fictions readily explains the appeal of fairy tales to the Indian mind.

Some Indian "romances" rather closely resemble the *Märchen*, with their indefinite time-settings, their supernatural atmosphere, and the close relationships in their plots between human beings and animals. Of this class I have given here only one instance, "Stink Lake," but others are in my notebooks; Alec Philemon told me of a woman who changed into a lion, and the man who courted a deer; Chief Welsh related a graphic tale of two boys born of a bear mother. For an analogous text and references to "Stink Lake," cf. The Son-in-Law Tests, in Thompson, *Tales of the North American Indians*, pp. 113–116 and note 170, pp. 324–325 (H310) and note 172, p. 325, *Ogre's Own moccasins burned* (K1615). The Timagami Ojibwa storyteller in the above text refers more politely than Alec Philemon to the malodorous water as "Burnt Moccasins Lake."

PART II: THE EUROPEAN TRADITION

CHAPTER 4: CANADIENS

The roots of French-Canadian folklore in the Upper Peninsula lie at first remove in the province of Quebec in Canada, and at second remove in France, especially in Brittany, whence the first habitants emigrated. A fine view of French-Canadian tradition can be gained from the new annual journal, *Les Archives de Folklore*, published at Laval University under the editorship of Luc Lacourcière (1946–). The extent and range of French-Canadian materials, which "seem to surpass the present-day resources of the motherland," are systematically outlined by Marius Barbeau in three articles on "Canadian Folklore" printed in the *French Folklore Bulletin* (New York) for November, 1945, February–March, 1946, and June, 1946, and separately issued as a sixteen page pamphlet. An excellent picture of Canadien storytelling which shows the general North American tendency toward tall tales, and also the overlap between the fantastic *conte* and the fabulous tall story, is given by William P. Greenough in *Canadian Folk-Life and Folk-Lore* (New York, 1897), ch. 4, "Amusements — Contes and Raconteurs," pp. 45–66. This chapter presents the tales of a conteur, Nazaire, who tells well-known frontier brags of hunting and shooting, along with regular *Märchen*. Nazaire's account of a notorious big eater closely parallels personal legends I collected in the Peninsula.

In Canadian story-telling there is a universal tendency to exaggeration that the listener soon learns to take into account . . . . Nazaire is fond of comparing our appetites in camp to that of the man (whose name and residence he gives) who was in the habit of eating a six-pound loaf of bread at noon while waiting for his dinner. He lived to be 105 years old, but is supposed to have died from having eaten at one meal three pan-cakes of the full size of a large frying pan and an inch thick, with an immense piece of fat pork imbedded in each. (p. 59)

Another collection from Quebec close in character to my material is Paul A. W. Wallace's *Baptiste Larocque: Legends of French Canada* (Toronto, c. 1923), which contains *Sagen* of the *loup-garou*, the *fifol-et*, the dance with the devil, and *contes* of Ti-Jean. Although Max Duhaim seems not to have entered print, feats of other Canadien strong men are retold in books: see Benjamin Sulte, *Histoire de Jos. Monteferrand* (Montreal, 1912), and A. N. Montpetit, *Nos Hommes Forts* (Quebec, 1884). The popularity of the tradition of the Chasse Galerie in Quebec is attested by H. Beaugrand, in *La Chasse Galerie and other Canadian Stories*, simultaneously published in French as *La Chasse Galerie — Légendes Canadiennes* (Montreal, 1900). He says of the story he reprints:

The narrative is founded on a popular superstition dated back to the days of the *coureurs des bois*, under the French regime, and perpetuated among the *voyageurs* in the Canadian Northwest. The shantymen of a later date have taken up the tradition, and it is in the French settlements, bordering the St. Lawrence River, that the legends of *la chasse-galerie* are specially well known at the present time. The writer has met many an old *voyageur* who affirmed most positively that he had seen bark canoes traveling in mid-air, full of men paddling and singing away, under the protection of Beelzebub, on their way from the timber camps of the Ottawa to pay a flying visit to their sweethearts at home. (p. 9)

Beaugrand speaks of the lutins in *New Studies of Canadian Folk Lore* (Montreal, n.d.), "The Goblin Lore of French Canada," pp. 9–22. An amusing account of a witless French-Canadian youth who tried to "sell the black hen" to the Devil appears in the *Proceedings and Transactions of the Royal Society of Canada*, Third Series, vol. XIII (1920), section I, 87–94, by Jules Tremblay, *"La vente de la poule noire (Anecdote canadienne)."*

Little has been done to record French-Canadian folklore in the United States, although a great deal certainly exists in northern New England and in the Great Lakes area. Harold W. Thompson gives accounts of the *loup-garou* and the *chasse-galerie* as they survive in New York, in *Body, Boots and Britches* (Philadelphia, 1940), pp. 115–118. Joseph M. Carrière demonstrated the striking survival of French fairy tales in a Missouri village, in *Tales from the French Folk-Lore of Missouri* (Evanston and Chicago, 1937). The same author surveys "The Present State of French Folklore Studies in North America" in the *Southern Folklore Quarterly*, X (December, 1946), 219–226.

The two *Märchen* of Trefflé Largenesse given here belong to Type 313 IIIc and 314 IVa, Obstacle Flight, and Types 1060–1114, Contest between Man and Ogre (Antti Aarne and Stith Thompson, *The Types of the Folk-Tale*, Helsinki, 1928). Trefflé's version of The Obstacle Flight modernizes the magic objects thrown in the path of the dragon; Frank Valin's Finnish text (in Chapter 6) gives the older form. For the variations in the objects in texts around the world, see the long list compiled by Johannes Bolte and Georg Polívka, *Anmerkungen zu den Kinder u. Hausmärchen der Bruder Grimm*, II (Leipzig, 1915), 140–146. An Americanized version of Tit-Jean's contest with the giant from the British tradition in Virginia and the Carolinas has been collected by Richard Chase, in *The Jack Tales* (Boston and New York, 1943), "Jack in the Giants' Newground." Many Tit-Jean stories appear in the series of "Contes Populaires Canadiens" which has run occasionally in the *Journal of American Folklore* from 1916 to 1950 (see the note in LXIII, 199). Trefflé told a number of other *contes*, some concerned with Tit-Jean and some independent types, like 326, The Youth Who Wanted to Learn What Fear Is. His crony, Charles Rivard, whom I found sitting on the steps with him, also told *contes*, giving a fine version of Type 1360 C, Old Hildebrand, and two jests from the group ridiculing parsons (see Stith Thompson, *The Folk Tale*, New York, 1946, pp. 212–214). Aunt Jane Goudreau too told me a parson joke, Type 1739, "The Parson and the Calf," although the priest had disappeared from her text (printed in *Western Folklore*, VI, 1947, 27).

On the subject of *Märchen*, I might say here that during my field trip I collected examples from five different groups, the Canadian-French, Finnish, Italian, Polish, and Indian. Some of these American importations help fill in the picture of a folktale's diffusion; for instance, Sam Colasacco, the Italian saloonkeeper, told me Type 735,

"The Rich Man's and the Poor Man's Fortune" (not included here) which Stith Thompson has reported as unknown outside Estonia and Lithuania (*The Folktale*, 142). The outstanding *Märchen* teller I met was Joe Woods of Crystal Falls, who related to me detailed texts of The Princess on the Glass Mountain, The Master Thief, and other traditional fairy tales, besides *novelle*, jests, heroic legends, and moral tales. (None of these are printed here; see my "Polish Wonder Tales of Joe Woods," and "Polish Tales from Joe Woods," *Western Folklore*, VIII, January and April, 1949, 25–52, 131–145.)

Dialect stories represent another fertile category in which I have given here only a small selection of what came my way. My article in the *Journal of American Folklore*, "Dialect Stories of the Upper Peninsula; A New Form of American Folklore," LI (April–June, 1948), 113–150, gives eighty-four texts, mainly French, Finnish, and Cornish, with some Swedish and Italian, which thus conform to the major ethnic strains in the Peninsula. It is the close mixture of these foreign-born groups with native-born Americans in upper Michigan that makes the dialect story so prevalent there, but the situation is characteristically American and the dialect tale undoubtedly flourishes in similar areas. In September, 1950, I heard recordings at Salt Lake City, from the archives of the Utah Humanities Foundation, of Danish dialect stories from Ephraim, Utah, that belong to exactly the same genre.

Apart from dialect humor, the legends and *contes* of the Peninsula Canadiens derive ultimately from France, and can most conveniently be traced in the encyclopedic work of Paul Sébillot, *Le Folk-Lore de France* (4 vols., Paris, 1904–1907). He refers frequently to the *loup-garou* (I, 284–5; II, 205, 206, 373, 437; III, 54–56; IV, 210, 240, 304); to *lutins*, as they appear in the air, in forests, on mountains (I, 90, 162, 230–32, 268–70, 283; II, 201–2, 308, 347, 417, 418, 422; IV, 16, 30–32); to the Diable and his tell-tale imprints (I, 239, 363–4, 369, 374, 378, 383, 385, 392, 394–5, 398); to ships and men borne in the air (I, 5–6; 175; II, 157); and to the various other common Canadien beliefs in apparitions, revenants, *fées*, miracles.

For the larger framework in which the French legends fit, Jacob Grimm's *Teutonic Mythology* (4th ed., 4 vols. translated by James S. Stallybrass, London, 1883) remains the most valuable discussion. Here the *loup-garou* is related to the whole continental theme of shape-shifting; the *chasse-galerie* is subsumed under the tradition of the Aerial Host; isolated fragments of black magic are fused into the folk cult of demonology (vol. III, chs. 31–35).

One curious title deserves mention here, for representing a direct connection between French folklore and the United States, and also in containing oral traditions from Brittany and Gascony similar to those in this chapter. Frank L. Schoell's *Le Folklore au Village: an Elementary French Reader* (New York and London, 1922) grew out of a lecture series in the United States that led listeners to suggest the French visitor print his simple and attractive folklore stories for language teachers. The stories used deal with saints, the Devil, miracles, *lutins*, revenants, and "histoires comiques," very much in the Upper Peninsula blend.

CHAPTER 5: COUSIN JACKS

The impact of the Cornishman on the northern mining states has received some attention from folk historians. Caroline Bancroft, "Folklore of the Central City District, Colorado," *California Folklore Quarterly*, IV (1945), 315–342, deals largely with the Cornish miner; Louis A. Copeland, "The Cornish in Southwestern Wisconsin," *Collections of the State Historical Society of Wisconsin*, XIV (1898), 301–334, studies the Cornish influx between 1825 and 1850; and James E. Jopling, "Cornish Miners of the Upper Peninsula," *Michigan History Magazine*, XII (1928), 554–567, gives some sketchy facts for northern Michigan. The humorous dialect anecdotes of the Cornishman are collected in Wisconsin by Charles E. Brown, in his booklet *Cousin Jack Stories* (Madison, Wisconsin, 1940), and in Colorado by Caroline Bancroft, "Cousin Jack Stories from Central City," *Colorado Magazine*, XXI (1944), 51–56. Since Cornish tradition in the United States mixes closely with mining lore, some references apply to both groups; in his article on the Butte miner, for example, Hand (see under Ch. 10, *Miners*) recognizes the distinctive folk contribution of Cousin Jacks underground. An unusual source for Cornish-American folkway is a long rhymed narrative by T. J. Nicholas, *Cornwall and the 'Cousin Jack'* (2nd ed., Ilfracombe, 1947), a folk document that describes his life in England and the Upper Peninsula in full and characteristic detail.

Contrasted with the meager bibliography for the United States, the literature of Cornish folklore in its home setting appears rich indeed. The outstanding collections include William Bottrell, *Traditions and Hearthside Stories of West Cornwall* (Penzance, 1870; Second Series, 1873; Third Series, 1880, titled *Stories and Folk-Lore of West Cornwall*); Mrs. Henry Pennell Whitcombe, *Bygone Days in Devonshire and Cornwall* (London, 1874); Robert Hunt, *Popular Romances of the West of England, or The Drolls, Traditions and Superstitions of Old Cornwall* (3rd ed., revised and enlarged, London, 1881); Miss M. A. Courtney, *Cornish Feasts and Folk-Lore* (Penzance, 1890; revised and reprinted from the Folk-Lore Society Journals, 1886–1887). These are all substantial volumes demonstrating the vigor of Cornish belief, custom, and narrative. Other works descriptive of life in Cornwall often contain folklore, as John T. Tregellas, *Peeps into the Haunts and Homes of the Rural Population of Cornwall, Being Reminiscences of Cornish Character and Characteristics* (Truro, 1868); and most recently, the writings of Alfred K. Hamilton Jenkin, collected under the title *Cornwall and Its People* (London, 1945).

For the background of Upper Peninsula Cornish lore, the following specific references can be given. The Cornish fondness for pilchards, scalded cream, and saffron cake is discussed by Hamilton Jenkin, pp. 400ff.; superstitions about pilchards (e.g., eating them from the tail up brings good luck) appear in Hunt, p. 368, Whitcombe, p. 140. Hunt gives an account of Whipping the Hake, p. 370. The particular affinity between the Cornishman and the "coo-coo," which ramifies into the whole cycle of Gothamite and "noodle" stories, is treated at length in John E. Field, *The Myth of the Pent Cuckoo* (London, 1913). Both the popular rhyme about the cuckoo months (as given me by Captain Arthur Williams) and the popular joke about Jan and Bill who tried to fence in the cuckoo with turfs, exemplify the common spirit between the silly bird and the naive Cousin Jack.

One finds in Cornish folklore examples of ill-wishing, blood-staunching, and other charmings, belief in piskies, divination, lore of the mines and the seas, and further categories that overlap with various chapters in this book. The distinctive feature about Cornish lore lies in its homogeneous character; each Cousin Jack reflects the parent stock. As William Bottrell, the pioneer Cornish folklorist, expressed it, "Cornishmen's clannish propensities are well known and are most apparent when they meet in foreign lands" (III, 182). The conservatism of Cornish tradition appears clearly enough in the Upper Peninsula.

CHAPTER 6: FINNS

The great repository of Finnish mythology and folk belief is of course the *Kalevala*, collected and polished by Elias Lonnrot in 1835, and translated several times into English, most recently in the fine prose rendition of my good friend from the Upper Peninsula, Aili Kolehmainen Johnson (Hancock, Michigan, 1950). A useful analysis of the structure and matter of the *Kalevala* is Domenico Comparetti, *The Traditional Poetry of the Finns*, translated by Isabella M. Anderton (London, 1898). John Abercromby, *The Pre- and Proto-historic Finns* (2 vols. London, 1898), provides both background data on Finnish origins and an anthology of Finnish charm-sayings with which the *Kalevala* abounds.

In spite of the rich folklore background of the Finns in America, and of the high level of Finnish folklore scholarship in Europe, little collecting has been done from Finnish Americans. Marjorie Edgar has published some material in *Minnesota History*; "Finnish Charms and Folk Songs in Minnesota," "Finnish Folk Songs in Minnesota," "Finnish Proverbs in Minnesota," (XVII, 1936, pp. 406–410; XVI, 1935, pp. 319–321; XXIV, 1943, pp. 226–228); and also "Ballads of the Knife-Men," *Western Folklore*, VIII (1949) 53–57; "Finnish Charmer from Minnesota," *Journal of American Folklore*, XLVII (1934), 381–383. Aili Johnson has written two fine articles on Michigan Finns, "Finnish Labor Songs from Northern Michigan," *Michigan History*, XXXI (1947), 331–334; and "Lore of the Finnish-American Sauna," *Midwest Folklore*, I (1951), 33–40. A purely historical account is John I. Kolehmainen and George W. Hill, *Haven in the Woods, The Story of the Finns in Wisconsin* (Madison, Wisconsin, 1951). For the general immigrant background, Kolehmainen's *The Finns in America, A Bibliographical Guide to Their History* (Hancock, Michigan, 1947) gives a classified list of published works, chiefly in Finnish.

The class-conscious tales about Jussi the Workman show some affinity with the Balkan cycle of Hodja Nasreddin, with its frequent note of discomfiting the aristocrats (*Tales of Nasr-ed-din Khoja*, translated from the Turkish text by Henry D. Barnham, London, 1923). The English cycle of Robin Hood, as the rough humor of the earlier Child ballads suggests, probably followed a similar pattern (Thomas Wright, "On the Popular Cycle of the Robin Hood Ballads," *Essays on subjects connected with . . . England in the Middle Ages* [2 vols., London, 1846], I, 164–211), and Janosik, the Polish Robin Hood (see my note in *Western Folklore*, VIII, April 1947, p. 135f.), shows a still closer similarity. Like all good proletarian heroes, Jussi is 50 per cent rogue.

A discussion of "The Shaman" among Old World Lapps by Una Holmberg can be found in Volume XIV of *The Mythology of All Races* (Boston, 1927), pp. 282–295. ("Shaman" is the closest translation for the Finnish *noita* and the Lappish *noidde*.) Holmberg, however, deals with pre-Christian magico-religious practice rather than the village wizard of the nineteenth century. Comparetti comments on the Europeanization of the shamanic idea (*op. cit.*, 227ff.) and Abercromby briefly describes "Wizards, Sorcerers, etc.," (*op. cit.*, I, 344–348).

The *noita* hero in Frank Valin's *Märchen* of "The Shoemaker and the Princess" gives a Finnish coloring to this well known incident, The Obstacle Flight, which Trefflé Largenesse rendered in a modernized form. Valin's other *Märchen*, "Cinders," is equally well known (Type 530, The Princess on the Glass Mountain). Von Sydow sees this form as a Teutonic oikotype, which alone has the glass mountain; the Slavs have instead a high tower, which in India becomes a high palisade (*Selected Papers on Folklore*, edited by Laurits Bødker, Copenhagen, 1948, p. 57). Where Valin has a modern touch in his text, in the photograph of the princess as the mountain-climber's prize, Norwegian and Swedish versions handed in to me by students have the princess toss the hero a golden apple. I collected a Polish text from Joe Woods at Crystal Falls, in which the princess marks Johnny with white chalk on his forehead, and by this the king's heralds later detect him (*Western Folklore*, VIII, 1949, 28–33). Cinders represents the so-called male Cinderella complex of this type, as Marian Roalfe Cox has worked it out in *Cinderella: Three Hundred and Forty-Five Variants* (London, 1893). The plots of three Finnish versions of "Tuhkimo" or "Tuhkamo" are summarized in *The Folk-Tales of the Magyars*, translated and edited by W. Henry Jones and Lewis Kropf (London, 1889), annotating the Slavic text, "Cinder Jack" (149–152, 389–390). See also *Yule-Tide Stories: A Collection of Scandinavian and North German Popular Tales*, edited by Benjamin Thorpe (London, 1880), "The Princess on the Glass Mountain" (pp. 86–97). An elaborate text secured by the Finnish collector Eero Salmelainen in 1852 (reprinted in Helsinki, 1920, in *Suomen Kansen Satuja ja Tarinoita* [*Tales and Legends of the Finnish Nation*], pp. 56–70), follows the Slavic oikotype in placing the princess on a high tower where she presses her ring on Cinders' forehead as an identifying mark. Stith Thompson remarks on the wide distribution of the tale, especially in northern and eastern Europe, in *The Folktale, op. cit.*, pp. 61–62.

Frank Valin told other *Märchen*, not included here, e.g., "Nies Nai," Type 532, The Helpful Horse; "The Poor Brother and the Rich Brother," Type 1535, The Rich and The Poor Peasant; "Jönkki Sailor," Type 313, The Girl as Helper in the Hero's Flight; "Old Man Lööpi,"

Type 461, Three Hairs from the Devil's Beard; "Tittirä's Truura," Type 500, The Name of the Helper.

The verified stories of the seers belong to a class with world-wide counterparts, but the most conspicuous area for second sight seems to be the Scottish Highlands. Andrew Lang contributed a good article on "Second Sight" to the *Encyclopedia Britannica*, 11th edition (1911), XXIV, 570–571, and he wrote a sympathetic introduction to the reissue of *The Prophecies of the Brahan Seer* by Alexander Mackenzie (Stirling, 1924), one of the most spectacular of the Highland mystics. In his *The Making of Religion* (3rd ed., London, 1909, pp. 65–83), he gives examples of visions among primitive peoples.

The wide range of Finnish folklore becomes evident in the salty tall tales of Herman Maki. Americans have no monopoly on such tales, and Maki fables in the spirit of any frontier boaster. "The Gun as Tobacco Pipe" (Type 1157, "The Trickster gives the ogre the gun to smoke") has already been reported from Finland; the New York *Spirit of the Times* printed a Welsh text, "Morgan Jones and the Devil" (XVI, July 4, 1846, p. 228), and the collection of Liars' Club tales by O. C. Hulett, *Now I'll Tell One*, gives an Oklahoma locale with a rugged Indian substituting for the Devil (Chicago, 1935, pp. 23–24).

Shortly after hearing Maki relate "How we caught the Silver Fox in Finland" I read the same yarn, applied to squirrel-shooting, in the *Saturday Evening Post* (November 9, 1946, p. 13), in an article by Barrows Mussey recalling his boyhood on a Vermont farm, where his granddad spun large stories. The Type-Index lists this plot under 1896, "The Man Nails the Tail of the Wolf to the Tree and Beats Him." "Hunting the Bear in Finland" finds a kindred exploit performed by the Maine guide, Ed Grant, who caught a bear in a trap, let it starve, and then gradually coaxed it out of its loose skin with a piece of liver (*The Tame Trout and Other Backwoods Fairy Tales*, narrated by Ed Grant, chronicled by Francis I. Maule, 2nd ed., Farmington, Maine, 1941), "A Remarkable Bear Skin." A variant of Maki's "An Unhappy Bear Hunt" appears in Charles E. Brown's booklet, *Whiskey Jack Yarns* (Madison, Wisconsin, 1940), "Hunts a Bear." Maki's clever hunting dog is matched by identical animals in Lowell Thomas, *Tall Stories* (New York & London, 1931), pp. 119–120. The profusion of partridges in Michigan that requires the hunter to fire two shots to kill a bird, has roots deep in American myth; John Clayton was describing back in 1688 how a cloud of turtledoves in the colonies would hide the sun and break great branches of trees when they alighted

(*America Begins*, edited by R. M. Dorson, New York, c. 1950, pp. 81–82).

A correspondent from Finland, Eeva Mäkelä-Henriksson, supplies the following information about Lapatossu. Lapatossu was a real person, born Kustaa Gustafsson in the village of Heinu in the middle of the last century. He ran away from his father's farm to work on the railway, and gained a reputation in the railway camps throughout Finland as a joker and wit. The name "Lapatossu" probably derives from a type of soft leather shoe worn by the Swedish workers, at whom Gustafsson poked fun, and in reprisal the word was applied to him. After his death about 1900, his fame still grew; any jester in a work camp was nicknamed "Lapatossu"; collections of stories attributed to him were published in popular editions; the well-known actor Aku Korhonen played Lapatossu in a motion picture and told Lapatossu stories over the radio during the war.

Lapatossu's retort that makes out the arrogant storekeeper to be a donkeyhead or a dumbbell turns up in nineteenth-century Yankee humor. His outwitting the ship captain is also an international jest; see Motif K. 263, "Agreement not to scratch. In talking, the trickster makes gestures and scratches without detection," which has several New World appearances, all Negro (Stith Thompson, *Motif-Index of Folk-Literature*, Bloomington, Indiana and Helsinki, Finland, 1932–36).

CHAPTER 7: BLOODSTOPPERS

The power to staunch the flow of blood from wounds or cuts belongs to a large group of verbal charms employed by their privileged possessors against disease, evil, witchcraft and the like. These date from pre-Christian times and are revamped to fit Christian tradition. Implicit in the efficacy of the charm is the belief in the power of sacred or magic words, such as "Jesus," but this idea has linked with shamanism, in that only specially gifted persons — those born with a caul, or the seventh son of a seventh son — can use the words effectively. For general discussions of charming, see Edward Clodd, "Cure-Charms," in *Magic in Names and in Other Things* (London, 1920), pp. 194–223; "Charms and Amulets (Christian)" in the *Encyclopaedia of Religion and Ethics*, edited by James Hastings, III (1910), an article by E. von Dobschütz, especially p. 424, "Charms of Non-Christian Origin (Words)"; Joshua Trachtenberg, "In the Name of . . . ," *Jewish Magic and Superstition* (New York, 1939), pp. 78–103; A. H. Krappe, *The Science of Folk-Lore* (New York, 1930), pp. 189–193, and Y. M. Sokolov, *Russian Folklore*, translated by Catherine R. Smith (New

York, 1950), pp. 246–256. The heathen origins of "Blood-Stanching" are, naturally, asserted by Jacob Grimm in his *Teutonic Mythology*, *op. cit.*, III, 1247–1248. G. L. Kittredge gives some English sources for bloodstopping in *Witchcraft in Old and New England* (Cambridge, 1929), p. 32, note 81, although here for once his references only scratch the existing collections; there is hardly a British county field book which does not contain examples.

Early texts can be found in D. G. Storms, *Anglo-Saxon Magic* (The Hague, 1948), pp. 292–294, 304–305, who comments, "Christ Himself, Who bled from the wounds made by the nails, the lance and the crown of thorns, is the central figure in most of these charms." The bloodstopping charms from the west of Ireland currently collected by the Irish Folklore Commission show the tenacity of this formula, e.g., "Ioleetish was the blind man's name who drove the spear through Christ's side, from which pale blood and water came. O Jesus, Mary, and St. Joseph, stop the blood that is flowing without pain. Stop it in the name of the Father and the Son and the Holy Ghost" (MS Vol. XI, p. 265). Reidar Th. Christiansen refers to this type in his review of F. Ohrt, *Da Signed Krist* (Copenhagen, 1927), in *Béaloideas*, I (1928), 412–415.

A good modern article is in the indispensable *Handwörterbuch des deutschen Aberglaubens*, I (Berlin and Leipzig, 1927), 1452–1465, "Blutsegen," which classifies the charms according to their qualities of resemblance and contrast to the things invoked. The same work contains, in its related article on "Jordansegen" (IV, 1931/2, 765–770) a bloodstopping charm from the fifteenth century very like the Finnish one of John Rantimaki: "Als Jesus über dem Jordan ging, da standen alle die Wasser still, ist das nicht wahr?" This article states that the charm involving Christ and the river Jordan is one of the oldest and best-loved invocations in North and Middle Europe. A similar Jordan charm, from the Swedish, goes, "Stand still, you blood! as Jordan's flood, when our Saviour let himself be baptized. In the name, etc." This appears in the rich collection of North European healing words, magic songs, formulas and prayers by John Abercromby, *The Pre- and Proto-historic Finns* (London, 1898), II, 39. For other word-spells against flowing blood see *ibid.*, 11 (Mordvin), 12–13 (Ceremisian), 16 (Votiak), 23–24 (Lettish), 34–35 (Great Russian), 38 (Latin), 144–147, 293–297 (Finnish). For burn-healing charms see 8–9 (Mordvin), 13 (Ceremisian), 24 (Lettish), 140–144 (Finnish). Abercromby's materials demonstrate the close relationships between the charm, the prayer, the incantation, and similar verbal devices to sway fortune.

A "fattura" case comparable though not identical with Sam Colassaco's can be found in Phyllis H. Williams, *South Italian Folkways in Europe and America* (New Haven, 1938), pp. 157ff. Here one *maga* uncovers the enchantment of another, who had rendered a bridegroom apathetic toward his wife — and interested in a pretty cousin — by concealing a knot of crumpled ribbons in his wedding clothes. (For oral charms against the Evil Eye see 155–156. The whole study is an all-too-rare investigation into the transference of ethnic folkways from Europe to the United States.) The *Handwörterbuch* treats the impotent bridegroom under "Nestelknüpfen" (VI, 1014–1016).

Relatively few examples of bloodstopping have yet been collected in America, simply for lack of inquiry. See "An Indiana Charm for Bleeding," *The Folk-Lorist*, I (1892), 75–76; Thomas B. Stroup, "A Charm for Stopping Blood," *Southern Folklore Quarterly*, I (1937), 19–20; and especially the important chapter on "The Power Doctors" in Vance Randolph, *Ozark Superstitions* (New York, 1947), pp. 121–161.

PART III: THE NATIVE TRADITION

CHAPTER 8: TOWNSFOLK

The bibliography on legends of local history is surprisingly limited. What the Germans call *Sagen* represent chiefly supernatural-geographical tales, of spirits or curses attached to rocks, hills, streams and castles. That tradition grows around local events and characters seems not to have occurred to the continental folklorists, preoccupied with mythological origins. Two early English folklorists however, working on their own, dealt with folk history. Robert Chambers, the publisher, in the first edition of his *The Popular Rhymes of Scotland* (1826) collected the proverbial sayings and jingles that frequently synopsized village legends (see especially the sections, "Rhymes on Localities" and "Characteristics of Localities"). Hugh Miller, the geologist and journalist, set down the historical traditions of his home town, Cromarty, in *Scenes and Legends from the North of Scotland* (1835 and 1858) in a rich variety that embraces anecdotes of the starving year of 1740, the invasion of the Highlanders in the "forty-five," the wonders that befell Methodist ministers, and lurid memories of the French Revolution. American folklorists could profitably plough in this field.

The curse motif in "The Lynching of the McDonald Boys" still turns up in contemporary events. A news item run by the Associated Press on November 27, 1948, stated that Jake Bird, a Negro vagrant sentenced to death in Tacoma, Washington, for an ax slaying (he confessed to forty-four other murders), cursed all those connected with his case. Five persons died between the time of his curse and his execution, his lawyer, two policemen, the court clerk, and the judge; Joe had cursed them by saying: "All you guys who had anything to do with this case are going to die before I do."

In the autobiography of Tomás Ó Crohan, *The Islandman* (translated from the Irish by Robin Flower, London, 1951) occurs a curse tale connected with hated bailiffs from the mainland. "Some forty of them came to this Island in the days of the persecution to collect rent, and not one of them died in his own house except one man who lived out there in Coumeenhole. They all died in want in the poorhouse; and that was only just. Thanks be to God that they are all dead and we are alive still" (p. 57).

The rivalries between towns for the county seat or the state capitol, for railroad stations and business capital, and all the freaks that have determined the growth and death of communities, are ubiquitous themes in American local history. As yet they lie unnoticed in the marchland between historian and folklorist.

From Ireland Tomás Ó Crohan in his grim tale of "The Boat of Gortadoo" (*op. cit.*, 49–51) tells how boats from Dunquin and Ballyferriter quarreled to the death over a prize wreck, and the two parishes feuded ever after. The rivalry between the sister channel islands of Guernsey and Jersey gave rise to jocular anecdotes, reported by Sir Edgar MacCulloch in his *Guernsey Folk Lore*, edited by Edith F. Carey (London, 1903), pp. 426–432. Once three inebriated Jersey mariners tied a hawser to a Guernsey rock and attempted to pull the enemy island alongside their own.

The legends behind place names have received better attention. George R. Stewart's *Names on the Land* (New York, c. 1945) popularized this subject; *Western Folklore* runs a regular department on "Names and Places"; the New Mexico Folklore Society is currently compiling a place-name dictionary for its state.

CHAPTER 9: LUMBERJACKS

For the human side of north-woods logging operations, Stewart Holbrook's *Holy Old Mackinaw* (New York, 1938) broke new ground in picturing the rugged atmosphere of lumbercamp life. Richard Lillard, *The Great Forest* (New York, 1947), looks at the trees more than the men, but provides a valuable historical background for the northern lumberjack. Rare personal histories by old-time woodsmen dealing with the Upper Peninsula area are *The Life of a Lumberman*, by John Emmett Nelligan, as told to Charles M. Sheridan (n.p., c. 1928), and *Recollections of a Long Life, 1829–1915*, by Isaac Stephenson (Chicago, 1915). Several collections of lumberjack ballads exist, the most recent being that of Earl C. Beck, *Songs of the Michigan Lumberjacks* (Ann Arbor, 1942; revised and erroneously retitled *Lore of the Lumber Camps*, 1948), but the narrative traditions of lumbering life in various parts of the country are largely uncollected. Harold W. Thompson gives some lumbermen tall tales from New York State in *Body, Boots and Britches* (Philadelphia, 1940), pp. 266–274. An unusual and relatively early collection of tales about mythical woods animals, with which old-timers gulled greenhorns, is William T. Cox, *Fearsome Creatures of the Lumberwoods* (Washington, D. C., 1910).

Some of the Con Kulhane stories, including variants of ones I collected, were printed in *Michigan History*, XXXI (1947), 437–442, by Ida M. Spring, "White Pine Portraits: Con Kulhane." In *Michigan: A Guide to the Wolverine State* (New York, 3rd printing, 1946) mention is made of the legend of the Seney stockade, of P. K. Small's dietary habits, and of some old-time maulers (pp. 559–560). Several volumes of Paul Bunyan stories purportedly gathered in Michigan have been published; I regard none of them as authentic.

CHAPTER 10: MINERS

Mining is the best collected of all the American occupations. The lore of the anthracite and bituminous coal miners of the East is presented in George Korson's *Minstrels of the Mine Patch* (Philadelphia, 1938), and *Coal Dust on the Fiddle* (Philadelphia, 1943). Wayland D. Hand has interviewed California gold miners, Utah silver miners, and Montana copper miners and recorded their traditions in a fine series of articles, in the *California Folklore Quarterly*, I (1942), 24–46, 127–153; *ibid.*, V (1946), 1–25, 153–178; *Journal of American Folklore*, LIV (1941), 132–161. Both these collectors ably relate miners' folklore to the patterns of life in the mining towns. Korson discusses such social institutions as the coal-camp doctor and preacher, the saloon, the union, and the company store, as background for mining legends and ballads. Hand has worked out a useful finding list for mining lore, dividing the material into "above-ground" tales of lucky

discoveries and lost mines, and "below-ground" superstitions concern-
ing women, rats, whistling, the last shift, and similar hoodoos and
hunches. Both Hand and Korson emphasize the miner's concern with
accidents and death, around which revolve so many of his songs and
superstitions.

The Upper Peninsula material follows closely Hand's motifs: the
mines found by boob's luck and those missed by a hair; the bitter
legends surrounding the great disasters; the craft traditions. I ran onto
a number of ghost stories as well (only one is given here, but note
Aaron Kinney's ghost-laying exploit in Chapter 12), which corroborate
Korson's and Hand's reports that the old-time miners feared underground spooks, and were easy prey for practical jokers utilizing the
eerie sounds and shapes under the earth.

CHAPTER 11: LAKESMEN

A useful survey of Great Lakes lore in the days of sailing ships can
be found in Ivan Walton's chapter, "Marine Lore," in the *Michigan
State Guide, op. cit.*, pp. 113–134. He comments on weather beliefs,
great feats of navigation, ghost ships, tales of sunken treasure, and
songs of the lakes. As Professor Walton indicates, the Lakes traditions
have an affinity with those of the ocean; see e.g. the too little known
work of Lieutenant Fletcher S. Bassett, founder of the Chicago Folk-
Lore Society, *Legends and Superstitions of the Sea and of Sailors in
all Lands and at all Times* (Chicago and New York, 1885). Angelo S.
Rappoport, *Superstitions of Sailors* (London, 1928), and Frank Shay,
A Sailor's Treasury (New York, 1951), are patchworks.

An account of "The Bull at the Soo," similar to the two versions I
collected, but lacking the folklore touch of the amazed English traveler
aboard the *Manitoba*, is printed by Dana T. Bowen in *Memories of
the Lakes* (Daytona Beach, Florida, 1946), "The Soo Lock Accident,"
pp. 248–252. He also gives a factual account of "The Wreck of the
Western Reserve," pp. 201–204.

Serpents and monsters are reported on America's inland waters
with scarcely less frequency than the sea serpent is spied in the Atlantic. I have a Vermont example in *Jonathan Draws the Long Bow,
op. cit.*, pp. 135–137. Charles E. Brown sets down some Wisconsin
appearances in his eight-page booklet *Sea Serpents* (Madison, Wisconsin, 1942), and Austin Fife describes some Utah specimens in "The
Bear Lake Monsters," *Utah Humanities Review*, II (1948), 99–106.

Captain Truedell's premonitory dream of shipwreck can be matched by a much older Lakes tale, which I ran onto in a family scrapbook filled with clippings from early Ontonagon newspapers. John Parker's dream predates the building of the Soo locks in 1855, and hence his story talks of portaging around the St. Mary's River, and of shooting the St. Mary's Rapids for sport. Parker dreamed of his own calamity and thereby saved himself from drowning.* The newspaper story follows:

CAPTAIN PARKER'S DREAM

Last week's Menominee *Herald* contained the following interesting article regarding one of Ontonagon's oldest settlers, which was gathered from a conversation had with the captain while he was visiting in that city.

Capt. John G. Parker, one of the pioneers of the Lake Superior region . . . was born in Winchester, New Hampshire, in 1821.

It was during his stay at the Sault, awaiting the *Fur Trader's* (schooner) turn to be taken across the portage, that Capt. Parker met with quite an adventure. The schooner *Merchant,* lying at the Sault, was anxious to continue on her way without the delay of being hauled over the portage. It was necessary for the channel to be sounded before the vessel started on her perilous voyage, and this was done by a small boat in which was Capt. Brown, steersman; Capt. John Stannard, pilot; with Tom Ritchie, John Flynn and John G. Parker as oarsmen. Dr. Prouty, who was staying at the Sault; Mr. Seymour, a son-in-law of Father Bingham, a Baptist preacher well known in the early days of the Sault; Dr. Prouty and Mr. Seymour going for the fun of shooting the rapids.

As the boat entered the rapids, Capt. Parker remembered a dream of the night before in which he had seen a boat-load of men put off from one of the vessels, himself being one of the party. He saw them enter the rapids and go a short distance when the boat capsized and all were thrown into the water.

The captain quietly removed his heavy coat and boots and prepared for the worst, which soon came. The boat was caught by the foaming water, and her oarsmen being unable to keep her in the proper channel she was overturned, her crew being plunged into the ice-cold waters. As Captain Parker rose to the surface he still held in his hands a heavy oar, which proved a life-preserver to himself and four men he was able to reach by swimming. The others, being encumbered by their heavy boots and coats, were unable to help themselves and so perished.

If it had not been for the strong impression made by his dream the captain would have found a watery grave. Himself and companions managed to reach the boat to which they clung until assistance came from shore. Doctor Prouty was past all help, but Mr. Seymour was resuscitated after a long effort. While they were working over his body an Irishman known as Uncle Tom came running toward them shouting, "Rowl Seymour! rowl him! He owes me tin dollars!"

* Parker describes this dream in his diary, which J. K. Jamison quotes in *Michigan History* (XXIII, 1939, pp. 253–254). The date of the dream was June 1, 1847, and Parker places the sinking nine days later.

CHAPTER 12: SAGAMEN

The noted Swedish folklorist, C. W. von Sydow, has recognised the marvelous personal narrative as a distinct form of folk tradition, which he proposes to call the "memorat" (*Selected Papers on Folklore*, Copenhagen, 1948, pp. 73–74, 87). A fine description of a sagaman akin to Charlie Goodman and Swan Olson can be found in Hugh Miller's autobiography *My Schools and Schoolmasters* (Edinburgh, 1907), pp. 208–211, in the wonderful stories of the stone mason Jock Mo-ghoal. Miller, with his untrained but astute folkloristic instinct, properly appreciated and classified Jock.

During the whole season a newspaper never once entered the barrack door. At times a song or story secured the attention of the whole barrack; and there was in especial one story-teller whose powers of commanding attention were very great. He was a middle-aged Highlander, not very skilful as a workman, and but indifferently provided with English . . . . Of all Jock Mo-ghoal's stories Jock Mo-ghoal was himself the hero; and certainly most wonderful was the invention of the man. As recorded in his narratives, his life was one long epic poem, filled with strange and startling adventure, and furnished with an extraordinary machinery of the wild and supernatural . . . . The workmen used, on the mornings after his greater narratives, to look one another full in the face, and ask, with a smile rather incipient than fully manifest, whether "Jock wasna perfectly wonderfu' last nicht?" (pp. 208–209)

And then followed the text of one such narrative, fully justifying Miller's plaudits. I completely agree with Miller's recognition that Jock "belonged to a curious class, known by specimen, in, I suppose, every locality, especially in the more primitive ones . . . ." (p. 211).

John Hallen's narratives differ from those of his redoubtable fellows in embodying psychic or mystic rather than heroic experience, and they add the salt of supernaturalism to the regular saga of frontier adventure.

INDEX

INDEX

INFORMANTS

PLACE NAMES: OLD COUNTRY

PLACE NAMES: UPPER PENINSULA

TALES: TITLES, TYPES, TRAITS

* Logical Chess
Move by Move   ) CHERNEV

* The Complete Chess Player
        REINFELD

Ideas Behind Chess Openings
    * FINE

Chess Openings Theory + Analysis